THE MIRACLE OF
SALT

ALSO BY NAOMI DUGUID

Burma: Rivers of Flavor

*Taste of Persia: A Cook's Travels
Through Armenia, Azerbaijan,
Georgia, Iran, and Kurdistan*

WITH JEFFREY ALFORD

*Beyond the Great Wall:
Recipes and Travels in the Other China*

*Mangoes & Curry Leaves: Culinary Travels
Through the Great Subcontinent*

*Home Baking: The Artful Mix of Flour and
Tradition Around the World*

*Hot Sour Salty Sweet: A Culinary
Journey Through Southeast Asia*

Seductions of Rice: A Cookbook

Flatbreads & Flavors: A Baker's Atlas

THE MIRACLE OF
SALT

Recipes and Techniques to Preserve,
Ferment, and Transform Your Food

NAOMI DUGUID

ARTISAN | NEW YORK

Salt pans near Petchaburi, southern Thailand

CONTENTS

THE WIDE WORLD OF SALT

SALT IS AS FAMILIAR AS WATER AND THE AIR WE BREATHE, AND IT'S JUST as essential to us. Salt is our most important ingredient, the only food that we all need.

These days we are able to take salt for granted. Modern production techniques and transportation have made salt both plentiful and inexpensive. Our forebears weren't so lucky: salt was scarce and often heavily taxed. Families depended on salt for preserving food (for example, large catches of fish, the cabbage harvest, the meat from the pig that was butchered in late autumn) so that they had a supply to last them through lean times. Salt was an essential tool for preserving then, and it still is.

This book celebrates salt's essential role in helping us make the best use of our food by preserving it and enhancing it, so that it not only keeps well but also tastes delicious.

In the first part of the book, The Salt Larder, I take you on a journey through the realms of salt preservation, to explore techniques and foods that cooks have developed over the centuries as brilliant solutions to the twin problems of food scarcity and food oversupply. I've included recipes for many salt-preserved foods that are easy and fun to make at home, along with descriptions and information about others that you can buy ready-made. In the second part, From Larder to Table, you'll find recipes for simple dishes that make use of salt-preserved ingredients in many enticing ways.

All warm-blooded animals need salt to survive, and because salt is not distributed evenly throughout the world, humans and animals have to seek it out. Archaeological remains show evidence of salt trading and salt travel among the earliest peoples. And once humans developed agriculture and large settled communities, control of salt and trading for salt became both causes of conflict and major sources of revenue.

My research for this book transported me to many places and took me time-traveling to many other eras. The field of salt archaeology has developed over the last thirty years, generating research and papers about early peoples and

Quechua woman walking in the salt terraces of Maras, Peru (see page 313)

salt technologies in many parts of the world (you'll find some of these papers and other works listed in the Resources). It's a fascinating field.

Another resource for salt history is older cookbooks. They are a reminder of how much salt-dependent food preserving went on until relatively recently, when refrigeration became widely available. I learned so much from these books, from Dorothy Hartley's *Food of England*, which takes us back to nineteenth-century practices and wisdom, to William Shurtleff and Akiko Aoyagi's groundbreaking *Book of Miso* and *Book of Tofu*; Catherine Parr Traill's freshly edited and reissued 1854 cookbook for settlers in Canada, *The Female Emigrant's Guide*; and Jane Grigson's *Charcuterie*, published more than fifty years ago (see the Resources for these books and more).

We walk in others' footsteps. We reinvent the wheel in some ways in each generation, most often without knowing that we are doing so. In salt terms, the recent rise of interest in fermentation and in specialized artisanal salts is a good example. None of this is completely new, it's just new to those of us who were not aware of the historical context. I'm pleased that we're retrieving and honoring long-standing knowledge and putting into practice some of the insights that our forebears gained in earlier times. I hope that this book will help home cooks and professionals alike discover that making salt-preserved foods is easy and interesting, and that salt-preserved foods of all kinds, both homemade and store-bought, can transform our cooking.

SALT PLACES

While salt occurs in various forms in numerous regions around the world, some regions have none. That unequal distribution of salt has led to trade and cultural exchange as well as to all kinds of hardship. There are salt stories almost everywhere, some of them about plenty, many about scarcity.

All salt originates in the ocean, but some of it was deposited long ago in what is now dry land. That is what we refer to as rock salt, or halite. It is found underground as solid crystals or dissolved in groundwater in the form of salt springs or salt wells.

Humans have been seeking out salt and evaporating salty water to get salt for thousands of years. Since animals seek salt too, people have long followed the cues from animals to find salty places. Whether from seawater (the oceans are on average 3.5 percent salt) or inland and/or underground sources, salt must be extracted, and that almost always requires an energy source to evaporate the water the salt is dissolved in. Over millennia, people have figured out many ingenious ways of doing so.

Along seacoasts, people learned to create shallow ponds for seawater so that the sun—i.e., solar energy—would evaporate the water until the salt precipitated out. The most well known of these are on the Atlantic coast of France, in the Mediterranean (for example, at Trapani in Sicily and Malta's Gozo Island), and in the Rann of Khatch, but there are many more. In less sunny climates, such as those of coastal Japan or Oregon or England's Essex County, where there is not adequate solar energy for evaporation, the

"Flor de sal" from Maras, Peru

seawater has to be boiled over fires powered by wood or natural gas or coal to precipitate out the salt.

Inland, where there are salt wells and springs, the salty brine is pumped up to the surface and then boiled in large containers over fires. Less frequently—for example, on solar evaporation terraces in Maras, near Cusco, Peru, and in Añana in the Basque Country—solar energy is used to evaporate the water from salt springs.

Inland salt is also found in the form of salt lakes or salt crusts in arid places, such as much of Utah, the Tibetan plateau, the Danakil Depression in Ethiopia, central Iran, and a few locations in the Sahel and Sahara in Africa. The salt from these desert-area deposits at the edges of salt lakes or in hollows where salt lakes once existed can often be extracted without special machinery; the salt is there for the taking.

There are also large deposits of salt underground in Poland, Colombia, New York State, Ontario, Pakistan, and many more places. This salt has historically been extracted with pick and shovel, as still happens in the small salt mines in the Atlas Mountains in Morocco. But in most mines, machines now do the excavating. These days much extraction of underground salt deposits is by solution: Water is injected into the ground, the salt dissolves in the water, and then the brine is pumped out and filtered to remove impurities before being boiled (these days in a vacuum to make the process more efficient). The water evaporates, leaving the salt behind.

You'll find descriptions of salt places and salt history in stories and photographs throughout this book and some more technical explanations at the back of the book (page 366). For further explorations of salt history, chemistry, and salt preservation, have a look at some of the references in the Resources.

FERMENTATION

When the idea for this book first came to me, it felt exciting and full of promise. And as I progressed into recipe explorations, I realized that a book about salt is inevitably also a book about fermentation. It's the careful use of salt that permits us to preserve foods safely through fermentation. By preventing the development of unwelcome bacteria, salt enables fermentation by lactic acid bacteria (LAB). And because salt makes an inhospitable environment for spoilage bacteria, it is a primary tool for preserving food and ensuring food security.

Fermentation has become a big theme in the food world in recent years. But it has in fact underpinned food processing, and hence human survival, for millennia. We're only now returning to an appreciation of its remarkable impact on flavor and nutrition. And that has led to a growing fascination with the process of fermentation and an exploration of the many ways it can be used in both home kitchens and restaurants.

Fermentation involves the transformation of plant or animal materials by bacteria or yeasts, small microscopic actors that break down organic material as they feed on it. Bacterial activity lowers the pH level of most foods to 4.5 or 4.0, creating a more acidic environment. Yeasts thrive in an acidic environment and bring flavor. Examples of the process include the fermentation of fruit into alcoholic drinks such as wine or cider; of grains into leavened bread or beer; of beans and grains into miso; of raw meat into cured products; of fish and seafood into shrimp paste or fish sauce; and of milk into cheese. Much fermentation is anaerobic, meaning that it takes place in an environment that has no oxygen. (The absence of oxygen prevents the growth of some bacteria while encouraging the development of yeasts and other helpful organisms.)

KITCHEN ANXIETIES AND KITCHEN TOOLS

Many of us are anxious when we embark on a new technique. That anxiety can be magnified when the outcome lies days or weeks or months away, as it does with many salt-preserved foods. We can't adjust the seasoning as we go, as we could for a salad or a soup. And we won't know for some time how well our efforts have succeeded. It's a familiar and age-old reflex, like hesitating before jumping into cold water.

I felt that anxiety hovering when I was starting work on the preserving recipes for this book. What if my kimchi didn't work? Or my salt pork? It was important to look myself in the eye and say firmly, "Well, then, there will be a bit of food wasted. But I'll have learned something, and I'll be able to pass it on."

The testing that went into these recipes should save you from a lot of such worries. You can rely on the recipe instructions and measurements. And that brings me to tools—specifically, kitchen scales. I usually hesitate to ask people to use specialized equipment. I believe in improvising and working freely. But with salt preserving, kitchen scales

are important, because exact measuring is important.

I urge you to get yourself two scales: a regular kitchen scale that measures up to one kilogram/two pounds or more and a scale that can measure as little as tenths of a gram, often called a jeweler's scale. You'll find it relaxing to be able to rely on exact measurements.

Precise measurements are needed when salt is used for preservation, especially for meat, where the proportion of salt to the basic ingredients and/or water is critical. Another reason to get a jeweler's scale is that salts differ widely, so that a given volume of some salts will weigh less than others. For example, fine table salt is generally heavier per volume than coarse salt; and even within those two categories, there are large variations.

It's the weight of salt, not the volume, that tells you how much salty flavor you are adding. The differences aren't as critical when you're talking about single spoonfuls, but with any larger volumes, small differences add up to something significant. To give you an idea of the range: ¼ cup kosher salt weighs from 45 to 62 grams, depending on the brand, while ¼ cup fine table salt weighs about 75 grams. And the same volume of some flake salt weighs only 32 grams.

PART ONE

THE SALT LARDER

IN PAST TIMES, PEOPLE WHO FACED THE chore of putting up crocks and jars of salted meat or kimchi or sauerkraut for the winter had to get it right the first time. The job of preserving much of their food for the next five to ten months by salting and brining was actually a matter of life and death for many. Knowledge was passed down through the generations, and people learned by doing.

Adapting traditional recipes to the smaller quantities that seem practical today has been a reminder to me to feel grateful that I live in an easier time. Preserving food is far less fraught now. If I mess up, I won't starve, nor will my family. The worst that can happen is that I waste a little food. I can go out and buy another cabbage or piece of pork belly and try again.

But as I make pancetta or kimchi or miso and then later turn to it, in my salt larder stash, to use in my cooking, there's a great sense of satisfaction. It comes from feeling a greater autonomy—I'm taking control of more of my food supply by doing my own processing—and also from the realization that I can now explore all kinds of cooking with a larder that is richer in flavor and possibility.

When I preserve food this way, I feel that I'm in conversation with, and learning from, cooks and dairymaids, farmwives and charcutiers, and many others past and present who have worked with, and still work with, salted foods. I'm grateful to them all.

Engaging with salt-preserved ingredients can be life-changing; it has been for me. It has given me real respect for our forebears, and it has enriched my kitchen and my cooking. Instead of a huge larder and cold cellar full of a winter's worth of salted meats and brined vegetables, though, as I might, with luck, have had in centuries past, I have a "flavor larder"—small amounts of salted flavorings and salt-preserved ingredients that I can rely on to enhance my cooking. There's a feeling of wealth when I put up sauerkraut or miso or salted lemons or salt pork: all that real food and flavor, made from scratch and so useful.

Many of these foods are delicious on their own, as well as part of that larder of flavors that can be used to heighten a meal or a dish. In the second part of this book, From Larder to Table, you'll find recipes that make wonderful use of the ingredients in The Salt Larder.

SALTS & SALTING

WE HAVE AN INTIMATE RELATIONSHIP
with salt, grain by grain, in our fingers as a pinch,
between our teeth as we bite into a crystal, on our
tongue as it melts. We have salts we prefer, salts we
seek out.

The variety of salts available today to cooks in the
developed world would have astonished our forebears.
The differences in their tastes and textures are subtle
but marked. There's the intense harsh saltiness of
refined sea salt, pure white sodium chloride with all
impurities removed, in contrast to the more complex
taste of "raw" (unrefined) salt from land or sea, whether
gray or white or pink. Coarse pickling salt has medium
even crystals. Coarse sea salt crystals are generally
larger, and sometimes irregular in shape. Table salt is
quick to dissolve and doesn't cake or clump. It's worlds
away in flavor and texture from the cracking, melting
fragility, and delicate aroma of the flat crystals of the
flake salts often referred to as fleur de sel.

Black salt (kala namak) in two forms: finely ground and in large pebbles (see page 23)

WHAT DOES SALT DO?

The salt that we depend on to season our food and to maintain our health is sodium chloride; NaCl is its chemical formula. One molecule of salt is about 40 percent sodium and 60 percent chlorine by weight. In our bodies, sodium is an electrolyte that controls fluid balance and is necessary for the transmission of electrical impulses in our nerves and muscles. Sea salt or salt from underground deposits may contain small amounts (up to 10 percent) of other salts, mainly potassium chloride, calcium chloride, and magnesium chloride.

Salt is a key to flavor and, in some dishes, to texture. It heightens flavors, lessens bitter elements, and enhances sweetness. In food preservation, it's a contributor to the processes that give fermented and cured foods their enticing umami flavor.

But how does salt enhance or heighten flavors? Scientists tell us that sodium stimulates the sensors in our taste buds, or awakens them, you could say, so that they are more sensitive to other flavors in food. Without salt, more subtle flavors often go undetected. That's why unsalted food tastes flat.

The exception to this is bitter: salt mutes our receptors for bitter flavors. This is one of salt's gifts to us in the mouth: by lessening bitter tastes, it allows other tastes (often sweet) to become more noticeable. Why do we salt greens? Originally it must have been as a way of making them taste less bitter. (The English word *salad* has its root in the Latin term for salt or salted: *salata*.) We salt eggplant, and the salt mutes the eggplant's bitterness, as well as draws out bitter liquid.

That's also the reason why the pinch of salt traditionally added to campfire coffee (where the coffee boils in a pot of water until strong and dark) makes it less bitter.

When salt is added to vegetables or meats, it draws out water, and that frees some of the aroma molecules. For example, when we add salt to chopped scallions, they start to smell stronger because as the salt draws out water, some of the volatile aroma molecules are released and then reach our noses. Since what we taste comes partly from our sense of smell, this is another reason why salted food has more flavor. And it's also a reason for holding back and doing a final salting just before serving, so that appetizing aromas will be released as the food comes to the table.

Salt also serves as an antibacterial agent by drawing water out of plant or animal tissues so that pathogens cannot flourish. (This is true for bacterial cells also; through osmosis, salt draws water from these cells, causing them to die.) After light salting, chopped vegetables such as cabbage, cucumber, and radishes lose water and become inhospitable to all but the friendly, naturally occurring lactic acid bacteria that make fermentation happen. The result is preserved vegetables with enhanced flavor (think sauerkraut or kimchi). In contrast, heavy salting of vegetables draws out most of their liquid and the salt then dissolves in it to make a very salty brine that prevents the growth of all bacteria so that no fermentation will take place. The brine is reabsorbed by the vegetables, which will stay crisp and well preserved in sealed containers for a long time.

Salt's effect on the texture of foods is noticeable in a number of situations, from bread-making to pre-salting meats. Apart from the traditional salt-free bread of Tuscany, leavened bread all over the world is generally made with some salt. In addition to adding taste, the salt slows down the growth of the yeasts and also strengthens the gluten strands in wheat and rye doughs so that the dough can rise and hold its shape.

Salting leafy vegetables briefly to draw out liquid (rubbing salt into kale leaves, for example) causes them to wilt and become more tender.

Salting meat or poultry before cooking causes excess water to be drawn out and firms the flesh, intensifying flavors. Brining meat by immersing it in salted water for a longer period before cooking seasons the interior of the meat as well.

TASTE AND AROMA

The differences in taste among various salts are often extremely subtle. In many cases, it's only when you taste them side by side that you can clearly note what distinguishes one from another.

The way in which sea salt is produced has an effect on both its taste and its texture. Seawater contains trace amounts of calcium, magnesium, and potassium, as well as sodium chloride, and so do many rock salts (since they originated in ancient seabeds). Phytoplankton and other microscopic creatures found in salty water can also affect the taste and color of salt.

The crystals of unrefined sea salts from different salt producers have discernibly different tastes and characteristics. Some of this depends on their place of origin and the water in which they were dissolved, and some on the technique used by the people who produced the salt (by solar evaporation or boiling or a combination), as well as on their skill and judgment. Those differences involve both taste and the shape of the crystals; see more on texture below.

In Tokyo, I visited a remarkable store called Ma-Suya that carries many kinds of salt, a place to test and taste as much salt as you are able to handle. As with trying perfume, most people, including me, hit their tasting/testing limit pretty quickly. It was rather overwhelming. I ended up trying only six or seven and then opting to buy just four.

I did ask myself what I was looking for, apart from the chance to see how many salts there were in the store. Yes, I could taste differences between them, but what difference would the taste of a particular salt make in my own cooking? With rare exceptions, the role of salt is not to be tasted on its own as the star of the show but instead to alter and enhance the foods it is added to. Salt plays a supporting role, an essential one, it is true, but like a good actor, its job is to blend seamlessly, to be there, but not so obtrusively that it becomes too noticeable, or the main flavor.

Nevertheless, the taste and smell of some salts can give us enormous pleasure. The aroma of unrefined solar-evaporated sea salt is evanescent. You get a tantalizing whiff of it when you open a sealed container, but it's so delicate that it's quickly overcome by the taste and smell of any food you sprinkle it on. Still, the gift of that aroma is one good reason for using natural sea salt.

For the eater and, in some ways, for the cook, the finishing salt is the most important. You want the crunch of fleur de sel, perhaps, or the color of a tinted salt. Or maybe the aroma of the sea, or of a flavored salt such as vanilla salt (see page 39) or spruce tips salt (see page 40). All these are useful for finishing, for being noticed as you bring a mouthful of food up to your mouth and then take it in. That's when aroma is most important.

I have come to love the clean taste of salt evaporated from the cold waters of the northern Pacific and northern Atlantic, from Iceland and Ireland to Oregon, Nova Scotia, and Vancouver Island. It's especially noticeable when flake salt is sprinkled on at the last moment by the cook or at the table, for then, with luck, the flakes stay intact long enough that you taste the individual salt crystals as you crunch down on them.

I was introduced to sea salt when I lived in France for a year as a teenager. I tasted salt from the Guérande and from the Ile de Ré,

At Wajima market, on Japan's Noto Peninsula, you're invited to taste salt.

both on France's Atlantic coast. My preferred unrefined sea salt, both coarse and fine, is still the gray salt from that coast. Madame J, who cooked wonderful meals for her *pensionnaires*, including me, would deftly add a pinch of fine sea salt to finish a dish, or a spoonful of coarser salt to a pot of soup. None of those salts had the off-putting smell or taste of the iodized table salt that my mother used and that is still the standard in many kitchens in Canada and the US.

TEXTURE AND WEIGHT

Texture is easier to talk about than taste, which can be so subjective.

The texture of a given salt is determined during its harvesting and/or production. Crystal shape and size depend on the methods used to evaporate the seawater and process the salt. Salt that rises to the surface of the brine during solar evaporation, if undisturbed by wind, can form large, flat crystals—e.g., fleur de sel. Salt that is evaporated by boiling the brine in vats can also be gently simmered toward the end of the process to produce a flake salt like fleur de sel. Apart from artisanally produced salts, though, most salt is machine-processed after evaporation or extraction to create evenly sized grains or crystals—fine, medium, or coarse—and crystals with distinctive shapes or properties.

Crystal shape and size affect many things: the feel of the salt between your thumb and finger when you take a pinch; the size of pinch you take; the speed with which the salt dissolves in liquid; and, importantly, how much a given volume of salt weighs, which is actually another way of saying how much saltiness a tablespoon of that salt will add. The texture of salt you prefer will depend on what you're using it for as well as on your own kitchen habits.

FEEL, AND JUDGING YOUR PINCH OF SALT

Medium-sized salt crystals, such as those of kosher salt or coarse pickling salt, are the easiest to pick up quickly as a pinch between your thumb and forefinger. That's why I generally use coarse pickling salt when adding a pinch of salt. For the same reason, many chefs choose kosher salt in the kitchen because its industrially produced crystals are medium to large, easy to pick up, and of even size, so a pinch gives a consistent amount of saltiness. Fine salt can be trickier because it can stick to your fingers, especially if it's unrefined sea salt. Coarse unrefined sea salt, and many flake salts, have irregularly sized crystals, which can make them uncomfortable to pick up and also make it difficult to judge amounts consistently.

DISSOLVING SPEED

Large crystals generally dissolve more slowly than small grains of salt. (Large crystals used to be called "corns," which is how corned beef got its name.) Old-style salt cures, sometimes known as salt-box cures, in which the meat is buried in salt for a number of days, traditionally used very coarse salt because it was cheaper. Kosher salt, the salt used for koshering—the process in the Jewish tradition of drawing the blood out of freshly slaughtered meat—is somewhat different. It's not intended to infuse meat with flavor but to create a salty environment at the meat's surface that will draw out liquids through osmosis. Its crystals cling easily to the surface of the meat.

Sometimes you want the salt to dissolve as quickly as possible. That's true when you're fine-tuning the seasoning of a dish as it finishes cooking. You want the adjustment to dissolve right into the dish, so fine salt is the best choice. And when you're baking, whether it's bread or pastry or cakes or cookies, you want to use fine salt, which will dissolve evenly into the dough or batter. When you add salt to a pot of water for cooking pasta, or when you're salting the cooking water for potatoes or other vegetables, it will dissolve more quickly if you add it once the water is hot. And you don't want large salt crystals sitting on the bottom of the pot, so avoid coarse unrefined sea salt, which often takes longer to dissolve. I find fine sea salt or fine or coarse pickling salt are both good choices here.

When you're sprinkling a finishing salt onto food as you serve it, you don't want it to dissolve but instead to keep its delicate crunch and to have its flavor still concentrated, so that your guests get an intense little hit of salt with their first bite. A good choice here is flake salt, a colored salt, or, perhaps, a smoked salt—or one of the flavored salts in the following chapter.

When you're doing a salt cure of meat or vegetables with a measured amount of salt, the salt starts drawing liquid out of the meat or vegetables. Fine salt crystals will dissolve in that liquid, making a brine, a little more quickly than coarse crystals will, though that difference is usually inconsequential.

To recap, the pinch of salt used to adjust the seasoning as you finish cooking should be a fine salt that dissolves quickly, and it should be a salt with which you're familiar so that you know how much salt flavor you're delivering in that pinch. Salt sprinkled on at the last minute to give surface crunch or a quick salt hit as part of the dish (or put out at the table as a condiment) should be a flake salt, unrefined fine sea salt, or, perhaps, a colored salt. A generous spoonful of salt tossed into the water when you are cooking pasta or boiling potatoes should be an inexpensive refined salt, which in my case is coarse pickling salt, my generic kitchen salt.

Custom and habit play a big role in my salt usage and preferences. There may well be other salts I would like as much as those that I have in my kitchen, but the familiarity of the ones I know is important to me. You may feel the same way. I am used to judging how much salt to use in a given situation by eye and by feel. I do believe that because we so often use our fingers to add salt, that act becomes a question of intimacy, of intimate physical knowledge and connection. That's why switching to another salt can feel disorienting.

WEIGHT, DENSITY, AND SALTINESS

Crystal size and shape affect the density of a salt—in other words, how much a given volume of salt weighs. Density varies widely among different salts. Because it is the weight of the salt that determines how much sodium a given volume of salt contains, and thus the amount of salty taste it will add, using volume measures for salt rather than weighing it can give wildly different results. Table salt tends to be the densest (heaviest

per volume) because of the shape of the crystals, which pack tightly together. Flake salts are the lightest (least dense), because their large irregular crystals don't pack tightly, leaving gaps in the measuring cup or spoon.

When the volume in question is small—a teaspoon, say—such variations are less important. But when you're working with larger amounts, for example, ¼ cup or more, these differences matter. This is why it's especially important to measure salt by weight rather than by volume when preserving and pickling, especially if the quantities are significant. These preservation

SALT MEASURES AND WEIGHTS

	1 tablespoon	¼ cup
Iodized table salt	19 grams	76 grams
Unrefined sea salt (such as Noirmoutier)		
fine	11 grams	45 grams
coarse	13 grams	52 grams
Refined sea salt		
fine	15 grams	60 grams
coarse	17.5 grams	70 grams
Pickling salt		
fine	14 grams	56 grams
coarse	16 grams	65 grams
Kosher salt		
Diamond Crystal	11 grams	45 grams
Morton's	15.5 grams	62 grams
Flake salts		
Maldon	12 grams	48 grams
Sal de Añana "flor de sal"	7 grams	29 grams

techniques rely on the taste and antibacterial strength given by the sodium, and that amount, which needs to be reliable and consistent, will vary if you measure the salt by volume.

If you always use the same salt, you'll have developed an intuitive sense of how much you need to add to a soup, for example, as you adjust the seasoning. But when you're doing salt-curing, or following a recipe that's new to you, or using a salt that is new to you, it's best to measure salt by weight rather than by volume. That's where your jeweler's scale (see page 162) can be a reassuring tool.

SALTS AND SALT TERMS

ALAEA SALT: This red salt from the Hawaiian island of Kauai is colored by the addition of the red volcanic clay called *alae*, which contains iron oxide (hence the color) and various minerals.

BLACK SALT: True black salt, known in Hindi as *kala namak*, comes mainly from Central India and from Pakistan. Large crystals of it are charcoal-colored to black, but when it's finely ground, it has a pinkish hue. It has a sulfurous aroma. Other "black salts" are colored with the addition of charcoal.

BLUE SALT: A rare and expensive salt from Iran, blue salt is mined in the Albourz Mountains east of Tehran. Its blue tint comes from the potassium chloride in the rocks in which it is found.

COARSE SALT: Coarse salt, or *gros sel* in French, refers to large crystals of salt that may be manufactured and regular in shape or, if unrefined sea salt, rough and irregular.

COLORED SALTS: Pure salt crystals are white. Colored salts are usually tinted by other earth substances, local silt, or trace elements. The pink salt from Khewra Mine in Pakistan, for example, is tinted by trace minerals (see Pink salt, below). Some salt is colored by the production process, such as the gray sea salt from the Guérande and pink salt from Maras, which pick up color from the clay in the evaporation basins. In other cases, the salt is mixed with a coloring material after it has been extracted. Other salts are colored by the addition of various ingredients for flavor and sometimes to make them more eye-catching as a finishing salt.

FINE SALT: Fine salt refers to the small size of the salt crystals. There are refined and unrefined versions of fine salt; table salt is a fine salt, for example. The crystals of most fine salts pack tightly together, so that in general a measured volume of fine salt weighs more than the same volume of a medium or coarse salt.

FINISHING SALT: Finishing salts are intended to be sprinkled on a dish just before it is served and they are meant to be noticed, because of their distinctive color or texture. Flake salts and colored salts are both used as finishing salts.

FLAKE SALT, FLEUR DE SEL: Flake salts are defined by the shape of their crystals, which can be flat and quite brittle, or pyramid-shaped. Most flake salts are modern versions of the traditional fragile salt flake crystals called fleur de sel. This French term translates literally as as "flower of salt," and it was originally a description of the lacy-looking flat salt crystals that float on the surface of a saturated seawater

GRAY SALT: Often called by its French name, *sel gris*, this is unrefined sea salt that gets its color from the clay that lines the evaporation basins on the western Atlantic coast of France. There's also a Korean gray salt, which is a little drier than French gray salts. I use the fine version of the French gray salt in my cooking, usually when using a measuring spoon to scoop it up; it dissolves very quickly. The salt is usually a little moist, like many sea salts, so that it sticks to the fingers, which is why I tend not to use it when I'm reaching for a pinch of salt.

brine as it evaporates slowly in traditional evaporation ponds. It's an ancient form of salt that is traditionally gathered by hand because of its fragility. Fleur de sel (known in Spanish and Portuguese as *flor de sal*) is produced in places with an ancient sea salt history, such as the Guérande and the Ile de Ré on the western coast of France, as well as a number of saltworks on the coasts of Portugal and Spain.

Producers in many places, using more modern methods of salt production, make flake salts that mimic the texture of fleur de sel crystals more or less successfully. There's a narrow band of size and thickness that is ideal for flake salt. You want a slightly pyramidal crystal, not too thick, so that you can crush it with your fingers if you wish, or crunch it between your teeth, without getting too strong a dose of salt.

Flake salts and fleur de sel are used as finishing salts to add a hit of salty crunch to a dish.

Flake salts command a premium price; true fleur de sel is even pricier.

HAWAIIAN RED SALT: *See Alaea salt, above.*

IODIZED SALT: In most countries today, table salt is iodized either with potassium iodide (in North America) or with potassium iodate (elsewhere). Iodizing is a public health measure introduced internationally over the last seventy-five years (for more see page 367). The iodine gives salt a distinctive smell and taste. Iodized salt should not be used for pickling or preserving.

KOSHER SALT: Koshering meat means drawing out the blood and impurities from it immediately after slaughter. The salt crystals of kosher salt are shaped so they cling to the surface of the meat during koshering. Kosher salt has been refined to remove trace minerals, but some kosher salts contain anti-caking ingredients. The weight per volume of kosher salts can vary widely among brands.

MEDIUM-GRAIN SALT: There are many salt crystals that fall between the descriptions fine and coarse. Medium-sized crystals, with various crystal shapes, are made by boutique producers as well as by large manufacturers. These include coarse pickling salt, most kosher salts, and some finishing salts.

PICKLING SALT: Pickling salt is most often fine, but it also comes in medium-sized crystals, labeled "coarse pickling salt." It is refined salt with no additives—no anti-caking products or iodine—that might interfere with the pickling process. I use coarse pickling salt for much of my daily cooking as well as for preserving.

PINK SALT: The best-known pink salt is Himalayan pink salt, a rock salt from deep underground in one of the world's largest salt mines, the Khewra Mine in Pakistan, north of Islamabad. It is primarily sodium chloride with other trace minerals (the pink is said to come from iron). The pinkish "rosada" salt produced near Maras, Peru, is tinted by the ocher-colored soil that lines the evaporating basins. Black salt, kala namak (see above), is pinkish colored when it's finely ground.

REFINED SALT: Most of the salt we consume, either in commercially prepared foods or our own cooking, is refined salt. Refined salt with no additives is almost odor-free. It may have started as rock salt from a mine or as sea salt, but it's been cleansed of all other minerals or impurities, leaving only sodium chloride, pure white salt. When you taste it, the "salty" taste is direct, without any bitterness or other flavors. Refined salt may be labeled sea salt, rock salt, kosher salt, or pickling salt. The differences among these refined salts lie in the differing shapes and sizes of the crystals (or grains). The crystals of different refined salts have been processed for

uniformity of size and shape. Some refined salts are iodized or have added anti-caking agents (see pages 366–367).

ROCK SALT: Most of the salt used around the world comes from underground salt deposits that originated as ancient seabeds. In that sense, all salt is sea salt. Before the twentieth century, rock salt was generally viewed as less desirable than sea salt because it often contained impurities. Modern processing techniques have eliminated that concern. Note that today the term *rock salt* can also mean road salt, the coarse unrefined salt used to melt ice on roads and sidewalks; road salt is sodium chloride, but it should not be eaten because it can contain additives and impurities.

SEA SALT: Seawater has a salinity level of about 3.5 percent—1 liter (about 1 quart) of seawater contains 35 grams (about 2 tablespoons) salt. Sea salt is harvested from seawater by the process of evaporation, either by solar evaporation or by boiling the water over a heat source (see page 371).

Once the salt has been extracted from the brine, it may be further refined to eliminate trace elements and impurities, or left unrefined. Some unrefined sea salts have a distinctive, if ephemeral, aroma, from trace minerals in the salt. Unrefined sea salt is often off-white to gray in color and a little moist because of traces of magnesium. Many cookbooks published before 1900 call for "bay salt," an older term for sea salt.

TABLE SALT: Table salt, the salt most commonly used by home cooks, is refined, fine-grained, and usually iodized. It contains anti-caking agents to ensure that it is free-flowing. The crystals pack together tightly, so that it is denser than other salts: i.e., a given volume of table salt will weigh more (and therefore give more saltiness) than the same volume of most other salts.

UNREFINED SALTS/NATURAL SALTS: Some rock salts and sea salts are available in unrefined form, also called natural salt. Often named for the region they come from, they may be fine or coarse, grayish or tinged

with another color, the color indicating the presence of substances other than sodium chloride. Some unrefined salts have a strong smell of iodine (which would make them too strong to use in pickling, for example); others may have a touch of bitterness from trace amounts of magnesium or potassium.

WHEN AND HOW TO SALT

We all need salt, and health experts tell us that about 1 teaspoon (6 grams) per day is a good target (see page 369 for more detail). Most people consume more than that, given the chance. At the same time, we have a limited tolerance for saltiness. Too much salt in a dish and we find it inedible.

One way of ensuring that you do not oversalt your food is to use restraint when you add salt during cooking. Salt added early is infused into the food; salt added late has more of an impact on the tongue when you first put the food in your mouth. In her book *My Bombay Kitchen*, Niloufer Ichaporia King describes the dance with salt and salting this way: "Everything depends on salt. With Indian food particularly, judicious salting can make the dish, giving it its meaning and its anchor. Without the right amount of salt, spices float around in search of a leader. To ensure depth of flavor and seasoning, we add a small amount of salt at the start of a dish as well as at the end, tasting as we go."

SALTING VEGETABLES TO CHANGE THEIR TEXTURE AND FLAVOR

When and how you salt affects both flavor and texture. Salting a short time before cooking can modify the taste of ingredients, drawing out liquid in order to intensify flavors, as with a steak, or drawing out bitterness from a vegetable such as bitter melon. But salting in advance can affect

texture too. When we want ingredients to retain their crispness, such as salad greens, we salt very late, so the salt doesn't have time to draw out water and wilt the leaves. If you want to draw out a vegetable's bitter flavors, salt it 10 minutes ahead, but no earlier; any longer risks making it too salty, because it will have absorbed the salty brine. You can also salt sliced onions to soften them and take away some of their harshest edge (see page 65). Bitter melon is often sliced and salted to draw out its bitterness (see page 242), and some cooks use the same technique for eggplant. The easiest way to do this is to toss the sliced vegetables with salt and lay the slices on a rack placed over a tray or over the sink so the liquid can drain off. After 10 minutes or so, rinse the

Chunks of pink salt from Khewra Mine in Pakistan

slices briefly in cold water to wash off any remaining salt and brine and pat them dry with a cloth or paper towel.

SALTING STEAMED VEGETABLES

The spinach recipe on page 240 offers an example of salting leafy vegetables as they start cooking to encourage them to wilt and cook more quickly.

SALTING COOKING WATER FOR PASTA, POTATOES, OR OTHER VEGETABLES

Bring the water to a rolling boil before adding the salt. Bring the water back to a boil, then add the pasta or potatoes or other vegetables. They will absorb a little salt while cooking, a light seasoning that penetrates them as they cook. Then you add another layer of seasoning with the pasta sauce, or the way you dress and season the cooked potatoes or vegetables. I use a scant 1 tablespoon/18 grams salt per quart/liter of cooking water.

SALTING DRIED BEANS DURING COOKING

Add about 2 teaspoons/10 to 12 grams salt per quart/liter of water when your pot of beans has come to a boil. The salt will be absorbed as the beans cook, and the salting will help shorten the cooking time because the sodium in the salt molecules replaces the magnesium in cell walls of the beans, making them soften more easily. Do your final adjustment of seasoning, if necessary, just before serving.

SALTING GRAINS

Although I don't usually salt my plain white rice, I do salt brown rice and other grains such as farro or freekeh, using about 1 teaspoon/6 grams salt per each cup/180 to 200 grams of raw rice or other grain.

SALTING A SLOW-COOKED DISH, SUCH AS A STEW OR A SOUP

You want some salt to be drawn into the meat or other ingredients during cooking, but you also want fresh late-added salt. The best way to do this is to add about half the salt called for in the recipe early on and then add the balance toward the end of cooking, with a final adjustment of the seasoning just before serving if necessary.

SALTING A CHICKEN BEFORE ROASTING

I like rubbing a whole chicken with salted onions (see page 65) or herbes salées (see page 49) or with coarse pickling salt or sea salt before roasting it. I do this about 30 minutes before putting the bird into the hot oven, breast side down, and then flipping it over after about 20 minutes (see Roast Chicken with Celeriac and Lemon-Apricot Sauce, page 276). The salt draws a little moisture out of the skin so that when the chicken comes out of the oven, the skin is crisper and more delectable. And the seasoned skin bastes the meat with flavor as it cooks.

BRINING A CHICKEN

Brining a chicken for 12 to 24 hours before roasting or grilling makes it moister, and because the brine seasons the meat right through, it also makes it more flavorful. Note that a brined bird will cook more quickly (in about 25 percent less time) than one that has not been brined, because the resulting extra moisture in the meat helps conduct heat to the center of the bird as it roasts. It's critical, for food safety reasons, to make sure your brine has cooled completely before submerging the chicken in it.

The proportions for the main ingredients for the brine are 2 quarts/2 liters water to ⅓ cup/90 grams additive-free salt; I use coarse pickling salt or sea salt. Like most cooks, I include some sugar or honey in the marinade to soften the flavors: an amount equal to or slightly less than the salt is a good ratio. Other optional ingredients, which will lightly perfume the brining water and thus add touches of flavor to the meat, may include a combination of aromatics; see the Brined Chicken recipe on page 176.

SALTING STEAK OR OTHER SMALL CUTS OF MEAT BEFORE COOKING

The reasons for salting meat ahead of cooking it are to season it and, if you salt well ahead, to change the texture too. If you salt meat just before cooking, it will flavor the surface of the meat; it will also draw out some meat juices during cooking, helping to create a delicious crust. If you salt a steak or similar cut of meat well ahead, the salt will draw liquid out of the meat. That liquid, in turn, will dissolve the salt, creating a little brine that will then be drawn back into the meat by osmosis, remoistening it and seasoning the interior. In addition, the brine will tenderize the meat by starting to relax and denature some of the proteins.

So you can either salt the meat immediately before cooking it to season it or season it far enough ahead that there's time for a brine to be created and for that salty liquid to be drawn back into the meat to season the inside.

For steaks and similar cuts, if you are seasoning them ahead, the general rule of thumb is 30 minutes ahead for each ½ inch/1 cm of thickness. Then, before cooking, pat the surface of the meat dry so that you will get a good browned surface.

SALT-RUBBING ROAST BEEF OR PORK

My mother made brilliant beef roasts using less-expensive but more flavorful cuts. An hour before putting it into a 375°F/190°C oven, she'd rub the roast with a mixture of salt and hot mustard powder, then smear on some bacon fat to keep it moist. I don't cook roasts (beef or pork) often, but when I do, my impulse is always to salt them ahead and perhaps include some other flavorings in the rub, then seal that in with a smear of lard or chicken fat or even duck fat before roasting it. I start it in a relatively hot (400°F/200°C) oven and then lower the heat after about half an hour to a more moderate 375°F/190°C.

SALTING GROUND MEAT

Unlike a single piece of meat, such as a pork chop, which can be salted to taste on the surface, ground meat—for burgers, meatballs, meatloaf, stuffings, etc.—needs to have the salt incorporated before cooking. I use the ratio of 1 teaspoon/6 grams salt per pound/450 grams meat. It's a reliable yardstick.

SALTING KEBABS

As in the kebab recipe on page 293, I generally season kebabs early, about an hour ahead, with a marinade of fish sauce and pomegranate molasses. The fish sauce seasons them perfectly. You can use a plain or flavored salt or a blend of flavored salts instead, rubbed on well ahead. But if you're not using a marinade, cut your cubes of meat smaller and sprinkle on a little salt just before you cook the kebabs. The salt helps draw out some of the meat juices to create a crust. As the cubes of meat start to soften and yield their juices, shortly before they're done, sprinkle on one of the pepper salts (page 37) or Svan Salt (page 31), or a mix of salt and ground cumin. This is the technique used by the grill masters I've seen in small street stalls in Iran and in Xinjiang in western China.

SALTING BREAD DOUGH

When you're making roti/chapati, the proportions are very simple. For every 2 cups/260 grams of atta flour (finely ground whole-grain durum flour), use 1 teaspoon/ 6 grams salt and a scant cup/240 ml of lukewarm water. You'll need a little extra flour for kneading and surfaces, but not much. This ratio gives you the freedom to make as much or as little dough as you want and have it taste as it should.

A useful guideline for just about all bread doughs is 1 teaspoon/6 grams salt for every cup/240 ml liquid. Knowing this proportion gives you the freedom to make bread dough freehand, without a recipe. The question of salt is the critical one: if you undersalt or, worse, oversalt your dough, your bread won't taste good to you or anyone else. If you forget to add the salt with the flour (as has happened to me), you can remedy the problem after the dough is mixed and kneaded, or partially kneaded, by mixing the salt you need into a little water and kneading that into the dough.

Traditional salt production beside the Sea of Japan on the Noto Peninsula:
vats of concentrated brine boiling, heated by woodstoves

JAPANESE SALT TRADITIONS

In traditional Japanese culture, salt is a metaphor for purity, for death, for eternity. It's tossed by wrestlers in the sumo ring before a bout, and many Japanese

restaurants have a cone of salt on either side of the entrance to signify cleanliness and purity. On the shores of the Noto Peninsula, I caught a glimpse of why salt is so honored and respected: Harvesting salt the traditional way was laborious and unforgiving. People hauled seawater onto the shore and poured it onto smooth-raked fine sand, over and over. The salty sand would then be shoveled into a fine filter placed over a large vat and rinsed with seawater to produce a strong brine. The brine would be boiled down slowly to make salt.

That method is still being used by one salt maker on the Noto Peninsula (although now at least there's an electric pump to draw the seawater up from the ocean and onto the sand, in place of the labor of hauling buckets of water). Another salt maker along that coast is working with a modern variant, spraying seawater onto vertical screens so that the salt clings to the screens and concentrates there. It can then be rinsed off and the brine boiled down. Both of these brine-concentrating methods save on wood or other fuel.

For the last seventy-five years or so in Japan, table salt has been made with a modern process that eliminates all impurities and trace minerals, leaving pure sodium chloride. For most of the twentieth century, salt making was a government monopoly and consumers had no choice about where their salt came from. Most of the artisanal old-style salt makers on Noto and elsewhere eventually stopped production because they could not charge a premium for their special salt. Since the monopoly ended, there's been a revival of traditional salt making in many parts of Japan. You can find salt from Okinawa or Hokkaido, hand-rubbed salt crystals, *moshio* salt made from seaweed, and many more choices. Salt is once again a tangible link with the past.

FLAVORED SALTS & SALTED FLAVORINGS

THERE'S AN AMAZING VARIETY OF SALTS and saltiness possible if we look past salt on its own to salt blended and flavored with aromatics or other ingredients. Salt also plays a role as a preservative in many salted flavorings, allowing us the pleasure of herbs and aromatics out of season. Flavored salts and salted flavorings are versatile seasoning tools for the cook, and many can be put out on the table as condiments as well. These blends extend the possibilities of seasoning and give plenty of choice to cook and diner alike.

The recipes in this chapter include, among others, simple combinations of salt with ground dried red chiles, Sichuan pepper, and black pepper, or with only one or two of them, as well as Japanese *gomasio* (salt with toasted sesame seeds), and spiced mountain salts from Uttarakhand in India and Svaneti in Georgia. Then there's *chaat masala*, a complex Indian blend of various spices with black salt that is a versatile larder ingredient. Finally, salt can be blended with chopped scallions or herbs to create jars of useful kitchen flavorings.

FLAVORED SALTS

THREE-PEPPER SALT

Sichuan pepper is the fruit of a species of prickly ash that is related to the Japanese spice *sansho* (see Glossary). The peppercorns are usually a reddish brown. You may see some shiny black seeds in with them; if so, discard the seeds. While the premium in this versatile condiment is on heat, both chile heat and the numbing aromatic heat of Sichuan pepper, the black peppercorns bring a warm, fruity complexity to the mix. *See photo, opposite.*

Makes a generous 3 tablespoons

---

3 dried red cayenne chiles

2 tablespoons coarse sea salt or coarse pickling salt

1 teaspoon Sichuan peppercorns

1 teaspoon black peppercorns

You will need a small heavy skillet, a spice grinder or mortar and pestle, a small bowl, and a glass jar for storage.

Toast the chiles briefly in a small heavy skillet over medium heat until softened, about a minute. Remove from the pan and let cool slightly.

Remove the chile stems and discard, along with the seeds. Coarsely chop the chiles. Transfer to a spice grinder or mortar, add a little of the salt, and grind or pound to a powder. Set aside in a small bowl.

Toast the Sichuan peppercorns and black peppercorns in the same skillet over medium heat until aromatic, about 2 minutes, stirring or shaking the pan to prevent scorching. Transfer to a spice grinder or a mortar, add a little more of the salt, and grind or pound to a powder. Add to the bowl with the chiles and stir in the remaining salt. Let cool.

Store in a glass jar, well labeled, in a cool place, out of the sun. The flavors may fade after about 6 months.

CHILE AND SICHUAN PEPPER SALT

This flavor combination is called *ma-la* in Mandarin, meaning numbing (*ma*) and chile-hot (*la*). Use it as a rub for meat before roasting or grilling, or as a table condiment. Follow the recipe for Three-Pepper Salt, but omit the black peppercorns.

SICHUAN PEPPER SALT

This blend is handy as a finishing salt or as a rub for meat, and it's also good seasoning for grilled or steamed vegetables. The numbing qualities of the Sichuan pepper are balanced by its heat and aromatic fruitiness, and all the flavors ride on the back of the salt.
Follow the recipe for Three-Pepper Salt, but omit the cayenne chiles and black peppercorns, and use only 1 tablespoon of salt.

CHILE SALT

The simplest of these flavored salts, this is a basic seasoning in Thailand and India, commonly used as a dip or sprinkle for slices of sour fruit, such as green mango or pineapple. A little sugar is often added in Thailand to give a combined hit of hot, sweet, and salty.

Follow the recipe for Three-Pepper Salt, but omit the Sichuan peppercorns and black peppercorns, and use only 1 tablespoon salt.

GOMASIO

Shio means salt in Japanese, and *goma* is sesame. This blend of lightly toasted sesame seeds and salt adds a subtle nutty aroma and taste to cooked vegetables, and it is also a pleasing condiment for rice dishes.

Makes about ½ cup/110 grams

½ cup/75 grams white sesame seeds

2 tablespoons coarse or fine sea salt

You will need a medium heavy skillet and a glass jar for storage.

Toast the sesame seeds in a heavy medium skillet over medium heat, stirring or shaking the pan occasionally to prevent sticking, until they start to jump and pop and give off a toasted aroma. Add the salt and cook, stirring or shaking the pan, for 30 seconds or so, then remove from the heat and continue stirring for another 30 seconds, or until the pan has cooled a little. Let cool completely in the pan or transfer to a bowl to cool.

Store in a glass jar, well labeled, in a cool, dark place. The flavors will fade after a month or so.

NOTE: *You can use this mixture as is, but it has much more flavor if you follow tradition and coarsely grind it just before you use it. You don't want a powder, just a crushed-seed texture. If you have a ridged bowl-shaped Japanese mortar, called a* suribashi *(see photo), use it for grinding. Or use a spice grinder: Pulse briefly, only two or three times.*

VANILLA SALT

This vanilla-salt blend is delicious and heady, especially when sprinkled onto sliced ripe tomatoes—umami on umami. Or try it sprinkled on raw or lightly cooked scallops, or lobster.

Makes about ¾ cup/180 grams

¾ cup/180 grams fine sea salt or fine pickling salt

2 good, moist vanilla beans

You will need a wide bowl, a sharp knife, a spoon, and a glass jar for storage.

Place the salt in a wide bowl.

Split each vanilla bean lengthwise with the tip of a sharp knife. Use the edge of a spoon to scrape out all the goopy seeds inside. Cut or pull apart, add to the salt, and mix well, rubbing the seeds between your fingertips to break them up and blend them into the salt. Transfer to a glass jar and label clearly. After just a few days, the salt will be wonderfully perfumed.

SPRUCE TIPS SALT

If you're walking in a forest or a grove of spruce trees in springtime, it's easy to break off some of the fresh bright green spruce tips and harvest them in a bag. Spruce tip salt is aromatic with notes of resin, citrus, coriander seed, and more. Sprinkle on roasted or grilled vegetables, or onto fruit or ice cream. Or serve it as a condiment at the table. I like to put the salt into small jars to give as presents for friends.

Makes about 1½ cups/330 grams

1 cup/80 grams spruce tips (see headnote)

1 cup/280 grams coarse sea salt or coarse pickling salt

You will need a medium bowl, a spice grinder, and a glass jar or jars for storage.

Mix the spruce tips and salt together in a bowl, then transfer to a spice grinder. (You may have to work in batches.) Pulse to grind; if necessary, pause to stir, then grind again until evenly ground. It's very quick.

Transfer to a glass jar or jars and store, clearly labeled, in a cool, dark place.

POT-BUD SALT

If you have access to cannabis buds, let them dry out if they're freshly harvested, then grind to a powder. Rub a little of the mixture onto meat before grilling or frying.

Makes about 4 teaspoons

2 teaspoons ground cannabis buds

Scant 2 teaspoons coarse sea salt or coarse pickling salt

You will need a spice grinder and a glass jar for storage.

Place the buds and salt in a spice grinder and grind to a fine powder.

Store in a well-labeled jar in a cool, dark place. The flavor will start to fade in about 4 months.

NOTE: *You can work with other dried greens to make flavored salt using the same method: Dry the greens (for example, wild garlic/ ramps or young nettle leaves) in the sun or in a dehydrator, then grind them to a powder with the salt in a spice grinder or mortar. It's easiest to work by volume: start with 2 parts dried powdered green to 1 part salt, then increase the salt a little if you want.*

ETHIOPIA

In one of the hottest places in the world, Ethiopia's Danakil Depression, more than 400 feet below sea level, men cut chunks of salt out of the ground, salt

left there over the millennia by the evaporation of salt lakes in that desert environment. The men shape it by hand into flat blocks, like large thick tiles, weighing nearly 9 pounds/4 kg. For centuries, the salt blocks have been loaded onto camels to be carried out across the austere landscape. These days some of them are transported by truck.

I was thrilled when I caught sight of a pile of salt blocks at the Saturday market in the mountain town of Lalibela some years ago. The market was busy, under a hot bleaching sun, with vendors shaded by small black nylon umbrellas selling teff and barley, vegetables, meat, donkeys, bright fabrics, and tools. The salt blocks weren't spectacular looking, but they started me thinking about times past, when blocks of salt (called *amoleh*) were used as currency in the country.

Those salt blocks in Lalibela are as close as I've come to the Danakil and its salt trade: to the brutal temperatures there, the painful working conditions, the long trains of camels plodding uphill to the rest of the country.

At the market in Lalibela, in the highlands of Ethiopia, blocks of salt cut from the desert crust in the Danakil

SALTED FLAVORINGS

CHAAT MASALA

Chaat is the word for a class of snacks in India, deftly made by street vendors and often eaten right there in front of the street stall. Chaat masala is a powder, a mix of freshly roasted and ground spices with salt. It's a kind of use-everywhere seasoning that improves almost anything you want to sprinkle it on, from an omelet to roast potatoes to raita to fresh fruit.

Chaat masala is made with a special salt—kala namak, black salt—that has a slight sulfurous aroma and adds an important note to the mix. Kala namak is available online and in South Asian grocery stores. Finely ground, kala namak is grayish pink. See the Glossary for information about any unfamiliar ingredients.

If you're not familiar with kala namak, or with chaat masala, you may cringe at the idea that a whiff of sulfur can improve and heighten flavors, but here it gives the blend a subtle hit of funk that makes it a great addition to the salt larder.

Makes about 1½ cups/170 grams

3 tablespoons coriander seeds

1½ tablespoons black peppercorns

2½ tablespoons cumin seeds

1 tablespoon ajwan seeds

1 tablespoon fennel seeds

Pinch of asafoetida

1½ tablespoons ground ginger

1 teaspoon cayenne, or to taste

3 tablespoons kala namak (black salt; see headnote)

2 tablespoons dried mint

¼ cup/42 grams amchoor powder (dried mango powder)

You will need a large heavy skillet, a wooden spatula, a medium bowl, a spice grinder, and one or more glass jars for storage.

Place a large heavy skillet over medium heat. When it is hot, add the coriander seeds and peppercorns and toast them, shaking the pan from time to time and using a wooden spatula to move them around and prevent them from scorching, until they start giving off an aroma. Immediately lift the pan off the heat and continue to shake it and keep the spices moving around for another 10 or 15 seconds.

Transfer the coriander seeds and peppercorns to a medium bowl, place the skillet back on the heat, and toss in the cumin and ajwan seeds. Because they are finer-textured, you'll need to shake the pan and stir fairly constantly until the seeds start to become aromatic, then remove from the heat and continue stirring for a short while. Add them to the bowl.

Repeat with the fennel seeds, toasting them briefly, just until aromatic, and then adding them to the bowl. Let the spices cool completely.

Add the toasted spices to a spice grinder, along with the asafoetida (in batches, if need be), and grind to a powder.

Return the powder to the bowl, add the ginger, cayenne, salt, and mint, and mix well. Transfer to the grinder again (in batches if necessary) and grind until fine. Return to the bowl and stir in the amchoor.

Store in one or more glass jars, clearly labeled, in a cool, dark place. The flavors will fade after about 6 months.

NOTE: *After you've made this a couple of times, you may want to adjust the proportions a little to suit your taste. If you can find Kashmiri red chile powder, do try it; it's mild and a little sweet. Add 1 tablespoon of it instead of or in addition to the cayenne. This recipe calls for less cumin and more coriander than many versions do, because I love coriander and find cumin a little intrusive.*

Powdered ingredients (from bottom): ginger, cayenne, amchoor, salt, and mint

HERB AND
GINGER SALT

Uttarakhand is the Indian state that lies just west of Nepal in the steep Himalayan foothills and mountains. Salt was traditionally an expensive and valued ingredient that had to be carried into the region from Tibet, China.

There's a tradition in Uttarakhand of making flavored salt, called *pisi loon*, that is salt ground with various spices and/or herbs. Perhaps, like Svan salt (opposite page), this was a way of making the salt supply go further, as well as adding a lift of warmth and flavor to many dishes. There are classic combinations (for example, with dried red chile and cumin) as well as creative individual versions.

Here is one of my riffs on the possibilities. It's a beautiful bright green, and it has aromatic herbal heat from the combination of green chiles and mint and coriander leaves. In Uttarakhand, the blends are ground using a flat stone mortar with a heavy pestle that the cook rolls and grinds across the stone.

Makes 6 to 7 tablespoons/about 125 grams

1 teaspoon cumin
  seeds, lightly
  toasted

2 green cayenne
  chiles, stemmed,
  halved lengthwise,
  stripped of seeds
  and membranes,
  and coarsely
  chopped (to yield
  about 2 ounces/
  60 grams)

1 small garlic clove,
  smashed, peeled,
  and coarsely
  chopped

4 or 5 sprigs
  fresh coriander
  (cilantro)

About 10 fresh mint
  leaves

A ½-inch/1.25 cm
  piece fresh ginger,
  peeled and minced

3 tablespoons
  coarse sea salt or
  coarse pickling salt

*You'll need a spice
grinder or mortar
and pestle, a small
food processor
or a stone mortar
(see headnote), a
parchment paper–
lined tray or a plate,
and a glass jar for
storage.*

Use a spice grinder or mortar to grind the cumin to a powder. Transfer to a small food processor or a stone mortar, add all the remaining ingredients, and process or pound to as smooth a paste as possible.

Spread the mixture out on a parchment paper-lined tray or a plate and set aside to dry for a day or two, stirring and turning the mixture occasionally to expose all of it to the air.

Store in a clearly labeled glass jar in a cool, dark place. The flavors and color will fade after about 6 months.

SVAN SALT

The intensity of this delicious salt mirrors the intensity of the people who live in Svaneti, high in the mountains of Georgia by the Russian border. People there are self-sufficient, and they're proud of their reputation as the repository of Georgian tradition. For centuries, the region had no road access to the rest of Georgia, just tracks; in winter, it was completely isolated. There's a remarkable 1932 documentary called *Salt for Svanetia* that shows the harshness of life at that time and the suffering in winter, when there were often severe shortages of salt. Perhaps the flavored-salt tradition developed as a way of extending the precious supply.

Svan salt incorporates the perfume of spice and the fragrance of the herb garden, and it is used to season all kinds of savory dishes, both vegetarian and meat-based. Every household has its own version. I like it in simmered meat stews and in bean soups. You can also put it out as a table condiment.

Feel free to alter the proportions here; individuality is the hallmark of Svan life, so suit yourself. The recipe makes a lot, but it keeps for months and also makes a great gift for friends.

Makes about 4 cups/650 grams

1 large or 2 small heads garlic

1 cup/280 grams coarse sea salt

1 cup/50 grams dried dill

1 cup/180 grams ground coriander

¼ cup/45 grams ground fenugreek

½ cup/35 grams powdered dried fenugreek leaves (see Glossary)

½ cup/35 grams powdered dried marigold

3 tablespoons ground caraway

3 tablespoons cayenne or other dried red chile powder

You will need a large cleaver or knife, a food processor or large mortar and pestle, and several glass jars for storage.

Soak the head(s) of garlic in lukewarm water for 20 minutes; this will make it easier to peel. Separate and peel the cloves, then smash them with the side of a cleaver or large knife. Set aside.

Place the remaining ingredients in a food processor or a large mortar and process or pound to a fine powder. Add the garlic and process or pound to blend it in completely.

Spread the mixture out on a parchment paper-lined tray and set aside to dry for several days, stirring it occasionally to expose it all to the air. Store in several glass jars, clearly labeled, in a cool, dark place. The flavors will fade after about 1 year.

ACADIAN SALTED SCALLIONS

Salted scallions—*oignons salées*—are a staple of the Acadian pantry. The Acadians are descendants of colonists from France who, in the early 1600s, settled fertile areas of present-day Nova Scotia, creating prosperous farm communities. The British took control of the area about a century later, and then in the years 1755 to 1763, the Acadians were deported by the British and their lands seized. Many died as they were transported to various English and French colonies. Some ended up in Louisiana (the term *Acadian* is the origin of the word Cajun), while others returned and settled in more isolated and generally less fertile parts of Nova Scotia and New Brunswick. Acadians have a distinctive culinary culture and their language is a distinctive version of French.

In the Acadian kitchen, salted scallions play a role similar to that of Svan salt in Georgia (see page 45) or herbes salées (see page 49) in Quebec: they are a taste of summer in winter, and they can be used as an aromatic seasoning all year round. Simon Thibault says that although fresh scallions and salt can be substituted in any dish, there's something about the long, slow marriage of the greens and salt that gives these a special flavor. I urge you to take a moment in the summer to chop scallions and mix them with plenty of coarse pickling salt.

Simon tells me that these days most Acadian cooks use less salt in their oignons salées than was traditional, because they can now be stored in the refrigerator.

But I prefer to follow the traditional approach, using a large amount of salt, and to keep my jar of oignons salées out on the counter instead of in the fridge.

Makes about 2½ cups/400 grams

½ pound/225 grams scallions, well washed and trimmed

Generous ¾ cup/ 225 grams coarse pickling salt (see Note)

You will need a sharp knife, a large ceramic or glass bowl, and one or more glass jars for storage.

Finely slice the scallions crosswise with a sharp chef's knife or other large knife. Transfer them to a large ceramic or glass bowl and add about one-third of the salt, to cover them completely. Use your hands (my preference) or a wooden spoon to mix the scallions thoroughly with the salt, kneading them a little. The green parts of the scallion will look as if they're well speckled with white crystals. Then add another one-third of the salt and mix again very thoroughly. Set aside overnight to let the salt do its work of pulling moisture out of the scallions.

The next morning, you'll see some liquid at the bottom of the bowl, a salty brine, and the volume of scallions will have shrunk a little. Add the remaining salt and mix well, so that once more the scallion greens look dotted with white crystals.

Transfer the mixture and its liquid to one or more clean glass jars, packing it in, seal with the lids, and label clearly. Store in a cool place, out of the sun. The flavors will fade after about 1 year.

NOTE: *If you'd like to make a larger quantity of salted scallions, know that you need a weight of salt that is about equal to the weight of the scallions. If you don't have a scale, that translates into about 4 packed cups/250–275 grams chopped scallion to 1 cup/ 260 grams salt.*

HERBES SALÉES DE MON JARDIN

Québécois herbes salées, like Acadian oignons salées (page 46) and Georgian green *ajika* (page 92), is a way of preserving summer flavor into the winter. Like them, it depends on heavy salting.

An assortment of fresh herbs is finely chopped and combined with chopped carrot and a portion of the salt and then refrigerated overnight; the next day, the brine is drained away and the remaining salt is added to the herbs. The traditional mixture of herbs in Quebec includes the local favorites: *sariette* (summer savory), celery or celery leaves, scallions or leek and/or chives, parsley, a little oregano or thyme, and sometimes some rosemary.

After making the classic version, I decided to develop my own recipe, using the herbs from my back garden, because those are the ones I like and use in my cooking. For the ingredients and proportions in the classic recipe, see the Note.

This recipe calls for about 4 packed cups herbs (see the Glossary for any unfamiliar herbs). You may prefer other herbs and other proportions; I invite you to play with your favorites. Just keep the scallions or chives and parsley, along with the chopped carrot, as a base, and improvise from there. If you include stronger-tasting herbs such as rosemary and thyme, use smaller quantities of them.

Use this as an herbal flavoring and a salty seasoning. If you are using it to flavor a soup, for example, don't season with salt until after you have added your herbes salées.

NOTE: *I hand-chop the herbs as fine as I have the patience for. You could instead do a coarse chop and then grind them in a food processor or blender.*

Makes about 4 cups/650 grams

1 cup/30 grams finely chopped sorrel

1 cup/50 grams finely chopped scallions (white and light green parts)

½ cup/20 grams finely chopped fresh flat-leaf parsley leaves and fine stems

½ cup/24 grams finely chopped garlic chives

½ cup/15 grams finely chopped fresh shiso (perilla)

¼ cup/10 grams finely chopped fresh tarragon

¼ cup/5 grams finely chopped fresh basil

1 tablespoon finely chopped fresh lovage

1 small to medium carrot, peeled and finely chopped

1½ cups/390 grams coarse pickling salt

You will need a medium bowl, a fine sieve, and a few glass jars for storage.

Place the chopped herbs in a bowl and add the carrot and ½ cup/130 grams of the salt. Mix very thoroughly with your hands, then cover and refrigerate overnight.

The next day, transfer the mixture to a fine sieve set over a bowl and press the herbs against the mesh to drain them. Discard the brine and return the mixture to the bowl. Add the remaining 1 cup/260 grams salt and mix well. Transfer to one or more glass jars and label clearly.

Store in a cool, dark place for the first week. After that, you can keep your jar(s) of herbes salées out on the counter.

NOTE: *Proportions for the classic Quebec herbes salées are 1 cup each chopped scallions and parsley; ½ cup each chopped celery leaves, chives, and summer savory; and 1 cup chopped carrot. Combine with 1¼ cups/ 325 grams coarse salt in two stages.*

VEGETABLES & FRUITS

SALT WORKS IN FRUIT AND VEGETABLE preservation by drawing liquid out by osmosis. The liquid mixes with the salt and creates a brine, which is then reabsorbed by the fruits or vegetables and transforms them in various ways.

A low-percentage salt environment (2 to 5 percent salt) discourages spoilage microbes and encourages the growth of lactic acid bacteria (LAB), which do the work of fermentation. The result is a complex, tangy flavor and a softer texture.

A high-percentage salt environment (about 20 percent salt) prevents all microbial activity and results in crisp vegetables whose original water content has been replaced by brine.

Several of the ingredients in the recipes here—in the cucumber pickles, pickled mustard greens, and salted onions—are transformed by brief salting. Many of the useful larder ingredients in this chapter, including the chopped red chiles, kimchi, salted lemons, and green mango pickle, are salted *and* fermented; the salt controls and protects the fermentation.

HUNAN-STYLE SALTED RED CHILES

The jars of bright red chopped chiles that result from this simple recipe, freely adapted from the recipe for *duo la jiao* in Fuchsia Dunlop's excellent *Revolutionary Chinese Cookbook*, are a joy to look at and a larder treasure. They come from Mao Zedong's home province of Hunan. After they've fermented for two weeks, the chiles have a mild heat, a slight sweetness, and a pleasurable depth of flavor. They have become regulars on my table. Put them out as a condiment with any meal, add a few to dishes as you cook, or toss a few slices of chile into hot noodle soups just before serving.

Makes two 2-cup/500 ml jars (about 500 grams)

1 pound/450 grams blemish-free red cayenne chiles (25 to 30 long chiles), washed and dried

¼ cup/65 grams coarse pickling salt

You will need a medium bowl and two 2-cup/500 ml glass jars.

Trim the stems off the chiles and discard. Cut the chiles crosswise into approximately ½-inch/1 cm slices, leaving the seeds in. Place in a bowl, add 3 tablespoons of the salt, and mix well.

Transfer the salted chiles to two clean 2-cup/500 ml glass jars and top with the remaining salt. Seal tightly and store in a cool place, out of the sun, for about 2 weeks before using. The chiles will soften and give off a little liquid as they ferment, and the salt will control the bacteria, leaving them sweet tasting.

Once you open the jars, store in the refrigerator, where they will keep for many months.

SPICED GREEN MANGO PICKLE
with Mustard Oil

Mango trees are big, and when a mature tree is in fruit, that means a lot of mangoes! One way of dealing with the abundance is to preserve some of the green fruit, tart and firm, in a delicious spiced pickle like this one. People in the West associate green mangoes with sweet chutneys; this is instead a salt pickle, and delectable. There are many different green mango pickle recipes from across India, because the seasonal overabundance of mangoes is something all communities take advantage of. This Punjabi-style recipe, with its intense spiced flavors and tartness, has joined my list of favorite condiments.

The classic pickling method, used here, is to let the salted spiced chopped mango sit in a jar in the sunshine for 4 or 5 days. During that time, the salt draws moisture out of the fruit, resulting in a thick spiced liquid that coats the fruit as the flavors mature and blend. The classic version uses only mustard oil, but in deference to those who find mustard oil very pungent, I have cut it with sunflower oil. Use whatever proportion of oils you wish.

Makes about 7 cups/2 kg

2¼ to 2½ pounds/1 to 1.2 kg green (unripe) mangoes, well washed

¼ cup/60 grams fenugreek seeds

¼ cup/55 grams mustard seeds

¼ cup/36 grams fennel seeds

¼ cup/34 grams nigella seeds

2 tablespoons ground turmeric

¼ cup/28 grams cayenne

½ cup/130 grams coarse pickling salt

2 cups/480 ml mustard oil, plus more if needed

1 cup/240 ml sunflower or other vegetable oil, plus more if needed

You will need a vegetable peeler, a paring knife, a large bowl, a small heavy skillet, a medium bowl, a spice grinder or mortar and pestle, several spoons, and a 2-quart/ 2 liter glass jar or two smaller jars, preferably widemouthed.

Peel the mangoes with a vegetable peeler. Cut the flesh off the stones with a paring knife and chop into ¾-inch/2 cm pieces; discard any discolored parts. Set the flesh aside in a large bowl.

Lightly toast the fenugreek seeds in a small heavy skillet over medium heat until just aromatic. Set aside to cool a little.

Use a spice grinder or mortar to coarsely grind the mustard seeds. Transfer to a medium bowl. Coarsely grind the toasted fenugreek seeds and add to the bowl. Add the fennel seeds, nigella seeds, and turmeric and stir well. Add the cayenne and salt and stir again.

Add the spice blend to the mango pieces and stir and turn to coat all the fruit. Add ¼ cup/60 ml each of the mustard oil and sunflower or other oil and stir and turn to distribute the oil throughout the mixture.

Transfer the fruit to a 2-quart/2 liter glass jar or two smaller jars, squeezing it in a little to fit. Top with the lid(s) and place in the hot sun in a window, or outside, for 4 to 5 days. Each evening, take off the lid(s) and stir the fruit with a clean spoon, bringing the liquid and flavorings on the bottom back up to the top. After the first day, the fruit will have given off liquid and shrunk. After 4 or 5 days, taste the fruit. It should be somewhat salty, but the spices will still taste quite raw.

Because the fruit will have shrunk, you may want to transfer the pickle to a smaller jar or jars. If you are switching jars, empty the pickle out into a large bowl, with all the liquid, add the remaining 1¾ cups/420 ml mustard oil and ¾ cup/180 ml sunflower or other oil and mix well, then transfer to one or more clean jars. If not, add the remaining oils to the mangoes, distributing them evenly if you used two jars. The oil should cover the pickle by at least 1 inch/2.5 cm. Add more oil if needed.

Set aside for a month to mature, then eat with pleasure. This pickle does not need to be refrigerated and keeps indefinitely.

QUICK CUCUMBER PICKLES

I learned this easy salted cucumber pickle from my friend Gord Sato. This take on his mother's recipe is a fine example of *shiozuke*, or Japanese salt pickles.

The cucumbers have a nice little crunch even after being brined and bathed in a dressing, which makes them an excellent accompaniment to many meals, from Japanese breakfasts to quick sandwich lunches to substantial dinners.

Thin-skinned very fresh small cucumbers, either Japanese cucumbers or the cucumbers labeled Persian or Lebanese or Turkish, work best here. If necessary, you can substitute English (seedless) cucumbers, although they won't keep their crispness as well. Avoid regular thick-skinned cucumbers: the flesh is too soft and watery, and their skin is too tough.

The cucumbers are sliced, salted, and brined for at least 8 hours, or overnight. The next day, they're rinsed and then soaked for 6 or more hours in a tart-sweet dressing. There are two dressings here for you to try. The first is slightly sweeter, with a more pronounced soy sauce flavor, while the second has a smoother, more blended taste. Any leftover pickle will keep in the refrigerator for up to a week.

Makes about 4 cups/700 grams

2 pounds/1 kg Japanese or Persian cucumbers (see headnote)

2 tablespoons/35 grams coarse sea salt or pickling salt

One or two pinches dried wakame (seaweed) strands, soaked in water to cover for an hour (optional)

DRESSING #1

1 tablespoon rice vinegar

1½ teaspoons sugar

1 tablespoon soy sauce

½ teaspoon toasted sesame oil

DRESSING #2

1 tablespoon mirin

1 tablespoon rice vinegar

¼ teaspoon sugar

2 teaspoons light soy sauce (see Note)

½ teaspoon toasted sesame oil

2 teaspoons toasted sesame seeds

You will need a knife, a bowl, a small tsukemono (Japanese pickle press; the top has a spring in it to maintain pressure on the salted vegetables) or a glass or other nonreactive container and a small lid or flat plate, a tray, a small bowl, a small saucepan, and a storage container.

Wash the cucumbers. Cut off both ends of each one, slice crosswise on a slight diagonal into ⅓- to ½-inch/1 cm slices, and put in a bowl. Add the salt and mix with your hands to distribute it well.

continued

Transfer to a tsukemono (Japanese pickle press) or a bowl or other nonreactive container. Close the press, or cover the slices with a small lid or flat plate, then top with a weight such as a full can or jar (the weight needs to be just heavy enough to keep the cucumbers submerged but not to distort or flatten them). Place on a tray to catch any overflow and refrigerate for at least 8 hours, or overnight.

The cucumbers will have given off a lot of water and be sitting in brine. Drain off and discard the brine. Rinse the slices thoroughly in cold water and gently press out the water. Have a taste; they'll be fresh and slightly briny. Transfer to a nonreactive container with a lid. If using the wakame strands, drain and add now.

If using Dressing #1: Mix together all the ingredients in a small bowl and pour over the cucumbers. Stir carefully to ensure that all the slices are coated.

If using Dressing #2: Combine the mirin, rice vinegar, and sugar in a small saucepan and bring to a boil over medium heat. Let simmer for several moments, then pour into a small bowl and let cool to room temperature. Add the soy sauce and sesame oil to the cooled liquid and stir, then pour over the cucumber slices and stir and turn gently to ensure all the slices are coated.

You can serve these right away, but they are best if you refrigerate them for at least 6 hours so they can steep in their dressing. Just before serving, sprinkle on the toasted sesame seeds. Leftovers can be stored in the fridge for up to a week, although the texture will start to soften after 4 or 5 days.

NOTE: *Light soy sauce is milder tasting and often less intensely salty than regular soy sauce. I use Kikkoman low-sodium soy sauce, which is widely available, for this pickle.*

JAPANESE SALT-PRESERVED PLUMS AND PLUM PASTE

Just thinking about umeboshi plums makes my mouth water. Their salty tartness is a great way to wake up your palate. When I was in Japan long ago doing research for *Seductions of Rice*, Mariko Doi, the friend I stayed with near Kyoto, suggested that we take a cooking class together with a teacher she admired named Mrs. Marayama. She had lived through the privations of the Second World War and was steeped in the vegetarian tradition. I learned so much in those few hours, but my most vivid memory is of the teacher encouraging us to switch from white rice to brown, and to start our day by eating one or two umeboshi with our morning rice to wake up our digestion, which would lead to better health.

I don't eat umeboshi every day, but I do turn to them often, especially if I am feeling lethargic. They call me to order in some way, bringing my tongue, my whole mouth, and then my spirits, to life.

Preserved plums are traditionally made in June, when *ume*—a Japanese plum-like fruit that is closely related to apricot—are in season. The fruits are rinsed and carefully picked over to make sure they are perfect, with no breaks in the skin. They are soaked in water overnight and then mixed with 10 to 12 percent salt by weight and put in a barrel or other large container. They're topped with a heavily weighted lid and sealed off from the air. The salt and the pressure of the lid cause the fruits to release their sour liquid and shrivel, and the liquid mixes with the salt to make a brine that gradually immerses the plums. Sometimes red shiso leaves are added to the brine for color and another layer of flavor. After two to three weeks, the fruit is lifted out and dried in the sun. The brine is saved to make vinegar (*ume-su*). If red shiso is part of the process, the brine and plums are red-tinted. Otherwise, the plums are a medium brownish color.

Once they're ready, the plums can be stored whole in a glass or plastic container, or they can be pitted and mashed into a paste.

You can find umeboshi plums and umeboshi paste in Japanese and Korean grocery stores. I usually buy the shiso-flavored plums.

OPTIONS: *If you'd like to try making your own umeboshi, there's a detailed recipe in Nancy Singleton Hachisu's* Preserving the Japanese Way *(see Resources).*

SALTED SHISO LEAVES

Shiso is the Japanese name for an herb that is also known in English as perilla, or beefsteak plant. The fresh and the salted leaves, but also the salted seeds and the oil pressed from the seeds, are all traditional Japanese ingredients. Because shiso grows for only a few months in the year, having a way of preserving its intense flavor is a real bonus.

The salting takes a few days. After that, use the leaves either as wrappers for onigiri (rice balls) or as you would treat fresh shiso: finely chopped in salads, sprinkled onto grilled fish, or sprinkled onto pasta or noodles.

You can also dry the salted leaves; see below.

30 or more red or green shiso leaves, or a mix	**Fine sea salt or fine pickling salt**	*You'll need paper towels or a fine-mesh wire rack, a nonreactive container with a lid, plastic wrap, and something to weight the leaves.*

Rinse the leaves and lay them out on a flat surface lined with paper towels or on a rack to dry completely. Sprinkle the bottom of a glass or other nonreactive container lightly with salt and then layer the leaves in the container, sprinkling a little salt on each layer. You don't need a lot of salt: I use 1½ to 2 teaspoons/9 to 12 grams fine salt for about a hundred leaves.

Cover the leaves with plastic wrap, then top with a weight of some kind to press the leaves. Cover and refrigerate. The leaves will give off some liquid as they stand, so after a few days you'll see them sitting in a little tinted brine.

At this point, remove the plastic, seal the container, and refrigerate. The brined leaves will become soft and beautiful within a few more days. After a couple of months, the leaves will start to disintegrate a little; they can still be chopped and used in salads and other dishes.

To make dried salted shiso leaves: Remove the leaves from the brine after 4 or 5 days, place them on a rack or parchment paper-lined surface, and let dry out completely, in the open air or in a warm, sunny, well-ventilated space indoors. Alternatively, dry them in a very low oven, 150°F/65°C, with the door propped slightly ajar.

Once the leaves are completely dried out and papery, store them in a brown paper bag in a cupboard until you are ready to tear them up and grind them to use as a sprinkled seasoning (*furikake*), on their own or with other flavorings; see Salted Shiso and Sesame Furikake, page 197.

SALT-PRESERVED LEMONS

I first read about salt-preserved lemons, known as *citrons confits* in French, in Claudia Roden's groundbreaking and now-classic *Book of Middle Eastern Food*. There are two versions in her book, one in the recipe section for Moroccan-style preserved lemons, and the other in a note about sliced salted lemons in the small glossary of flavorings.

The jars of whole preserved lemons on display in markets in Morocco look beautiful. Those lemons are quartered but not completely sliced through, so that the quarters stay connected at the base of the fruit. The cut surfaces are rubbed with salt before the lemons are stuffed into jars.

If instead the lemons are cut crosswise into slices—a style more common in the eastern part of North Africa—they are much easier to pack tightly into a jar and to remove when you need them; I find it a more practical option.

There are only two ingredients: coarse pickling salt or sea salt and lemons, preferably organic. The preservation depends only on salt, not on pressure-canning or cooking. I call for regular (tart thick-skinned) lemons here.

After they've been in the jar for a few months, preserved lemons will be very soft, despite their thick skin, and sweeter tasting. They are a very versatile pantry staple, available to give flavor to everything from sauces to roast chicken to cake (see the Index).

For every pound of lemons, you will need about ¼ cup/65 grams coarse sea salt or pickling salt. I find it easiest to make one large jar at a time, using just under 2 pounds/900 grams lemons. I've found that if instead I use smaller jars, I can't fit in quite as much lemon, even if I cut the slices in half.

Makes about 2 pounds/1 kg

About 2 pounds/900 grams lemons (7 to 10 medium-large lemons), preferably organic

About ½ cup/130 grams coarse sea salt or coarse pickling salt

About 1 tablespoon mild-tasting extra-virgin olive oil or nut oil

You will need a cutting board, a sharp knife, and one 1-quart/1 liter or two 2-cup/500 ml wide-mouthed glass jars.

Sterilize one 1-quart/1 liter or two 2-cup/500 ml widemouthed glass jars and their lids in the dishwasher or in boiling water, then air-dry.

Wash the lemons; if using nonorganic fruit, scrub them well in hot water, then rinse. Trim off and discard the small nubs at both ends of each lemon.

continued

Cut several of the lemons into ¼-inch/½ cm slices, flicking out any seeds you encounter. Sprinkle a little salt on the bottom of the large jar or one of the smaller jars. Add a layer of slices to cover the bottom of the jar, then sprinkle on some of the salt. Continue to layer the lemon slices and salt, slicing more lemons as needed. Press down occasionally on the slices to force out air and give you more room, and tuck smaller slices into the gaps to even out the layers. Continue to pack the slices and salt to just short of the top of the jar, and press down again to compress them. The lemon juice given off by the slices should now come up to the top of the jar. If it does not, then squeeze a lemon or two and add the juice so that the slices are covered. Add the oil (or half the oil if using two jars) to help seal off the lemons and juice from the air. Put on the lid. Repeat with the second jar if using. Set aside, away from direct sunlight.

The lemons will be transformed after about 1 month, and they will continue to evolve after that and become sweeter. Refrigerate after opening. They keep indefinitely.

NOTE: *Claudia Roden includes a dash of cayenne with each layer of lemon slices; follow her example, if you wish. I prefer to leave them without extra flavoring, for greater flexibility. I can always add spices or aromatics when I use them.*

SALTED RED ONIONS

Salt tames onions. They sweeten and soften, lose most of their raw pungency, and become a very useful and adaptable ingredient. Salted onions add flavor to sandwiches and to various dishes as a garnish, and they can also take center stage, as in a Central Asian–style salad (page 230).

Makes a generous 1 cup/about 200 grams

About 2 cups/225 grams thinly sliced red onions (about 2 medium onions)

1 tablespoon/16 grams coarse sea salt or coarse pickling salt

You will need a colander, a large bowl, and a storage container.

SALTED CABBAGE AND SALTED KALE

Salt can also tame the somewhat tough texture of many greens, such as raw kale and cabbage, allowing them to shine in salads. Salting softens them and brings out their sweetness.

Coarsely chop the leaves, then sprinkle a little coarse sea salt or coarse pickling salt over them and massage them firmly with your fingers for several minutes. Transfer the leaves to a colander and set aside (in the sink or over a bowl) for 15 to 20 minutes. The leaves will give off some water and become softer. Rinse them, chop them finer if you wish, and use in a chopped mixed salad or in stir-fries and other cooked dishes. For example, substitute several large handfuls of the salted cabbage or kale for the Brussels sprouts in Brussels Sprouts and Potatoes with Salt Pork (page 310). Or toss into a soup.

Place the onion slices in a colander, sprinkle on the salt, and massage it into the onions a little with your fingertips. Set the colander over a bowl to catch the drips and set aside for 30 minutes. The onions will soften as they shed some of their liquid.

Rinse the onions thoroughly, squeeze gently, and pat dry. Transfer to a container and store in the refrigerator for up to 2 days before using.

To use the onions as a topping or flavoring: Add the juice of 1 lime to the bowl and toss to mix well. Use as a topping for hamburgers, sandwiches, or gravlax (page 142), or as an accent in chopped tomato salads.

QUICK SALT-PRESERVED MUSTARD GREENS

Mustard greens are one of the workhorses of the kitchen (and garden). They can be tossed into a stir-fry or eaten raw, they lend themselves to pickling, and they survive cold weather. This recipe is adapted from one by Carolyn Phillips, author of *All Under Heaven*. The preserving technique is an easy way to get extra flavor and longer shelf life from tender mustard greens.

In the springtime, when the first mustard greens become available, start with a few bunches (about 1 pound/450 grams). The only other ingredients are salt, turmeric, cayenne, if you like, and a little patience. Though the purely Chinese version does not include either turmeric or cayenne, I like to include turmeric, and I sometimes add cayenne to give the greens a little warmth.

Makes a little less than
1 pound/400 grams

About 1 pound/450 grams
tender (young) mustard
greens

About 1 tablespoon/15 grams
fine sea salt

About ¼ teaspoon ground
turmeric (optional)

About ¼ teaspoon cayenne
(optional)

You will need a large bowl, several tea towels or other cotton cloths, a large bowl, a small bowl, gloves, a cutting board and knife, and a glass or ceramic container with a lid.

Fill your sink or a large bowl with water and toss in the greens. Swirl to wash well, drain, and repeat twice more, or until no longer gritty.

Lay a couple of kitchen towels on a counter or other flat surface, in the sun if possible. Lift the greens out of the water, shake off excess water, and lay them on the towels. Use another towel or two to pat them dry. Turn them over and keep patting and drying for a good 5 minutes, until all surfaces are dry. (This will go more quickly in the sun, of course.)

Transfer the greens to a large bowl. Mix the salt with the turmeric and cayenne, if using, in a small bowl. You will want to wear gloves for the next step to protect your hands from the turmeric, which will dye them yellow. Sprinkle on about half the mixture and rub it onto the greens with your fingertips as thoroughly as you can. After a few minutes, sprinkle on the remaining mixture and continue to rub it onto the leaves and stems for 3 or 4 minutes more. It may feel as if you're not achieving much, but in fact the salt is already working on the greens to draw out water. You'll feel them start to wilt.

Flooded rice terraces in early springtime, on the Noto Peninsula, above the waves of the Sea of Japan

JAPANESE OVERNIGHT MUSTARD GREENS PICKLE

When I stayed on the Noto Peninsula, a friend of my host brought over an even quicker salt-pickle of mustard greens that had a fresh clean taste. Start with tender young mustard greens. Toss them into boiling water and blanch them for about 1 minute, then drain and squeeze dry. Chop into short lengths, place in a bowl, add fine sea salt (about 2 teaspoons/10 grams per pound/450 grams), and rub it in. Cover and let stand at room temperature for 1 day before using. Serve as a vegetable side after rinsing off the salt and squeezing dry (allow about ¼ pound/110 grams per person). Refrigerate any leftovers.

Turn the greens out onto a large cutting board and chop into roughly ½-inch/1 cm lengths. Transfer to a glass or ceramic container, cover tightly, and refrigerate for 2 days.

Pour off the accumulated liquid from the greens. They are now ready to use, but they will keep for at least 10 days in the refrigerator.

Before using, rinse the greens well with cold water and squeeze dry. Chop more finely if you wish. Use as a side condiment/pickle or include in stir-fries.

OLIVES

Olives are a bit of a mystery. An olive picked ripe from the tree is bitter and astringent, not at all edible. How did early humans figure out that olives could be made edible, not just pressed for their oil?

The phenolic compound oleuropein (together with other phenolics) in olives makes them very bitter when first picked (oleuropein makes up about 14 percent of the fruit, including leaves and seeds). To draw it out, olives can be soaked in water, salted, or brined, or a combination. The simplest and oldest method is to wash and dry them, then layer them with salt.

Here are the instructions for dry-salting olives in case you have the good luck to be near an olive tree when the olives are fully ripe (they'll have turned black). You can scale the recipe up or down according to the amount you have; the basic proportion is 40 grams salt to 100 grams olives. It takes about a month to yield slightly wrinkled cured olives, which can then be stored in olive oil. If you like, flavor the oil with rinsed and dried aromatics, such as several sprigs of rosemary, a couple of dried red chiles, or strips of (preferably organic) lemon peel.

Makes about 2 pounds/1 kg

2¼ pounds/1 kg ripe fresh (black) olives

1½ cups/400 grams coarse pickling salt

Extra-virgin olive oil for storing

You will need a cotton cloth, a sharp knife, a glass jar or jars for curing, and several glass jars for storage.

Carefully wash the olives, then pick over them and discard any stems or leaves and any bruised or damaged fruits. Lay them out on a cotton cloth to dry completely.

Prick each olive with the tip of a sharp knife, to help the salt penetrate. Layer the olives with half the salt in a glass jar or jars: Start with a ¼-inch/½ cm layer of salt on the bottom, add a layer of olives no more than 2 olives deep, and continue alternating layers of salt and olives. Finish with a ¼-inch/½ cm layer of salt on top and put on the lid tightly.

Let the olives stand at room temperature, out of the sun, for about 10 days, turning the jar(s) upside down and back up again each day. As the salt draws out water, the olives will start to shrivel a little and the salt will become a mushy brine.

Pour off the brine and empty out the jar(s), then layer the olives again with the remaining salt. Let stand for about 10 days longer, again turning the jar(s) every day.

Girl harvesting olives, in the Atlas Mountains in Morocco

Rinse an olive and taste it. If it tastes a touch sweet with no bitterness, the olives are ready. If not, let them stand for another week or so, again turning the jar(s), before tasting again.

When they are ready, drain the olives, rinse quickly in a colander (you don't want them to reabsorb water), and lay out on a cotton cloth to dry completely; discard the salt and brine.

Sterilize one or more glass jars in the dishwasher or in boiling water and let dry. Fill the jar(s) with olives to come to about ¾ inch/2 cm below the rim(s), then pour in olive oil to cover them. Cover the jar(s) tightly and turn upside down and right side up several times to make sure that the olives are completely coated with the oil.

Store the olives in a cool, dark place for up to 6 months.

CAPERS

The flower buds of *Capparis spinosa*, a perennial bush that grows in the Mediterranean region and bears large white flowers, are preserved and used as a flavor accent. In Sicily, the buds are picked before they open and preserved in coarse salt. As they give off brine, the accumulated liquid is poured off and more salt added. Eventually they dry right out and look like dull green, wrinkled round seeds. In France, they are usually pickled in vinegar and salt, which gives them an acidic edge. If using salted capers, you'll need to soak them in a few changes of cool water; taste as you go and stop soaking once you like the salt level. If using pickled capers, simply rinse them briefly.

Capers can give a useful accent in salads or sprinkled on gravlax (page 142). Salted capers add an extra layer of intensity to cooked dishes such as the Spaghetti Puttanesca on page 333. Pickled capers are widely available; salted capers are more often sold in specialty shops.

SALTED WALNUTS AND SALTED ALMONDS

Soaking nuts in brine and then baking them transforms their flavor and their texture in wonderful ways. It also makes them more digestible. As they're such a favorite in my house, I often make a pound each of almonds and walnuts, working with two bowls and two baking sheets (and doubling the brine amounts). Plan ahead, because the nuts need to soak for at least 6 hours and take a good 8 hours to slow-roast.

Makes 1 pound/450 grams

4 cups/1 liter water

¼ cup/65 grams coarse pickling salt

1 pound/450 grams raw walnuts or almonds

You will need a scale, a large bowl, a cotton cloth or a lid for the bowl, one or two baking sheets lined with parchment paper, and glass jars for storage.

Combine the water and salt in a large bowl and stir until the salt is fully dissolved. Add the nuts. The water should cover them by at least half an inch; walnuts tend to float, so stir them to make sure that there's enough water for them to be fully submerged once they've absorbed a little of it. Let stand for at least 6 hours, or overnight, loosely covered with a cotton cloth or a lid.

Preheat the oven to 200°F/100°C.

Drain the nuts and rinse quickly under cold water. Spread out in a single layer on one or more parchment-lined baking sheets and bake for about 8 hours. Let cool completely before storing in a well-labeled glass jar.

NOTE: *Because nuts are rich in oils, these should be stored in the refrigerator or a cool place. Best eaten within 2 months.*

KIMCHI

Kimchi is a category of brined vegetable pickles from Korea, most often flavored with red chile powder and other aromatics. It's a cousin of the brined vegetables of China known as *suancai* (sour vegetable). Kimchi is eaten as a cross between a side salad and a condiment with many meals in Korea and used as an ingredient in stews and omelets, savory pancakes, and soups. Like many of the salt preserves in this book, kimchi originated as a way to safely store a harvest of fresh vegetables through the cold months of winter.

The world of kimchi is diverse and delicious. Though chile-seasoned napa cabbage (*baechu*) is the most common version, kimchi is also made with other vegetables, and it doesn't always include chile. The passion for kimchi, with its great flavor and flexibility, has now spread well beyond Korea.

Although baechu kimchi can be made anytime fresh napa cabbage is available, in Korea it is mostly made in late autumn, when large-batch kimchi making takes place in households all over the country. The kimchi is stored in heavy ceramic pots set into the ground or in a reliably cool place that is protected from frost. In addition to the winter stash, home cooks also prepare small batches at other times of year, like a kind of quick pickle, using whatever vegetables are in season; for example, cucumber, or the Korean radishes called *mu*. Commercially made kimchi is now available in grocery stores in Korea and many other places. Even so, kimchi is still prepared in many Korean households and then distributed to family members who live in small apartments and are unable to make their own.

The most familiar version of baechu kimchi is red with *gochugaru*, Korean chile powder, and sometimes with Korean chile paste, *gochujang*, as well. The heat varies, depending on the preferences of the cook, and so do the other flavorings. These most often include garlic, Korean soy sauce, and a little glutinous rice flour, along with one or more salt-fermented products from the sea, such as the anchovy-based fish sauce called *myulch aekjeot* (slightly thicker than Thai fish sauce) and salted shrimp, *saeujeot*. There is also a category of chile-free napa kimchi, called *baek kimchi*, or white kimchi, which is subtle and delicious. (For vegetarians, there are other options; see below.)

To make the kimchi, wedges of cabbage are immersed in a flavored brine and stored in a cool place while lactic acid fermentation takes place. There's good flavor after just a week, and it gets a little stronger as time goes on. The cabbage wedges are cut crosswise and served as a side dish.

Rather than making a large batch of kimchi each fall, you can make it in small batches from fresh vegetables in season and have a constant supply year-round. A small-batch project is less intimidating, and small batches give you the chance to experiment with different flavors.

I think the best "entry level" kimchi to try is radish kimchi, *kkakdugi*, made with Korean white radishes. The radishes are chopped into cubes and combined with salt and other ingredients to develop flavor. Radish kimchi is a quick-gratification preserve, as it's ready to taste in less than a week, though its flavor keeps evolving for a while.

I've also included two recipes for small-batch napa kimchi, one for the classic red kimchi and the other for a white kimchi that soaks in a brine delicately flavored with apple, pear, and onion.

Serve napa kimchi chopped up as a kind of cross between a condiment and a side salad, to complement a main course, or use it as a refreshing pickle or relish in a sandwich. It's also a great flavoring ingredient; see Kimchi Aioli (page 203), Kimchi Pancakes (page 321), and Kimchi Soup (page 216).

WHITE RADISH KIMCHI

The basic ingredient in this kimchi—kkakdugi kimchi is its Korean name—is the Korean white radish known as *mu*, which is round to oblong. It's smooth-skinned and white to pale tan, with a touch of pale green at the leafy end. The Korean white radishes available in North America tend to weigh a little more than 1 pound/450 grams each.

This recipe is a small one, calling for 2 average Korean radishes; or substitute the same weight of daikon. The radishes are cut into cubes, rubbed with salt to draw out some water, and then mixed with a paste of Korean chile powder, pureed apple and onion, minced ginger and garlic, and fish sauce (or soy sauce for a vegetarian version).

There's almost instant gratification with kkakdugi kimchi, as you can eat it with pleasure after only a few days, but it is really at its best after it's had about 2 weeks in the refrigerator. This version has medium heat and, once matured, a pleasing hint of sweetness.

Makes 1½ quarts/1.5 kg

2½ pounds/1.2 kg Korean white radishes or daikon (see headnote)

2 tablespoons/30 grams fine sea salt

1 tablespoon sugar

¼ cup/65 grams Korean red chile powder (gochugaru)

2 teaspoons rice flour or glutinous rice flour (or substitute all-purpose flour)

1 large or 2 small garlic cloves, minced

A ½-inch/1.25 cm piece of fresh ginger, peeled and minced

Greens from 2 or 3 scallions

Half a small yellow onion (1¾ ounces/50 grams), coarsely chopped

Half a medium apple (1¾ ounces/50 grams), cored and coarsely chopped

2 tablespoons Korean or Thai fish sauce (for a vegetarian version, substitute Korean or Japanese soy sauce)

You will need a knife, a large bowl, a medium bowl, a food processor or large mortar and pestle, a spoon, plastic gloves, a rubber spatula, three 2-cup/500 ml glass jars, and a tray.

Wash the radishes and trim off the stem ends and any little root hairs or blemishes, but don't peel them unless the skin is very damaged. Slice crosswise into about ½-inch-thick/1 cm disks, then cut those into approximate cubes (the Korean word *kkakdugi* refers to the fact that the radish is cubed). Place in a bowl, add the salt, and mix well with your hands. Set aside for an hour to give the salt time to draw water out of the radishes.

Meanwhile, prepare the flavor paste: Combine the sugar, chile powder, flour, garlic, and ginger in a medium bowl.

Cut the scallion greens into ½-inch/1 cm lengths and add to the bowl.

Place the onion and apple in a food processor or a large mortar and process or pound to a paste. Add to the other flavor paste ingredients, along with the fish sauce or soy sauce, and stir well to blend.

Drain the accumulated water from the radish cubes, but do not rinse them. Add the paste to the cubes and mix thoroughly with a wooden spoon or your hands (wearing plastic gloves to protect your skin from the chile heat) until all surfaces are coated with the paste.

Set three 2-cup/500 ml jars out on a tray. Using a spoon and/or gloved hands, transfer the coated cubes to the jars, pushing them down and forcing them in. It may seem impossible at first that they will fit, but they do in the end, with perseverance. Press down hard on the cubes to try to eliminate any remaining air pockets, then put on the lids.

Let the jars stand at cool room temperature (between 65 and 70°F/17 and 20°C) for 24 to 30 hours, then refrigerate. You might want to take a taste just before you refrigerate them, but they'll still taste a little raw then. You'll notice that flavors grow and deepen as you sample them over the next 10 days or so in the refrigerator. I find them delicious after a week has passed.

Keep the jars refrigerated, tightly sealed, and use clean tools—chopsticks or a fork or spoon—to lift the cubes out of the jars. This kimchi keeps almost indefinitely in the refrigerator.

continued

NAPA KIMCHI RECIPE NOTES AND BRINING INSTRUCTIONS

In Korea, napa cabbages grow to be enormous. Perhaps as a result, the recipes I have come across for "small batches" usually start with one large cabbage weighing about 5 pounds/2.25 kg.

Both of the napa kimchi recipes here are for small batches made with about 2.2 pounds/1 kg cabbage, the size the cabbages sold in North America usually are. You may want to make a bigger batch after you've made either of these for the first time. On the other hand, it's a nice thing to make smaller batches and prepare them sequentially, so that you always have some mature kimchi to eat and a fresh batch going. If you want to scale up, just increase the amounts proportionately.

For classic napa kimchi, the cabbage is sliced lengthwise into wedges. The salt is rubbed over all the layers of leaves at the start, and then later, after brining, the flavoring mix is smeared all over each leaf as well. Napa kimchi lovers swear that it tastes better when it's prepared with wedges, and I prefer the look of it too. But some people prefer to chop the cabbage into large bite-sized squares at the start, because it makes the process of flavoring the cabbage easier and quicker. (Instructions for both are given in the recipes.)

Brining the cabbage is a simple process: The leaves are first rubbed with salt and then left to soak in a 12 to 15 percent salt brine for at least 4 hours, or as long as overnight, until softened but not limp. If you can, use the coarse Korean sea salt called *cheonilyeom*. Then the cabbage pieces are rinsed and air-dried; I drape the wedges over a dish rack to drain and dry (see photo) for an hour or so. That gives me time to prepare the remaining ingredients for the kimchi, and to prepare my container(s). If you're making a smaller batch, using only one or two cabbages, it can all be done in less than 2 hours (and more quickly once you've had practice).

Makes enough for about 1 quart/1 kg Classic Red Kimchi (page 78) or White Baek Kimchi (page 81)

One 2- to 2½-pound/1 to 1.25 kg napa cabbage

About ⅔ cup/160 grams Korean sea salt or coarse sea salt

4 cups/1 liter water

You will need a knife, a small bowl, a large bowl, a board or other flat weight, plastic wrap or a tea towel, and a rack for drying, such as a dish rack.

Remove and discard any tough outer leaves from the cabbage. Cut it lengthwise into 4 or 5 wedges. If you are planning to make chopped kimchi, rather than kimchi in wedges, it's easier to do the brining in wedges and chop it later.

Put about 3 tablespoons of the salt in a small bowl and set it next to your work surface. Working from the outside in of each wedge, rub some of the salt vigorously onto the surface of each leaf. Set the wedges aside.

Put the water in a large bowl, add the remaining salt, and stir to dissolve it completely. Place the wedges in the brine and put a board or other flat weight on top to help keep them submerged. Cover loosely and set aside to brine for at least 4 hours, or as long as overnight. You don't want the leaves to wilt completely, just to soften.

Remove the cabbage from the brine and rinse it. Drape the cabbage wedges over a rack (such as a dish rack) and leave for an hour or two to drain and dry before proceeding.

CLASSIC RED KIMCHI

Traditional kimchi is given extra umami with the addition of fish or shellfish or other foods from the sea. I use kombu (seaweed) to flavor the brine and I also include both chopped saeujeot (Korean brined shrimp; see Glossary) and fish sauce. For a vegetarian version, use 2 tablespoons Korean or Japanese soy sauce instead of the fish sauce and brined shrimp. This recipe yields a mildly chile-hot kimchi; double the amount of chile flakes for more intense heat.

You will need to start at least 6 hours, and up to a day, ahead to prepare the brined and air-dried cabbage; see page 77.

Makes about 1 quart/about 1 kg

¾ cup/180 ml water

A small piece of kombu, rinsed

2 teaspoons glutinous rice flour (see Glossary)

¼ cup/25 grams Korean chile flakes

2 tablespoons finely chopped salted shrimp (saeujeot; see headnote for a vegetarian version)

4 teaspoons Korean or Thai fish sauce (see headnote for a vegetarian version)

4 medium garlic cloves, minced

A ½-inch/1.25 cm piece of fresh ginger, peeled and grated

1 teaspoon white sesame seeds

Scant ½ pound/225 grams Korean radish or daikon, peeled and cut into fine matchsticks (about 2½ cups/200 grams)

About one-third of a Korean pear (or substitute a whole Bosc or other firm pear), peeled, cored, and cut into matchsticks (about 1 cup/150 grams; optional)

2 scallions, trimmed, cut lengthwise in half and then crosswise into 1-inch/2.5 cm lengths, or 8 to 10 garlic chives, cut into 1-inch/2.5 cm lengths

One 2- to 2½-pound/1 to 1.25 kg head napa cabbage, cut into wedges, salted, brined, rinsed, and air-dried (see page 77)

Fine sea salt if needed

You will need two small saucepans, spoons, a small bowl, a large wide bowl, gloves, a knife, a widemouthed 1-quart/1 liter glass jar with a tight-fitting lid or two 2-cup/500 ml jars, and a rimmed tray to hold the jars.

Heat ½ cup/125 ml of the water in a small saucepan, add the kombu, and simmer over low heat (don't boil) for 5 minutes. Remove the kombu and set the broth aside to cool in a bowl (save the kombu for another purpose).

Stir the rice flour into the remaining ¼ cup/60 ml water in a small saucepan and heat gently, stirring, until the mixture thickens to a paste, about a minute. Set aside in a small bowl.

Mix the chile flakes, chopped salted shrimp, fish sauce, and rice paste in a wide bowl. Add enough of the broth to thoroughly moisten the chile flakes; set any remaining broth aside. Add the garlic, ginger, and sesame seeds to the bowl

and mix. Add the radish, the chopped pear, if using, and scallions or garlic chives and mix well. Let rest for 10 minutes to allow flavors to blend.

Wearing gloves to protect your hands from the chile heat, blend the chile mixture again to ensure that everything is well coated with flavor.

If you want to use cabbage wedges for the kimchi, trim the tough core off each one, leaving the leaves attached, and discard. Put one of the cabbage wedges in the bowl of chile paste and rub the paste mixture all over each of the leaves, starting with the outside leaves and working in. Then pull the wedge together into a tight bundle and place in a widemouthed 1-quart/1 liter glass jar. Repeat with the remaining wedges and chile paste, pressing them tightly together to eliminate air pockets. Top off the jar with any scraps or detached leaves.

Or, if you want to use chopped cabbage, cut out the tough core pieces and discard, then chop the leaves into approximately 1-inch/2.5 cm squares. Add them all to the bowl of chile paste and mix well, rubbing the pieces with your fingers to coat each one with flavor. Transfer to the jar, pressing down to eliminate air pockets, and cover the top with any scraps.

Use the remaining reserved broth, or water if you don't have any broth, to rinse out the chile paste bowl and then pour the liquid over the cabbage. Press down once more to compress the wedges or pieces tightly and eliminate air pockets. If the liquid does not cover the cabbage completely, add a little salted cold water (2 teaspoons/10 g fine sea salt per 1 cup/225 ml water). Make sure there is a 1-inch/2.5 cm space above the top of the liquid in the jar. Put on the lid tightly and set aside on a rimmed tray at room temperature, out of direct sun, for 2 or 3 days (2 days in warm weather, 3 in cooler weather).

After the first day, taste the liquid; it should taste a little salty. If it doesn't, add a little fine sea salt (about ½ teaspoon/3 grams).

After a couple of days at room temperature, the liquid should start to taste a little sour, indicating that fermentation has started. (If need be, leave it for an extra day and taste again.) That's the signal to store the jars in your refrigerator. The kimchi will continue to gradually ferment, growing a little sourer over time. You can start eating it anytime you like.

To serve, use clean chopsticks or another implement to lift one or more portions out of the jar. Cover the remaining cabbage again with any stray leaves, seal tightly, and refrigerate again. This kimchi will keep almost indefinitely in the refrigerator.

If after a couple of months your kimchi is getting too strong tasting, use it as an ingredient instead of serving it on its own: Finely chop it for an omelet or toss with boiled potatoes (see page 29). Or use it to make Kimchi Aioli (page 203), Kimchi Soup (page 216), or Kimchi Pancakes (page 321). You could also substitute it, finely chopped, for the bacalao in the Spanish tortilla on page 273.

WHITE (BAEK) KIMCHI

Baek kimchi cures in a brine flavored with fruit, nuts, and aromatics, a luxurious set of mild, slightly sweet flavors. The recipe doesn't use any chiles, or any fish sauce or salted shrimp—which might overpower the flavors of the brine—so it is suitable for vegetarians.

This mild-tasting kimchi is a real pleasure, especially for anyone who dislikes chile heat. Serve it to accompany foods with more delicate flavors (poached white fish, for example), or as a complement to dishes that include dandelion greens or endive or other ingredients with a bitter edge. It is a delicious addition to a chicken sandwich.

You will need to start at least 6 hours, and up to a day, ahead to prepare the brined and air-dried cabbage; see page 77.

Makes about 1 quart/1.5 kg

One 2 to 2½ pound/1 to 1.25 kg head napa cabbage, cut into wedges, salted, brined, rinsed, and air-dried (see page 77)

BRINE

3 cups/720 ml water

2 tablespoons/30 grams fine sea salt

PUREE

Half a Korean pear or 1 or 2 Bosc pears, peeled, cored, and coarsely chopped (1½ to 2 cups/250 to 325 grams)

½ medium apple, peeled, cored, and coarsely chopped (about ½ cup/60 grams)

½ medium yellow onion, chopped

2 medium garlic cloves, minced

2 thin slices peeled fresh ginger, minced

FILLINGS

Half a medium carrot, peeled and cut into 1-inch-long/2.5 cm long fine julienne (about ½ cup/45 grams)

½ pound/225 grams Korean radish or daikon, cut into 1-inch-long/2.5 cm long fine julienne

½ cup/25 grams fresh garlic chives or regular chives cut into 1-inch lengths (or substitute daikon shoots)

Half a small red bell pepper, cut into fine julienne (about ½ cup/75 grams)

4 or 5 pitted red jujubes (see Glossary), cut into matchsticks

About 2 tablespoons pine nuts, coarsely chopped, or 2 tablespoons coarsely chopped walnuts

You will need spoons, two large bowls, a food processor or blender, a cotton tea towel or cloth, string, a 1-quart/1 liter glass jar with a tight-fitting lid, a piece of plastic (such as the lid of a yogurt container) trimmed to fit inside the jar, and a rimmed tray to hold the jar.

To make the brine, stir the water and salt together in a large bowl until the salt is completely dissolved. Set aside.

To make the puree, combine all the ingredients in a food processor or blender and process to a puree.

continued

Place a clean tea towel or cotton cloth over the bowl of brine, with the edges hanging over the sides of the bowl and the center dipping into the brine so it gets moistened. Transfer the puree to the center of the cloth, letting that part of the cloth become immersed in the brine while keeping the edges dry. Lift up the edges of the cloth to shape it into bundle and secure it with string to keep it compressed, then drape the dry edges of the cloth over the side of the bowl while the bundle of puree sits in the brine. Give the puree a squeeze, then let it soak for 20 minutes or so while you prepare the filling.

To make the filling, combine all the ingredients in a wide bowl and toss them together. Place the bowl and a 1-quart/1 liter jar by your work surface.

Squeeze the puree again, then lift it out of the brine and, holding it over the bowl, squeeze again, twisting hard, to get out all the liquid and flavors; discard the debris and rinse out the cloth. Set the brine aside.

Roughly divide the filling ingredients into equal piles, as many as you have cabbage wedges. Place one wedge on your work surface and stuff a portion of filling between the leaves, starting with the outside layer and working inward. Gather the wedge of cabbage together, fold the tip over, and press to make a tight bundle. Transfer to the glass jar, pressing it down firmly. A few bits of filling will probably escape as you do so; don't worry. Repeat the process with the remaining cabbage wedges and filling, pressing down on them in the jar so they fit. The more tightly packed in the wedge bundles are, the better. Tuck in any stray bits of filling.

Stir the brine and pour it into the jar until the wedges are covered. Press down again to make sure there are no air bubbles. Make sure the cabbage is immersed in the brine, then press a piece of plastic (see above) on top to help seal the cabbage from the air and cover the jar tightly. Place on a rimmed tray or in a shallow pan to catch any liquid if it overflows a little during fermentation.

Let the kimchi stand out of the sun at room temperature for 2 to 3 days (2 days in the summer, 3 days in cooler weather), then taste the brine. Once it tastes a little sour, fermentation has started and it's time to move it to your refrigerator. (If need be, leave it for an extra day and taste again.)

You can start using the kimchi right away—I like the fresh taste of new kimchi—and then it will go on gaining flavor in the refrigerator, becoming fully mature after about a week.

Use clean chopsticks or a fork to lift out one wedge, or else cut off several leaves. Each time you take out some cabbage, press down the remaining kimchi to make sure that the liquid covers it completely before you seal the jar and refrigerate again.

The kimchi will be mild and slightly sweet to start. After 2 to 3 weeks, the extra fermentation will add an interesting and delicious tart note. The kimchi will keep well in the refrigerator for 2 months.

SMALL-BATCH SAUERKRAUT

I love sauerkraut, both the basic cabbage sauerkraut set out here and the classic hearty North European dish in which it is served with salt pork, sausage, and more, from France to Estonia. Perhaps it's genetic, this love of mine: my maternal grandfather was born and raised in Alsace. But I think it's probably because over the years I've had the luck of eating sauerkraut at the tables of people who prepare it with care.

Like many fermented foods, sauerkraut depends on a bit of patience. You do the work of making it and then wait a week or a month or more to taste the results of your efforts. But sauerkraut is actually one of the easiest and most flexible members of the preserved vegetable family. All it requires is a kitchen scale, cabbage, coarse salt, and a little care, as well as fermentation time. No cooking involved. The natural flora on the leaves cause fermentation, and the salt kills the spoilage bacteria as well as drawing water out of the leaves.

My first batch of sauerkraut each year is usually made with summer cabbages, round green ones that are small (a little less than 2 pounds/900 grams) and very fresh, with the distinctive hot, almost spicy taste that characterizes early cabbages. It takes two cabbages of that size to make a small batch that fits into a 2-quart/2 liter jar (or two 1-quart/1 liter jars). Later in the year, after the cabbages have been through a frost, their taste is sweeter. They're usually bigger too, about 4 pounds/nearly 2 kg each.

Once your sauerkraut is fermented to your liking, you have many options. Serve it with sausages or slices of corned beef, or next to a roast pork loin or goose. For vegetarians, it's a great complement to dal or other slow-cooked lentils or beans, and to grilled mushrooms. I like it with Thai fried rice and with bean soups. Or include it as a relish/pickle in meat or egg sandwiches. You can also use it to make Polish *kapusniak* (Hearty Sauerkraut Soup, page 220) or prepare hearty Sauerkraut with Meat and Potatoes (page 304), where the acidity of the kraut balances the richness of the meat.

Makes 3 to 3½ pounds/
1.3 to 1.5 kg

3½ to 4 pounds/1.5 to 1.75 kg
green cabbage (2 small or
1 large), preferably organic

**About 2 tablespoons/32 grams
coarse pickling salt (the
exact amount depends on
the weight of the trimmed
cabbage)**

*You will need a chef's knife, a
cutting board, a kitchen scale, a
jeweler's scale, a large bowl, one
2-quart/2 liter jar or two 1-quart/
1 liter jars, a rimmed tray to hold
the jar(s), and one or two smaller
jars or heavy plastic bags to use as
weights.*

Rinse the cabbage and trim off any discolored patches. Peel off 2 large outer leaves and set aside. Cut the cabbage into quarters, then cut out and discard the entire core from each quarter. (This way, when you shred or chop the cabbage, all the leaves will separate instead of remaining joined at the core end.) Use a long sharp knife to slice the cabbage very finely into shreds. Lift out any thick ribs and discard or set aside for another purpose.

Weigh the shredded cabbage. For every 1½ pounds/650 grams trimmed cabbage, you will need one 2-quart/2 liter jar or two 1-quart/ 1 liter jars. Or use smaller 2-cup/500 ml jars.

Place the cabbage in a large bowl and set aside. You need 2½ percent salt calculated by the net weight of cabbage. This translates in the case of a 1.25 kg cabbage into 30 grams salt, or with a 3 kg cabbage into 75 grams salt.

Add the salt to the cabbage and mix with your hands, massaging the cabbage a little and pressing and turning it. Set aside for 10 to 15 minutes; some water will already be starting to weep from the cabbage.

Using your hands, transfer the cabbage to the glass jar or the two smaller jars. Press the cabbage down firmly as you fill the jar(s), trying to eliminate any air pockets. This is critical: fermentation requires anaerobic conditions—in other words, no oxygen—so all the air must be pushed out. Add any brine that has accumulated in the bottom of the bowl.

Arrange the reserved cabbage leaves on top of the shredded cabbage to seal it off from the air. You need to weight down the cabbage to keep it immersed. Use one (or two) heavy resealable plastic bags. Fill the bag(s) with water to add weight, and add ½ teaspoon salt to each. (This is a precaution in case the bag leaks; you don't want the brine to be diluted with fresh water.) Place the sealed bag(s) on top of the cabbage to weight it down.

Put the jar(s) of sauerkraut on a rimmed tray to catch any overflow and set aside at room temperature, ideally 68 to 74°F/19 to 23°C, to ferment. Any colder, and it will not ferment completely; at hotter temperatures, fermentation will be faster but the flavors won't be as complex.

Taste the cabbage every 2 or 3 days. (Use clean chopsticks or a fork to lift out a taste; don't double-dip!) I find that 10 days at 72 to 74°/22 to 23°C will give a fermented kraut that is fresh tasting and not very sour. I usually leave it for another 5 to 7 days before I stop the fermentation. You can let yours go to just mildly sour or to very sour tasting.

Each time you taste, check the liquid. If it has sunk below the top of the cabbage, you need to top it up with a little more brine. If necessary, bring 2 cups/500 ml water to a boil, add 1 tablespoon/18 grams salt, and stir to dissolve it. Let cool to room temperature, then add enough brine to the jar(s) to cover the kraut.

When the sauerkraut is ready, remove the weight(s). Seal the jar(s) tightly and move to a cool (less than 60°F/15°C) place if you have one, or refrigerate. Sauerkraut keeps almost indefinitely in a cool place; refrigerate once opened.

Use a clean utensil (chopsticks work best) to lift the sauerkraut out of the jar as you need it. Each time you take out some sauerkraut, ensure that the brine level is high enough to immerse the remaining sauerkraut. Top up with more cooled brine, as described above, if you need to.

To prepare the kraut for serving as a side dish, Heat a large heavy skillet over medium heat. Add a generous dollop of duck fat, goose fat, or lard; or, if serving vegetarians, use butter or olive oil. (If you wish, finely chop an onion and cook it in the fat until softened.) Add the sauerkraut and heat, stirring occasionally, until thoroughly warmed and very soft. Taste and see if you want any more flavor (I rarely do, especially if using duck fat or goose fat). If you do, add some ground cumin or fennel seeds and/or black pepper, or several juniper berries. Serve hot or warm.

NOTE ON LARGE BATCHES: *The University of Wisconsin extension services department (like similar departments in many other universities) publishes guidelines for preserving, and particularly for making sauerkraut. What they imagine is the traditional task at a farm-family scale: starting with 25 pounds/ 11 kg or more of cabbage and putting it up for winter. The department publication says that a 5-gallon/19 liter crock holds 25 pounds of cabbage. Once you have discovered how easy it is to make a small batch, you may want to embark on large-batch sauerkraut making. If you do, you might want to buy or borrow a "kraut shredder" to make the chopping of the cabbage quicker and easier. And you'll need some ceramic crocks or 1-gallon/4 liter widemouthed jars, and a cool place to store them, once fermentation is finished.*

SALT-DRIED DAIKON STRIPS

Daikon is the Japanese name for a long white radish, known as *mooli* in northern parts of the Indian subcontinent. It's a kitchen staple in many cuisines, cooked as a vegetable in India, finely grated as a condiment in Japan, salt-fermented as a pickle in Japan and Korea, and quick-pickled as a condiment in Vietnam. Here, in a Chinese-origin version, it is salt-preserved as a larder ingredient that can add flavor and texture to many dishes.

Salt-dried daikon has an appealing crunchiness and saltiness. It's a great way to add vegetable texture at times when fresh vegetables are in short supply. I use it most often in an omelet or to give crunch to an otherwise soft dish such as fried rice. It's also an ingredient in Pad Thai (page 327).

Makes as much as you want; I recommend starting with at least ½ pound/225 grams daikon

Daikon

Fine sea salt

You will need a sharp knife or a coarse grater, a medium bowl, a scale, a jeweler's scale, two tea towels or other cotton cloths, a wire rack set over a tray, cheesecloth, and a glass jar for storage.

Peel the daikon and cut it into julienne strips, or use a coarse grater to make strips. Weigh the strips and place in a bowl.

Add 5 percent fine sea salt by weight to the daikon—e.g., if your daikon strips weigh 250 grams, add 12.5 grams salt. Rub the salt in well with your fingers and let stand for 30 minutes. The daikon strips will start giving off water.

Lay a cotton cloth on a wire rack. Squeeze a handful of daikon to release excess water and spread it on the cloth-lined rack. Repeat with the remaining daikon strips. Place the rack in a warm place, out of direct sun, drape a light piece of cheesecloth over top, and leave to dry. Depending on how warm and dry your environment is, it will take 1 to 3 days for the strips to dry out and shrink to about half their original weight.

Do not rinse off the salt! Weigh the semi-dried strips and place in a bowl. Calculate 1 percent of that weight (for example, if it is 125 grams, you need 1.25 grams fine salt) and add that weight of fine salt to the daikon, rubbing it on well. Spread the strips out on the rack lined with another clean cotton cloth and let dry at warm room temperature until they feel weightless. Again, depending on the humidity, this may happen in a day or might take as long as 3 days.

Store in a clean glass jar. The daikon does not need to be refrigerated.

To use, lift a clump of strips out of the jar, rinse off the salt completely, then finely chop.

BRINED TOMATOES

This distinctive Eastern European take on tomatoes is very simple to make and a refreshingly delicious accompaniment to a meal. There are many versions. Some include other vegetables as well as tomatoes, but I prefer them on their own.

Brined tomatoes, preserved by fermentation without vinegar, are a distinctive food, a great way to extend the summer. You can vary the flavors: some versions include a little chile, allspice, parsley, or celery, or all of them; some add a splash of vinegar. I like using several sizes and colors of tomato, because that makes the jars look so festive, and I include a chive flower or two in each jar for the same reason, as well as for flavor. I like tarragon, so I've included it here, but you don't have to use it. Dill is classic, the fronds or—even better—a flower head or seed head.

On one of my trips to the Republic of Georgia, my friend Tamar Babuadze took me to visit the grandmother of a friend. She had been a noted scientist, but with the fall of the Soviet Union she, like other academics and highly skilled professionals, lost her job and her pension. By the time I met her, she was in her eighties, and still every year she preserved fruits and vegetables for the winter including many jars of tomatoes.

If you love fizzy fermentation—the slight funk of kombucha, for example—you'll want to let your tomatoes ferment for longer before you seal the jars. I like less fizz, so I usually stop the process after 3 days. Store the jars in the refrigerator, labeled and dated. The tomatoes should be eaten within 2 months.

Use unblemished ripe tomatoes, smaller ones if possible, so they fit easily into the mouth of the jars. I use cherry tomatoes to help fill the gaps between the larger fruits. The exact amount of water and salt you need will depend on the volume of your jars. No matter what size batch you're making, use this ratio for your brine: 1½ teaspoons/9 grams salt per 1 cup/250 ml water.

Makes about 1 quart/700 grams

About 1 pound/450 grams organic tomatoes, preferably a mix of sizes and varieties, including some cherry tomatoes

1 or more dill flowers or a few dill fronds, or fresh lovage leaves

2 or 3 sprigs tarragon

2 chive flowers (optional)

1 grape leaf, torn in half, or several black currant leaves

About 1 tablespoon/15 grams fine sea salt

About 10 black peppercorns

2 bay leaves

1 tablespoon honey

2 garlic cloves, peeled

You will need two 2-cup/ 500 ml glass jars or one 1-quart/ 1 liter jar, a knife, a 2-cup/ 500 ml measuring cup, a saucepan, spoons, a jeweler's scale, plastic wrap and one or two sealable plastic bags to use as weights, a cotton cloth, and a rimmed tray.

continued

Wash the tomatoes, herbs, and leaf (leaves) well and set aside to dry completely. Sterilize two 2-cup/500 ml glass jars or one 1-quart/1 liter jar and lid(s) by washing them in boiling water, or running them through the dishwasher; set aside on a tray to dry.

Fill the jars or jar with the tomatoes: prick large ones a couple of times with the tip of a sharp knife and cut the largest ones in half if necessary so they will fit through the neck(s) of the jar(s); use the cherry tomatoes, if you have them, to help fill any gaps.

Add enough water to fill the jar(s) to the top and then, holding the tomatoes back with your hand, carefully pour the water out into a large measuring cup. Your salt measurement will depend on the volume of water: you'll need 1½ teaspoons (8 grams) fine sea salt per 1 cup/250 ml water.

Put the measured amount of water in a saucepan, add the measured salt, the peppercorns, and bay leaves, and bring to a boil, stirring to dissolve the salt. Remove from the heat and set aside to cool to lukewarm (about 100°F/40°C), then stir in the honey to dissolve it completely.

Add the garlic and the remaining aromatics to the jar(s) of tomatoes. If using two jars, lift the bay leaves out of the brine and tuck one leaf into each jar. Pour the brine into the jar(s) and add the peppercorns, dividing them fairly evenly if using two jars. Place the grape leaf or currant leaves on top. Make sure that all the tomatoes are submerged. Put the lid(s) on tightly and turn the jar(s) upside down and right side up several times to distribute the aromatics. Remove the lid(s).

To keep the tomatoes submerged in the brine (they will float upward unless they are really jammed in tightly), you will need to cover them with plastic wrap and then weight it down with a sealed bag filled with water. Cover the jar(s) with a clean cotton cloth or two layers of cheesecloth and set aside on a rimmed tray in a warm place, in the sun if possible, to ferment.

Timing will depend on the ambient temperature and your taste. You should see bubbles rising within 2 to 3 days. Once they do, you will know fermentation has started. If you like your brined tomatoes mild, as I do, leave them for just one more day. If you prefer more fermentation, let them ferment for another 2 or 3 days. Once they are to your taste, seal tightly with the lid(s), turn upside down and back a couple of times, and then refrigerate, labeled with the date. For best flavor, leave for another few days, then dive in! Eat within 2 months.

To enjoy them, make sure that you use clean utensils, not your fingers, to remove the tomatoes from the jar(s). You may notice a small amount of what seems to be creamy white mold on the surface of your jars, but don't worry! It is kahm, a harmless yeast that can form during this type of fermentation. Simply scrape or rinse it off.

CITRUS KOSHO

Kosho is a salt-fermented mix of citrus zest and chiles. The most well-known and traditional version is *yuzu kosho*. But yuzu is hard to come by outside Japan, and so other versions of kosho have come into being.

This recipe is a blend of Meyer lemon zest and pomelo zest mixed with a paste of red cayenne chiles and salt. Another delicious option is to use the zest of makrut (bumpy wild Thai limes) with red cayenne chiles and salt.

Kosho has a very intense chile-hot citrus taste, so you need only a tiny amount, whether using it as a condiment or as an ingredient, for example in a soup or a mayonnaise. The flavor sweetens and becomes more complex with time.

The traditional proportion of salt to the other ingredients is 10 to 15 percent of the combined weight of the zest and chopped chiles. I tend to like things salty, so I aim for 14 to 15 percent salt (in this case, 15 percent of 50 grams is 7.5 grams). Use whichever citrus juice you wish, say, juice from the fruit you zested.

Makes about ¼ cup/60 grams

1 tablespoon chopped fresh red cayenne chiles (about 4 medium, halved lengthwise and stripped of seeds and membranes)

1¼ teaspoons/7 grams fine sea salt

About 2½ tablespoons grated citrus zest (from 6 Meyer lemons and 1 medium pomelo, for example; see headnote)

½ to 1 teaspoon fresh citrus juice (see headnote)

You will need a jeweler's scale, a food processor or stone mortar and pestle, a medium bowl, a rubber spatula, and a glass jar for storage.

Weigh the chopped chiles and zest. Multiply that weight by 13 to 15 percent to calculate how much salt you need.

Grind the chiles and salt to a paste in a food processor, then add the zest and pulse a few times. Alternatively, pound the chiles and salt to a paste in a mortar with a pestle, then stir in the zest and pound briefly.

Transfer to a bowl, using a rubber spatula to scrape out every last bit of the mixture, and stir in enough citrus juice to make a looser paste. Transfer to a glass jar, label with the date, and store in the refrigerator for 10 days before tasting.

By then the kosho should have fermented enough to give it a hot citrusy-salty taste. Be sure to use a clean utensil when taking paste from the jar.

Kosho keeps almost indefinitely in the fridge.

GREEN AJIKA

Georgia may be a small country, but it has distinctive regional cuisines. This version of ajika originated in Migrelia. Green ajika is a delicious salt-preserved blend of leeks, garlic, herbs and spices, given heat by soaked dried red chiles. It's like a summer herb garden in a jar, with chile heat to intensify the taste, and is one of my favorite condiments. Start a day ahead so the dried chiles have time to soak.

Put ajika out on the table as a condiment, or mix with a little sunflower oil or olive oil and smear onto fish fillets (or into the cavity of whole fish) or onto vegetables (slices of eggplant or zucchini, for example) before grilling them.

Makes about 5 cups/1 kg

2 ounces/60 grams (about 150) dried red cayenne chiles

2 large bunches fresh coriander (cilantro)

1 bunch flat-leaf parsley

1 bunch dill

1 bunch celery leaves (see Glossary)

1 bunch basil

¼ cup/30 grams coriander seeds

¼ cup/35 grams dill seeds

4 heads garlic, separated into cloves, peeled, and trimmed of tough ends and blemishes

2 medium leeks, white and tender green parts, chopped and well washed, or 7 scallions, trimmed and coarsely chopped

¼ cup/70 grams coarse sea salt

You will need two medium bowls, a small heavy skillet, a food processor, a rubber spatula, a large bowl, a spice grinder or mortar and pestle, a wooden spoon, a cotton cloth, and glass jars for storage.

Remove the seeds from the chiles: It's easiest to work over a bowl for discards, with another bowl alongside. One by one, break open each chile, letting the seeds drop out into the bowl, then break off the stem if there is one and place the chile in the other bowl. When you've finished, add enough warm water to cover the chiles and set aside to soak and soften overnight.

The next day, remove the coarsest stems from the herbs and set the herbs aside.

Toast the coriander seeds in a small heavy skillet over medium heat until just aromatic, about 3 minutes. Set aside. Toast the dill seeds in the same way and set aside.

Drain the chiles and squeeze out the excess water. Place in a food processor and grind to a paste. Add the garlic and process to a paste, then add the leeks or scallions and process to a paste. Use a spatula to scrape down the sides of the processor as needed. Add some of the herbs and process, then continue adding the herbs in batches and processing until all are incorporated into the paste. Transfer to a bowl.

Using a spice grinder or a mortar, grind or pound the toasted spices to a powder. Add them to the herb mix, along with the salt, and stir in thoroughly with a wooden spoon.

Cover the bowl with a cotton cloth and let stand in a cool place out of the sun for 6 to 10 hours; give the paste a stir occasionally.

Sterilize your glass jars and lids by washing them in boiling water or running them through the dishwasher. Let dry completely, then transfer the ajika to the jars and seal tightly. Store in a cool place, and then, once opened, in the refrigerator. It keeps almost indefinitely.

Portrait of a working baker in the town of Rissani, in southeastern Morocco

SIJILMASA

Ibn Battuta, a Berber from Tangiers, Morocco, started on his epic travels in the year 1325 at the age of twenty. He set out toward Mecca, and in the end he

was away from home for about thirty years. A religious scholar, he visited every country where there were Islamic scholars and/or rulers, and he compiled a written record of his observations, titled *A Gift to Those Who Contemplate the Wonders of Cities and the Marvels of Traveling*.

From his writings, I learned of the city of Sijilmasa, south of the Atlas Mountains in what is present-day Morocco. For centuries, starting well before the Arab conquest of north Africa in 711, Sijilmasa was a rich and important center of trade and commerce in salt, slaves, gold, and more: Slaves and gold were brought north from sub-Saharan Africa to Sijilmasa, and from there transported to Egypt or to Fez. Salt, silk, and paper and other goods from the Mediterranean were carried south in large camel caravans across the desert to Timbuktu and beyond. Ibn Battuta wrote, "After this, I came to Sijilmasa, which is a very handsome city. It produces many very good dates."

Sijilmasa has been a ruin for about five hundred years now. It's a long two-day drive from Marrakesh over the Atlas Mountains and then eastward toward the Algerian border. The sand-colored ruins lie just outside the small town of Rissani, a date-palm oasis that is the main market town in the region.

When I was there in late October it was date harvest time. The bazaar has a seductively complicated geography, with narrow alleyways between shops displaying scarves or spices or cuts of meat. And then in one open area, lit by skylights, is the place of the date merchants. Heaps of dates, from red-brown to rich brown, some gleaming with sweetness, were piled on tables. Men gathered in clusters, tasting and discussing quality and price.

Despite its market, Rissani is a subdued place. Young people tend to move to the larger towns and cities of Morocco to earn a living, so there's very little active farming in the oasis these days. The land beneath the palm trees should be verdant with carefully tended vegetables, but instead it lies fallow. Because of the big sand dunes about twenty miles down the road, tourism is an important industry in the region. But Rissani itself doesn't seem to have much cachet, and for the moment, no fanfare sounds for the ruins of Sijilmasa.

Still, the place resonated for me. I wrote in my journal: "I keep imagining guys with loaded camels, who had been walking north through the desert for days, catching sight of the blue-edged Atlas Mountains one clear morning, with a lift of the heart, knowing they were only two days from Sijilmasa."

GRAINS & BEANS

WE ARE MORE LIKELY TO THINK OF SALT as a way of preventing spoilage of perishable foods such as meat or fish or vegetables, because grains and dried beans seem less in need of special preservation. But humans have figured out interesting ways of salt-preserving both grains and beans, and in the process, transforming them into spectacular agents of flavor and making them more digestible and more nutritionally valuable.

Rice is usually the main ingredient in *shio koji*, one of the oldest salt-preserved foods in Japan. It's an aromatic paste that is used as a flavoring and that brings umami to everything it touches. Shio koji is generally made through salt fermentation of freshly steamed rice, but it can also be made with other grains. In earlier times, before rice was widely cultivated in northern Japan, it was made with barley, and probably also with millet.

Miso, which we most often think of as based on soybeans, is made with grains as well as, or instead of, beans: shiro white or sweet miso is made with rice and barley, usually with some soybeans too, and red and dark misos are made with wheat or barley or a mixture, most often also with soybeans. It's possible as well to make miso out of whole-grain bread. I found the idea so intriguing that I've included a recipe here for miso made from sourdough rye bread.

The bean that is most commonly salted or salt-fermented is the soybean. Fermented soybeans are an important ingredient in many parts of China. Black soybeans are cooked, cultured with koji spores, dried, salted, and fermented to make that agent of intensity, salted black beans. Soybeans are the main ingredient in Korea's *doenjang*, and the most common ingredient in miso, its Japanese equivalent. Soybeans also give us the liquid flavoring we call soy sauce or shoyu, which may have begun as a by-product of miso making. Soybeans are salt-fermented in many other places in Asia, including Nepal and northeast India, and the mountain regions of Burma and Thailand.

SHIO KOJI—
Japanese Salt-and-Rice Magic

Shio koji is a remarkable food that is close to "ground zero" in the world of salt-as-flavor-and-preservative. It is an umami-rich paste made of only three basic ingredients: rice or another grain, sea salt (*shio* in Japanese), and koji spores (dried *Aspergillus oryzae*, called *koji kin* in Japanese), and it has transformed my cooking. You can buy jars of shio koji in Japanese and Korean shops, but you can also make your own very easily.

The traditional way of making rice shio koji starts with steamed rice, koji rice, and salt. Koji rice is rice that has been inoculated with koji spores and then dried (just as fresh yeast is dried so it stays stable; see the sidebar below). The steamed rice, koji rice, and salt are mixed together and left to ferment in a jar for a month or more. The result is an aromatic sweet-salty paste, either white or yellowish.

The shortcut method combines measured amounts of koji rice, salt, and water into a paste and ferments for about 10 days. Shortcut shio koji lacks a little of the complexity of the longer-fermented version but is still a useful flavoring tool for the cook.

Over the last few years, koji rice and kojis made by inoculating other grains (such as barley) with aspergillus spores have become popular flavorings with chefs. For more on this trend, and the range of koji possibilities, have a look at *The Noma Guide to Fermentation*, by René Redzepi and David Zilber, and *Koji Alchemy*, by Rich Shih and Jeremy Urmansky (both listed in Resources).

KOJI KIN AND KOJI RICE

Koji kin is the Japanese term for the spores of *Aspergillus oryzae*. These are used to inoculate cooked rice or other cooked grains to create a grain koji, an easily accessible fermentation starter that can be dried and stored. Grain koji, most often rice, is widely used by cooks and food producers in Japan to make everything from miso to sake. And koji of various kinds has become a source of fascination and inspiration for many chefs and cooks in the West. The fermentation it activates results in the release of sugars, fatty acids, and amino acids, including glutamate, the source of umami. No wonder it entrances cooks—it is a wonderful flavor enhancer.

The recipes here for shio koji and the two miso recipes all call for dried koji rice. Koji rice looks like whitish or pale tan freeze-dried rice. You'll find it for sale in Japanese and Korean grocery stores, as well as by mail order. It should be light and dry when you buy it. The grains sometimes stick together, though, so you'll often need to separate the small clumps with your fingers. Store koji rice in the refrigerator or freezer, tightly sealed in doubled plastic bags.

AKO'S SHIO KOJI
from Rice and Koji Rice

One April evening when I was staying on the Noto Peninsula with the ceramic artist Caroline Watanabe, her good friend Akiko Matsuda came to supper. She arrived with a meticulously prepared shio koji lesson for us. She'd measured out the rice, koji rice, and salt, and she'd already steam-cooked the rice, then wrapped the hot cooked rice in a cotton cloth to bring it to Caroline's. By the time she'd arrived and unpacked the rice, she judged that it had cooled enough for us to mix in the koji rice and salt. We blended it all together with our hands, then packed it into containers to ferment for a month.

The lesson she taught us that evening was my entry into the world of koji fermentation. Since then, I've made shio koji many times in Toronto, because I use it so frequently in my cooking.

If you are curious about shio koji I urge you to try this traditional method to get a sense of the depth of flavor you achieve when you start with rice plus koji rice and salt and let them quietly ferment together. Instead of the water used in the quick recipe on page 102, this combo gets all its moisture from the cooked rice. And the rice, of course, provides a lot of carbohydrates for the aspergillus spores to feed on. This method of making shio koji uses much less koji rice in proportion than the quick method, and the long fermentation gives it a much more complex flavor.

The proportions needed are 3:5:8 measured by volume: 3 parts fine sea salt (with no additives) to 5 parts koji rice to 8 parts raw Japanese rice. Note that the recipe calls for polished (white) rice, meaning the Japanese rice that you might use for sushi. It must be soaked in cold water before steaming (use spring water if your tap water is very chlorinated or strong tasting).

Makes 4 to 5 cups/700 to 875 grams

---

2 cups/400 grams Japanese polished rice, soaked in cold water (see headnote) for 4 hours and drained

Water as needed for sprinkling

1¼ cups/300 ml koji rice

¾ cup/180 grams fine sea salt

You will need a rice steamer, muslin or cotton for steaming, a thermometer, a medium bowl, a large bowl, a rice paddle, three widemouthed 2-cup/500 ml glass jars, cheesecloth, scissors, and rubber bands.

To cook the soaked rice, place the rice in a steamer lined with muslin or coarse cotton and steam, covered, over boiling water, sprinkling on a little water from time to time. I find that the rice grains need water added fairly frequently until they suddenly start to soften in the steam. Once the rice is tender, after about 45 minutes, remove it from the steamer and set aside to cool to 150°F/65°C or less.

Place the koji rice in a medium bowl and break up any clumps with your fingers. Add the salt and mix well.

Place the cooled steamed rice in a bowl, add the koji rice and salt mixture, and, using a rice paddle or your hands, gently turn and fold and blend until uniformly mixed.

Transfer to clean glass jars. Cover each one with a lid. Set aside in a warm place, ideally 70 to 78°F/21 to 26°C.

After 4 or 5 days, the mixture will have become a little wetter as the salt draws water from the cooked rice and it starts to ferment. Give it a stir with a clean wooden spoon after a couple of days, then once the shio koji has all softened and has a sweet smell, 3 weeks to 1 month, you can start using it.

In a few more weeks, the shio koji should be a very moist paste, with an aroma that is both sweet and fermented. That's the sign that it has finished its fermentation. Store, tightly covered, in a cool place or in the refrigerator. Shio koji keeps well in the fridge; I've kept some for 3 years, just to test it, and it's fine.

QUICK SHIO KOJI
from Koji Rice and Salt

In this quick version of shio koji, all you need is koji rice (not plain rice), salt, water, and a little time, about 10 days. This recipe calls for 6 percent salt—that is, 6 percent of the combined weight of the water and the koji rice. You may want to experiment with a little more salt. Some recipes call for as much as 10 percent. I prefer the sweetness and subtlety of the lower level of salt.

This makes a small batch; if you'd like to double it, double all amounts. You will then need to make it in two jars or one larger (1-quart/1 liter) jar. The recipe calls for mixing the koji rice, salt, and water directly in the jar in which it will ferment, as I find this easier than pouring the mixture from a bowl into jars. If you make a large quantity, though, you'll need to mix it in a bowl and then divide it among your jars.

Makes about 1½ cups/500 grams

1½ cups/220 grams koji rice (see page 99)

1½ tablespoons/23 grams fine sea salt

1 cup/240 ml spring water

You will need a 2-cup/500 ml glass jar, cheesecloth or a cotton cloth, and a rubber band.

Mix the koji rice and salt in a very clean 2-cup/500 ml jar. Add the water and stir well. Cover the jar with a lid, and label the jar with the date.

Set aside at warm room temperature, ideally 70 to 73°F/20 to 22°C, out of the sun, to ferment for a week to 10 days. Stir it with a clean spoon every day or two. The shio koji will first taste a bit salty and then will start to sweeten and turn a little pasty and slightly yellower as fermentation gets going. When it is ready, it will have a delicately sweet, slightly funky aroma.

Store in the refrigerator, where it will keep indefinitely.

SHIO KOJI LARDER IDEAS

You can think of shio koji as a flavored salt: for every 1 teaspoon/6 grams salt, substitute 2 teaspoons/10 ml shio koji. It gives the bonus of umami as well as salt seasoning.

- Smear a little shio koji on top of fish fillets half an hour before grilling or frying, using a light hand. I find that just under a teaspoon spread onto a fillet weighing 1/2 pound/225 grams is about right. You will need no other seasoning. Scrape off any excess before cooking. (For more detail, see Shio Koji-Marinated Grilled Fish, page 253.)

- Smear some shio koji on a whole chicken an hour or two before grilling or roasting it. I use about 3 tablespoons on a large (4- to 5-pound/1.7 to 2.25 kg) bird, spreading it all over the skin.

- Spread a little shio koji on top of slices of eggplant or other vegetables about 10 minutes before grilling.

- Dissolve a tablespoon or more of shio koji in a saucepan of water before simmering cubes of kabocha squash in it.

- Blend a little shio koji into salad dressing instead of using salt as the seasoning.

SHOYU KOJI

This power combo of soy sauce with koji rice has a softened, appealing soy sauce flavor and can be used as a seasoning as well as an amplifier of umami. Use it in place of soy sauce.

Makes about 3 cups/720 ml

1⅓ cups/200 grams koji rice

½ cup/120 ml boiled and cooled water

1 cup/240 ml naturally brewed Japanese soy sauce (see page 115)

You will need a 1-quart/1 liter jar, a spoon, and cheesecloth.

Koji rice, with jar of shoyu koji

Separate the koji granules with your fingers. Place them in a clean 1-quart/1 liter jar, add the water and soy sauce, and stir thoroughly with a very clean spoon. Cover with a lid and set aside in a warm place, ideally 70 to 75°F/20 to 23°C, out of the sun to ferment. Stir every day or two.

After about 10 days, taste the mixture. The soy flavor will have softened and the umami intensified. Label with the date, and store in the refrigerator. It keeps indefinitely.

SALTED BLACK BEANS

Soybeans are loaded with protein. When freshly harvested, they are tender, like large green peas, but soon they dry into hard yellow (the most common) or black disks, depending on the variety. In that form, they can be stored for long periods if they are kept dry (and sealed off from hungry rodents). Many centuries ago, people in China, Nepal, Japan, and Korea began to ferment some of their soybean crops. They soaked and cooked the beans, set them aside to cool, and then salted and stored them in containers for months to ferment. A form of this first version of fermented beans is still an important food and flavoring.

Called *dou chi* in Mandarin, fermented black beans are made from cooked black soybeans that are inoculated with aspergillus spores, salted or soaked in an intensely salty brine, and fermented. (You'll find a recipe for them in Kirsten Shockey's book *Miso, Tempeh, Natto and Other Tasty Ferments*, listed in the Resources.) They're soft, a little wrinkled, and very strong tasting—salty and pungent, like a very aged hard cheese. They're a versatile larder ingredient, adding intense umami to any food they're combined with.

Salted black beans are the primary ingredient in black bean sauce, and both are widely available in East Asian grocery stores. I urge you buy salted black beans and make your own better version of black bean sauce; see the recipe on page 189. It's a versatile larder flavoring, especially useful for adding depth and intensity to stir-fries (see pages 242 and 282).

A different version of salted fermented soybeans, medium brown rather than black, and less salted, is a staple in northern Thailand. The beans are cooked and then only briefly fermented, for a day or two. They are the main ingredient in the important northern Thai flavoring known as *dao jiao*; in Vietnam, a similar soybean paste called *tuong* is used in vegetarian dishes. These soybean pastes are milder tasting than the intense Chinese salted black beans. Fermented soybeans are also used to make the flattened dried disks that form the flavor base in the cooking of many people in northern Thailand, where they are called *tua nao*, and in the hills of northern Burma and southern Yunnan.

Doenjang, the Korean salted fermented soybean paste, is made from cooked soybeans that are mashed, shaped into blocks, and left to ferment, then immersed in a salt brine for months. The process produces *ganjang*, Korean soy sauce, as well as doenjang.

MISO

Miso is an ancient fundamental of the Japanese kitchen, recently embraced by cooks from many countries and culinary traditions. You'll find the sweet-salty paste used in sauces, marinades, soups, and plenty of other dishes where a dose of umami is welcome. It is made from fermenting cooked beans or grains—rice, wheat, barley, millet, and soybeans are all candidates—with grain or bean koji, meaning grain or beans that have been seeded with aspergillus spores, called koji kin. The kojis are named for the grain or legume they're made of: for example, koji rice, koji wheat, or koji soy. (See page 99 for more.)

When I stayed at a farm in the mountains of Kyoto Prefecture at rice harvest time in the mid-1990s, I learned that most of the households in the village made their own miso and *amazake*, a low-alcohol rice drink, from the beans and grains they grew. In colder weather, the warm space under a quilt-draped kitchen table was the place various fermented foods were stored to develop.

The villagers there depended on the koji rice made by one family, who were by then the last local producers of koji rice in the region. Steamed rice that had been mixed with light-as-air spores of aspergillus was spread on straw mats on the ground in a small thick-walled stone building. The rice had to be raked frequently to ensure that the temperature stayed steady, for as the aspergillus spores started to grow, the rice would heat up. It looked like a rice version of a Japanese temple sand garden, deliberate and spare.

On the east side of Tokyo, in Koto City, there's a wonderful store called Sano Miso Kameido that stocks many kinds of miso, all available for tasting. It's a miso lover's dream. The only problem there is choosing which ones to buy. The variations include miso made with different kojis, from rice to soybean to wheat, and with a range of different main ingredients: soybeans, barley, wheat, etc.

The basic balance in miso making is this: more koji and less salt make for a quicker fermentation, less depth of flavor, greater sweetness, and less saltiness. At the other end of the scale, less koji and more salt mean a slower (it's slowed down by the salt) fermentation, a greater depth and complexity of flavor from that long fermentation, and more saltiness.

Color is a good shorthand way of keeping track of the different categories of miso. In general, the darker the color, the more aged, salty, and intensely flavored the miso will be. The light-colored misos, sometimes called "white miso" or "yellow miso," are sweeter, milder tasting, and often aged for only a few months. In between the extremes of dark brown and nearly white lie the reddish-brown misos, which are often called "red miso."

Dark brown *hatcho* miso, deeply flavored and heavily salted, is made of barley and is usually fermented with koji barley or koji made with soybeans. At the other end of the color scale, pale-colored shiro miso is usually made with rice and barley, along with some soybeans, and fermented with koji rice. Red miso, less salty and fermented tasting than dark miso, usually starts with a base of cooked soybeans that are fermented with koji rice. For a classic take on red miso, see page 109.

The Korean version of miso is a salty soybean paste called doenjang, meaning thick sauce. A by-product of the production of the salty Korean soy sauce known in English as soup soy sauce, it's made of naturally fermented soybeans (without the help of koji), salt, and water.

There are a number of sources that have helped me understand miso, starting with Willian Shurtleff and Akiko Aoyagi's groundbreaking work, *The Book of Miso*, as well as Sandor Katz's books on fermentation. For modern experimental approaches to miso, have a look at *The Noma Guide to Fermentation* as well as works by Kirsten Shockey (see Resources).

The two miso recipes that follow are examples of the way salt is used to control fermentation and transform plain staples into a delicious ingredient. The first one, miso made from cooked soybeans, is a way of preserving a staple high-protein food. The second one is a way to transform leftover bread into miso.

RED MISO

This recipe yields a classic mild-tasting, red-brown miso. The whole process takes about 10 months and over that time you can taste and smell your miso as it develops flavor and comes into being. It's exciting.

The recipe is based on 20 percent salt. It starts with roughly equal weights of raw soybeans (which are then cooked) and koji rice, and the amount of salt called for is 20 percent of their total weight. The other ingredient is a small amount of miso, store-bought or homemade, that is used as seed miso, to help get fermentation started. Apart from organic non-GMO soybeans and a good supplier of koji rice, almost all you need is a container to hold the miso as it ferments. In Japan, miso was traditionally made in ceramic crocks topped with heavy wooden lids. These days, plastic—less beautiful but very functional—has replaced the traditional vessels in many miso-making operations. I have used both a straight-sided food-grade plastic pail and a ceramic crock. The pail is semitransparent, so I can see the miso and make sure there are no air spaces in the paste, but the crock is much more beautiful, so I prefer it.

Makes about 3½ pounds/1.5 kg

1 pound/3 cups/450 grams dried organic soybeans

1 teaspoon red miso (as seed miso)

1 pound/about 3¼ cups/450 grams koji rice

¾ cup/180 grams fine sea salt

Vodka, sake, or shoju for wiping the inside of the miso container

You will need a scale to weigh out your ingredients, two large bowls, a large heavy pot, two small bowls, a food processor or large mortar and pestle, a thermometer, a 2½- to 3-quart/2.5 to 3 liter fermenting container such as a food-grade straight-sided plastic pail or a ceramic crock, a lid that fits inside the top of the container, cheesecloth or plastic wrap, weights to place on the lid (such as canned goods or jars filled with water), string, a large cardboard box, and sterilized glass jars with lids for storage.

Put the soybeans in a large bowl, cover with water by 4 inches/10 cm, and let soak overnight.

The next day, drain the beans, transfer to a large heavy pot, add water to cover by 3 inches/8 cm, and bring to a boil. Cook at a steady boil over medium-low to low heat, partially covered, until the beans are tender, 2½ to 3 hours; it's fine if the beans break up a bit. Add more water if they start looking dry.

Scoop about 1 cup (240 ml) of the cooking water into a small bowl and let cool, then drain the beans. You'll have about 7 cups/1.2 kg cooked beans.

Put about ½ cup/125 ml of the cooled cooking water in a small bowl and dissolve the red miso in it. Set aside.

continued

Working in batches if necessary, use a very clean food processor or large mortar and pestle (see Note) to process or mash the cooked soybeans to a paste. Leave it chunky if you wish; I like to try to get it fairly smooth. If the paste seems very dry, add a very small splash of the remaining cooking water. Transfer the paste to a large clean bowl.

By now, the beans should be just cooler than lukewarm, 90 to 95°F/32 to 35°C. Add the red miso mixture, koji rice, and ½ cup/120 grams of the salt to the paste and knead everything together very thoroughly with your clean hands, squeezing the mixture between your fingers until it is thoroughly blended.

Wash your fermenting container in very hot soapy water, then rinse with hot water and shake until mostly dry. Sprinkle about half of the remaining 4 tablespoons/60 grams salt into the container and shake it around to coat the sides and bottom with salt. (This is your anti-contamination strategy.)

You want the bean paste to go into the container as a solid mass, with no air pockets. Shape a small-lemon–sized ball of the paste and press it into the container. Then continue shaping balls and pressing them one by one into the container, making sure to avoid air pockets. Use your hands to press down on the balls as you work to eliminate any gaps.

When all the paste is in the container in a solid mass, sprinkle on the remaining salt. Moisten a clean cloth with the vodka or other spirit and rub down the inside surfaces of the container above the miso paste. (This further protects against contamination.)

Drape a clean cotton cloth (no fragrant detergent) or double layer of cheesecloth over the container and then press it lightly onto the paste. The edges of the cloth should hang over the edge of the container. Top with a layer of plastic wrap and a tight-fitting lid. Top the lid with weights (aim for the same amount of weight as your miso, about 3½ pounds/1.5 kg), so that it presses against the bean paste. Drape another piece of plastic (I use a large clean plastic bag) over the top of the container and secure it with string to protect the miso from contamination.

Put the miso container in a large cardboard box, close the lid, and let it sit in a relatively warm place (about 76°F/25°C) for 4 or 5 days to help get fermentation started.

Move the container to a cool, dark place (for example, a basement or the floor of a cupboard) to ferment. Check on it every 3 to 4 weeks (if the temperature is very warm, check it every 2 weeks or so). The coverings may now have some mold spores on them; if so, don't worry, simply replace them with fresh cloth or cheesecloth and plastic wrap after checking the miso. If there is any pale mold or kahm yeast (see Glossary) on the surface of the miso itself, carefully scrape it off and then wipe the inside walls of the container again with a clean cloth soaked with the vodka or other spirit. If there is any liquid on the surface of

the miso, stir it in with a clean spoon (you might try a little taste of it with another spoon; the liquid is a form of soy sauce). Press down on the miso to make sure there are no air pockets, then cover it again as before. After 3 months, remove the weights, leaving the remaining coverings.

After 4 to 6 months, you'll start to taste the miso coming into being—salty and aromatic, with a delicate umami-laden sweet edge. It should be ready in 8 to 10 months. Once it's ready, transfer it to clean glass containers with tight-fitting lids, label, and refrigerate. The miso should keep for at least a year.

NOTE: *Whatever you use to mash your cooked soybeans needs to be impeccably clean so that no other organisms have a chance to contaminate your beans.*

MISO FROM RYE BREAD

After I saw an Instagram post by Kirsten Shockey, coauthor of *Miso, Tempeh, Natto and Other Tasty Ferments* (see Resources) talking about making miso from leftover bread, I decided to try it using naturally leavened rye bread made by my brilliant baker friend Dawn Woodward.

Like the Red Miso on page 109, this starts with food for the koji—in this case, soaked softened bread—which is blended with koji rice and salt. The magic of koji fermentation in an airless environment yields a rich, sweet red miso in about 6 months. This is a remarkable way of fermenting bread, an already-fermented food, into new life.

The recipe below uses 1 pound of toasted trimmed bread, so you need to start with at least 3 pounds/1.35 kg of whole-grain naturally leavened rye. The important measurement is the weight of the bread *after* it has been trimmed of crusts and dried out in the oven; that weight will determine the amounts of koji rice and salt you need.

Makes 3¾ to 4 cups/1 to 1.1 kg (two 2-cup/500 ml jars)

About 3 pounds/1.35 kg naturally leavened organic whole-grain rye bread

Koji rice (50 percent of the weight of the toasted trimmed bread)

Fine sea salt (13 percent of the weight of the toasted bread)

Vodka, sake, or shoju for wiping the inside of the miso container

You will need a pot or kettle, a bread knife, one or two baking sheets, a kitchen scale, a jeweler's scale, a large bowl, 1½-to 2-liter straight-sided plastic or glass or ceramic container, a clean cloth, cheesecloth, plastic to cover the container, a heavy lid that fits inside the container, a plastic bag, string, a large cardboard box, and glass containers for storage.

Preheat the oven to 200°F/95°C.

Put a large pot of water or a kettle on to boil. (For better flavor, I like to use water that has boiled and cooled, or good spring water, to moisten the ingredients for miso.) Once it boils, set it aside to cool to lukewarm.

Meanwhile, trim the crusts off the bread and cut it into 1-inch/3 cm or smaller cubes. Place them on one or two baking sheets and toast them in the oven until very dry and lightweight. Remove from the oven and weigh the bread.

Measure out half that weight in koji rice. For example, if the weight of the toasted bread is 1 pound/450 grams, you want ½ pound/225 grams koji rice.

Calculate the salt: Add the weight of the toasted bread and the weight of the koji. Multiply that by 13 percent. So, with our example here, the total weight

would be 1¹/₂ pounds/675 grams. Multiply that by 0.13, to get 87 grams salt. Measure out the salt and set aside about one-quarter of it.

Combine the dried bread, koji rice, and the remaining salt in a large bowl. Add enough of the lukewarm (less than 95°F/35°C) water to just cover. Let it soak for a few minutes.

With clean hands, start to mash and knead the bread mixture. You want it well blended and softened to the texture of mashed potatoes, with no hard lumps. Discard any hard bits you come across. Add a little more of the water and set the mixture aside to soak for a few minutes, and then repeat as often as necessary. The process of getting everything just barely moistened but not mushy takes a good half hour or more. Your goal is a dryish pasty texture, so don't add too much water. The paste is ready when you can pick up a small-lemon-sized bit of it and shape it into a firm, round lump.

Wash your fermenting container in very hot soapy water, then rinse with hot water and shake until mostly dry. Sprinkle about half the remaining salt into the container and shake it around to coat the sides and bottom with salt. (This is an anti-contamination strategy.)

You want the bread paste to go into the container as a solid mass, with no air pockets. Form a small-lemon-sized ball of the paste and press it into the container. Then continue shaping the balls and pressing them one by one into the container, making sure to avoid air pockets. Use your hands to press down on the balls as you work to eliminate any gaps.

When all the paste is in the container, sprinkle on the remaining salt. Moisten a clean cloth with the vodka or other spirit and rub down the inside surfaces of the container above the paste. (This further protects against contamination.)

Lay a double layer of cheesecloth over the paste so the edges hang over the sides of the container. Top that with a piece of plastic (I cut a circle out of a used heavy plastic bag) to seal off the miso. Put a weight on top (a rock, a jar filled with water, or a very heavy lid) so the plastic presses down on the paste. Seal everything off from outside contamination by stretching a large plastic bag over the top and securing it with string.

Place the container in a cardboard box, close the lid, and let it sit in a relatively warm place (about 76°F/25°C) for 4 or 5 days to help get fermentation started.

Move the container to a cool, dark place (for example, a basement or the floor of a cupboard) to ferment.

Check the fermenting paste every 3 weeks or so (if the temperature is very warm, check it every 2 weeks). It will bubble a lot at the start. The coverings may now have some mold spores on them; if so, don't worry, simply replace them with fresh cloth or cheesecloth and plastic wrap after checking the miso. If there is any pale mold or kahm yeast (see Glossary) on the surface of the miso itself, don't worry. Carefully scrape it off and then wipe the inside walls of the container again with a clean cloth soaked with the vodka or other spirit.

After 3 months, using a large spoon, stir the mixture, turning the bottom up to the top, then press it all back down to push out all the air, seal it again, and cover again with the plastic, weight, and top layer of plastic. Continue to let the miso ferment, checking on it every month.

After 6 months, the miso should be ready—it will be salty with a rich, sweet umami flavor. Transfer to clean glass jars, label clearly, and refrigerate. The miso should keep for at least a year.

SOY SAUCE

Soy sauce is made from cooked soybeans that are mixed with aspergillus spores and usually also with lightly toasted cracked wheat berries (some soy sauces are made without wheat). The spores grow on the mixture in warm temperatures and then the whole mass is stirred into a salt brine and left to steep and ferment. (If you make miso, the liquid that forms on top is a form of soy sauce, and it is probably a precursor of the soy sauces we have today.) In earlier times, when salt was more precious, soy sauce would have been a valuable way of extending salty flavors, a tool of salt frugality.

When buying soy sauce, look for one that is naturally brewed and fermented, avoiding any made with caramel coloring, amino acids, preservatives, sugar, and/ or other added ingredients. All soy sauces have a salty taste, but the proportion of sodium ranges widely.

I've done a few parallel tastings of soy sauces, though not as many at a time as author Hsiao-Ching Chou. In her book *Vegetarian Chinese Soul Food*, she sets out a tasting chart with notes on eleven different soy sauces. The range of flavors is remarkable, and they change and evolve when the sauce is heated. The choice of soy sauce is especially important in vegetarian cooking, which relies a little more on soy sauce to give umami that could otherwise come from meat. You might like to try doing your own parallel tasting of soy sauces with friends.

I most often use Kikkoman regular soy sauce in cooked dishes, and Kikkoman low-sodium soy sauce for dressings because its flavor is less intense. Try exploring some of the new artisanally made soy sauces; you may find new favorites. You may already have your own favorite soy sauces. We all create a relationship with our staple ingredients, and that familiarity is precious.

I use a dash of soy sauce in some dals, and often in soups and stews, especially if they are meatless. It also goes into some stir-fries. To prevent the soy sauce from scorching on the surface of your hot wok or pan, be sure to add it to the ingredients or to any liquid already in the pan.

In Noto, Japan, I was told about soy sauce used as a preservative. When the fishing boats are out at sea, freshly caught squid are dropped into soy sauce and then flash-frozen. The term used for this technique is *okizuke*, literally, "on-the-sea pickle." The squid are delicious, they say.

Soy sauce can also be used to make a kind of superpowered version of shio koji, known as shoyu koji. See the recipe on page 104.

TRANS-HIMALAYAN SALT TRADE

Nepal has no salt, which is an age-old problem, but over the Himalayan passes lies the Tibetan plateau, where there are many salt deposits and salt lakes.

The passes are blocked with snow for many months of the year, and until recently, all loads needed to be carried by humans or animals along the ancient trading trails (there's now a rough road into western Nepal from the border).

The village of Burang has been a summertime trading center for generations. It lies on a trade route that is also a pilgrim route from India and Nepal. (The pilgrims are headed to Mt. Kailash, a holy mountain for Buddhists, Hindus, Jains, and various animists.) Every year after the passes clear of snow, sometime in May, Nepali traders arrive in Burang with goods to sell and trade: wheat flour, rice, small manufactured goods of various kinds, perfumes, glass beads, and more, all carried in by porters.

The annual summer market attracts Tibetan nomads and traders from all over the vast Tibetan plateau. They arrive on foot or get a ride in the back of rackety transport trucks. The nomads bring salt that they've gathered during the winter from the salt lakes. They also bring herds of sheep and goats, wool on the hoof. The animals are sheared right there in Burang, by the hundreds, and the wool is roughly sorted and wound into huge skeins. Once the deals are done, both wool and salt must be carried back over the mountains into western Nepal. From there, they'll be transported and traded in villages and towns, and eventually some will reach the capital city, Kathmandu.

In Burang at the summer market, a Nepali trader negotiates for salt.

DAIRY & EGGS

MILK AND EGGS ARE TWO VALUABLE foods that humans have depended upon since they first started domesticating animals. They're rich in calories and (for most people) very digestible.

Milk, of course, is extremely perishable. Herding cultures living in Asia, Africa, Europe, or the Caucasus long ago figured out how to preserve the milk given by their herds so that it could feed them in the seasons when milk was not available. Butter is one way that these pastoralists—whether nomadic or settled—store the fat from the milk of their animals. They also transform milk and milk fats into cheese and other dairy products.

Salt and fermentation play a complementary role in the creation of a wide range of preserved milk foods: the salt inhibits spoilage bacteria and helps control fermentation, while the fermentation gives flavor and also discourages spoilage.

Mongolian culture has probably the largest array of dairy-food preservation techniques. One of those techniques traveled west, perhaps with the Mongol invasions long ago, and is still used from Afghanistan to North Africa, in various forms, to produce a salted dried dairy product called *qurut* in Turkic languages and *kashk* in Farsi-related languages.

While people have been foraging eggs from birds' nests since the dawn of humankind, chickens were domesticated about five thousand years ago, in Southeast Asia, and ducks a little later. Eggs from domesticated chickens and ducks keep well for only a relatively short time without refrigeration. There are a few techniques that developed in China and elsewhere to preserve them for a longer period, including salting whole eggs by immersing them in brine. Brining whole eggs (page 127) or salting egg yolks (page 130) is a relatively simple way of preserving them, though brined eggs do eventually need to be cooked to keep even longer. The brine penetrates the shells as they soak, gradually flavoring and transforming both the whites and the yolks.

Huge blocks of fresh butter for sale in the Barkhor market in Lhasa, next to packages of incense

HOMEMADE BUTTER
Sweet, Salted, or Cultured

When I was a child, every couple of years we traveled west by train to visit my grandparents who farmed in northern British Columbia. My brother and I would get a chance to churn the rich milk from their Jersey cow, a magical but laborious task of transformation. In their butter churn, the cream was agitated by wooden paddles that went rapidly round a central pole, turned by a handle outside. The wet hollow sound of the paddles going round and round through the cream would eventually start to shift into a thicker, slower sound, *kthunk-kthunk*, as the fats emerged from the liquid and clung to them. The watery buttermilk released from the cream made light splashy sounds. Then it was time to scrape the butter off the paddles into a bowl, press it in our hands to squeeze out the last of the buttermilk, wash it with water, and add a little salt. The butter, a deep yellow from the grass the cow lived on in her summer pasture, tasted of rich cream and salt.

You can make your own butter quite easily using a food processor and starting with heavy cream (sometimes called heavy whipping cream), which in the US must contain at least 36 percent butterfat. (Cream labeled "whipping cream" or "light whipping cream" is only required to have between 30 and 35 percent butterfat, so it may not be rich enough for butter; check the label to determine the actual percentage of butterfat. If it's 35 percent, you're probably fine.) The instructions below give you options for making simple sweet butter, salted butter, or cultured butter.

Because the flavor of the butter depends on the quality of the cream, look for organic cream and, even better, cream from grass-fed cows. Avoid cream that has been treated by UHT (ultra-high temperature, also called ultra-pasteurized) processing or cream with any additives. If you're salting the butter, use a good sea salt with a pleasant aroma. If I'm salting only very lightly, I like using flake salt, with crystals that aren't too big or hard. Make sure all your tools and containers, and your hands, are very clean and free of odors. Butter picks up smells easily.

If you want to make cultured butter, start fermenting the cream a day ahead, as described in the Variation below.

continued

Makes about 7 ounces/190 grams butter, plus about 1¼ cups/ 300 ml buttermilk

2 cups/480 ml organic heavy cream (36 percent butterfat), well chilled (at or below 60°F/15°C)

About ½ teaspoon/3 grams fine sea salt, or more to taste (for salted butter)

You will need a food processor, a rubber spatula, a blunt knife, a container for the buttermilk, a medium bowl, a jeweler's scale (if salting the butter), parchment paper or wax paper, and plastic wrap.

Pour the cream into a food processor and start processing. The cream will spatter at first and then settle into a soft thickening mass; after a couple of minutes, you'll have whipped cream. Stop the processor, use a spatula to wipe down the spatters on the lid and sides of the bowl into the mass of cream (you don't want to waste any of it), then continue processing. After 5 to 7 minutes, the cream will break apart into fat and liquid; you will hear the sound change as it does, and you'll see that the fats have clumped together solidly and the liquid buttermilk has separated out.

Pour the buttermilk into a bowl or other container to save for baking or for drinking. Press on the butter with your spatula; it will give off a little more buttermilk, which you can pour into the bowl. Transfer the butter to a medium bowl. Press it again to push out as much buttermilk as possible, and add it to the rest.

To wash the butter, add about a cup of very cold water to the bowl and press and squeeze the butter with your hands to push out the liquid. Pour off the liquid and discard. Repeat several times, until the water runs clear. You now have sweet butter.

To make salted butter, sprinkle the salt over the butter and knead and fold the butter over and over on itself four or five times to distribute the salt well. My salt amounts are conservative, so taste and decide if you want a little more; if lightly salting the butter with flake salt, as I sometimes do, I use only 4 grams per pound. (Note: If you're making a different quantity of butter, use the proportion 7 to 9 grams fine sea salt per 1 pound/450 grams butter.)

Pull the butter together as you would cookie dough and roll it into a log. Roll it up in parchment paper or wax paper and twist the ends, or fold them over, to seal. Label with the date and store in the refrigerator as you would commercial butter. To freeze, wrap the butter roll in a second layer of plastic wrap or a well-sealed waxed cloth wrapper, to keep out smells and air.

Store the buttermilk in a glass jar in the refrigerator and use it to make pancakes or cake, or serve as a cooling drink, perhaps lightly salted.

continued

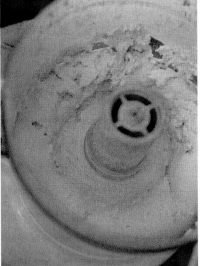

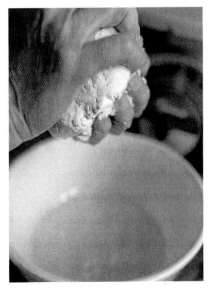

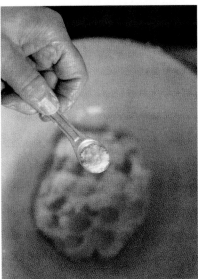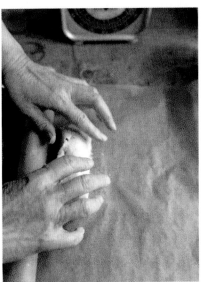

VARIATION

To make cultured butter, if using pasteurized cream, you will need an ingredient that gives you the lactic acid bacteria (LAB) necessary for starting fermentation. The easiest option for this is whole-milk yogurt that has no additives. Stir in 2 tablespoons/30 ml plain yogurt per cup/240 ml of heavy cream. (If you have access to unpasteurized heavy cream, you can rely on the LABs in the cream to start the culture; there's no need to add yogurt.) Another flavorful alternative is to use shio koji (page 100 or 102, or store-bought) to culture your cream; the proportions are 1 tablespoon/15 ml per cup/240 ml cream.

After you've stirred in the culture, if using, leave the cream out at room temperature, 68 to 72°F/19 to 21°C, in a covered container for 18 to 24 hours. It will thicken a little and smell slightly fermented. Move it to the refrigerator and chill it for an hour or two, then follow the instructions above to make butter.

SALT IN BUTTER

Traditionally, butter was salted to help it keep longer, as salt inhibits spoilage bacteria. Salt also brings out butter's flavor in the same way that salting vegetables or meat enhances their inherent flavors. **Sweet butter** is the term for butter that has no added salt; it may also be labeled "unsalted."

In most countries, butter is salted in a proportion of 1½ to 2 percent salt by weight. This translates to roughly 1 to 1½ teaspoons salt per pound of butter or 1.5 to 2 grams of salt per 100 grams of butter.

In France, there's also a lightly salted butter called **demi-sel** (half-salted). Some demi-sel is salted with flake sea salt or fleur de sel, and it is best eaten cool, on bread, each mouthful having a crunchy, salty hit embedded in the butter's smooth richness.

Cultured butter, which is the style of most butter in Europe, is made from cream that has been cultured with lactobacillus to give it a slight tang before it is churned into butter. The traditional system of culturing cream helped give butter a longer shelf life; it also adds a delicious flavor. (Traditionally the raw cream was left to sit out and culture naturally; now, with pasteurization the norm, most often there is a culture added, as in the recipe above.) Cultured butter may be salted or sweet.

FERMENTED SALTED DAIRY: KASHK/QURUT

Kashk is the Farsi name and *qurut* (sometimes transcribed as *qhoroot*) the term in Turkic languages and Arabic for a fermented dried milk, or milk and grain, product used in cuisines from Afghanistan to Iran to Greece to North Africa. Ingredients and preparation techniques vary. In Afghanistan and Iran, among other places, the whey from drained yogurt or the buttermilk from butter churning is salted, cooked down, strained, and then shaped into whitish disks or balls that harden as they dry out and ferment. In other places, the whey is cooked down and reduced to a paste, then mixed with crushed parboiled wheat and/or barley and dried in cubes, or crushed to a powder.

The pure dairy form (with no added grains) is usually quite salty and has a distinctive sour fermented taste. In Iran, the Caucasus, Turkey, and much of Central Asia, it's made in the summer and fall when pasture and milk are plentiful and then used in cooking during the winter months and early spring. The dried disks need to be soaked and ground into a paste before using. Powdered qurut/kashk is available in some Lebanese and other West Asian shops, as are jars of reconstituted kashk/qurut paste. The paste is not as shelf-stable as the disks or powder.

My experience with kashk/qurut has mostly been through Persian dishes such as eggplant with creamy kashk sauce (*kashk-e-bademjan*), where it gives a rich and funky depth to pureed grilled eggplant. There's also the Afghan dish called *kichidi-qurut*, in which the easy comfort of kichidi, a kind of simmered porridge made with a combination of green mung beans and plump central Asian rice, is topped with a thick sauce of qurut. Kashk, on its own or mixed with chopped walnuts and/or other flavors, is also used as a topping for supple flatbreads in Syria and other parts of West Asia.

CHEESE

Cheese is an important part of the world of salt-controlled fermentation. Whether a handcrafted farmstead cheese or an industrially produced cheddar, all the cheeses that we're familiar with in the developed world arose out of dairy cultures, primarily in northern Europe, from Finland to France and northern Spain, but also in Turkey and the Caucasus as well as in Yunnan in China.

Many of these cheese traditions originated with nomadic cultures; it's only in farming cultures that we find salted hard cheeses. Those cheeses are a very practical way of storing milk over the winter and of creating a supply of calorie-rich long-keeping food.

If a cheesemaker is starting with raw (unpasteurized) milk, then all she needs to add once the milk is heated is a coagulant (such as rennet or the equivalent). The milk will have enough naturally occurring lactic acid bacteria (LAB) to start fermenting. But if she is using pasteurized milk, she must also add a culture, because pasteurization strips milk of its LAB. After the milk has coagulated into a mass and the whey has been pressed out of it, the cheese-making progresses in various ways, all of which depend on salt brine or salting at some stage to help protect the fresh cheese from spoilage bacteria and to control fermentation as the cheese develops and ages.

Fresh cheeses such as feta are made of cheese curds that are salted and shaped, then stored in a brine, usually about a 7 percent salt solution, to age. Young feta is milder and softer, while aged feta is firmer and stronger tasting, but it still looks white and fresh, since the brine prevents the formation of molds on the surface or inside the cheese.

In contrast to feta, dry-aged cheeses (which are not stored in brine, as feta is) are firmer textured and stronger tasting, because they lose water during the aging process. The two most famous aged cheeses of Italy are strong tasting and salty: Parmigiano-Reggiano, made of cow's milk, and Pecorino Romano, made of sheep's milk. Parmigiano-Reggiano is aged for at least one and up to three years or longer, and Pecorino Romano for five months to a year. Aged Pecorino contains nearly 2000 mg sodium per 100 grams of cheese, compared to the 1529 mg sodium per 100 grams of Parmigiano.

If you're interested in exploring cheese-making further, I recommend *The Art of Natural Cheesemaking* by David Asher (see Resources). He describes how to use kefir grains and rennet with whatever milk you have (as fresh as possible) to make feta, cheddar, and many other classic cheeses.

BRINED EGGS

Brined eggs are immersed in salted water for about 3 weeks, a Chinese technique. You can leave the brine simple, but it's much more interesting to flavor it with aromatics. I'm grateful to Carolyn Phillips for the guidance in her cookbook *All Under Heaven*. This recipe is for chicken eggs, but you can use the same ingredients and method for duck eggs.

The first time I made these, I wasn't sure what to expect when I cracked one open, uncooked, after the weeks of brining. I'd read that the yolk would be firm, but I hadn't realized that it would also have become a beautiful deep-gold orb. The white was still liquid, so it poured off easily, leaving the yolk sitting in the shell like a large gemstone. I used the yolks from some of that first batch of brined eggs to make golden sand sauce, a rather magical flavoring from the Shanghai region for firm lightly cooked vegetables (see Zucchini in Golden Sand Sauce, page 244).

If you hard-boil brined eggs (see instructions below), they transform again: the yolks pale into a softer yellow, and the whites firm into a porcelain-like layer. The best thing about them, though, is their taste: the aromas in the brine are absorbed by the whites, so that each mouthful is a cascade of salty complex flavors. That makes them a handy ingredient, ready to add depth and richness to a variety of dishes: chop them and add to a salad, serve on top of plain rice or congee, or toss into fried rice . . . there are many possibilities.

Makes 12 brined eggs

About 6½ cups/1.5 liters boiling water

1½ cups/360 grams fine sea salt

12 large or extra-large fresh chicken eggs

A 2-inch/5 cm piece of fresh ginger, peeled and cut into matchsticks

1 tablespoon Sichuan peppercorns (optional)

2 teaspoons fennel seeds or 2 star anise

3 to 5 dried red chiles

3 large or 5 small garlic cloves, lightly smashed and peeled

2 tablespoons Shaoxing rice wine, mirin, or sake

You will need a 2-quart/2 liter glass jar or two 1-quart/1 liter jars, a well-washed round piece (or pieces) of stiff plastic about the same diameter as your jar(s) (such as one [or two] cut out of a plastic yogurt lid[s]), and a storage container.

continued

Pour the boiling water into a large clean bowl, add the salt, and stir to dissolve completely. Set aside to cool to room temperature.

If using one 2-quart/2 liter jar, lay it on its side and carefully put in the eggs one by one; tilt the jar slightly so that they roll gently down to the bottom and you don't risk cracking them. Stand the jar up and add all the aromatics and the wine. Pour in enough of the brine to come to about 1 inch/5 cm below the rim of the jar. Follow the same method if using two jars, dividing the aromatics and wine equally between them.

Slide the well-washed piece(s) of plastic (see above) into the jar(s) to submerge the eggs completely; they should not be exposed to air. Screw the lids on the jars and store in a cool place for 3 weeks.

After 3 weeks, test an egg: it should have a dense, solid yolk. If the yolk is not yet set, leave the remaining eggs in the brine for another week and test again.

Once the eggs are ready, drain them, transfer to a covered container, and refrigerate; discard the brine. Use the eggs for sand sauce (see page 244) within 2 weeks; hard-boil any eggs that you won't use within 2 weeks (see below).

To hard-boil the eggs: Place the eggs in a saucepan of warm water and bring to a gentle boil, then cook for 7 minutes. Remove from the heat. If using the eggs immediately, let cool slightly, then peel and slice; use as a topping for congee or in vegetable fried rice. Unpeeled hard-boiled eggs can be stored in the refrigerator for another 3 weeks.

QUICK-SALTED EGG YOLKS

A modern addition to the salted egg repertoire, these yolks are salted out of the shell. They have a flatter shape than the perfect round yolks from brined whole eggs. Because the yolks have no seasoning other than salt and time, be sure to start with the freshest eggs possible, ideally from a local farm.

Once salted and dried, the yolks keep well in an airtight container in the refrigerator. They can be grated like Parmesan (using a microplane) onto pasta or salads or vegetable dishes to add a layer of rich umami flavor and beautiful color. They're especially good on bitter greens: dandelion leaves, radicchio, broccoli rabe. Some chefs and cooks grate them onto desserts—fresh berries, for example—as a colorful salty-sweet garnish.

Makes 4 salted egg yolks

Fine salt as needed

Yolks from 4 large or extra-large fresh chicken eggs

You will need a small shallow glass container such as a baking dish, a spoon, a cloth, cheesecloth, and kitchen string.

Spread a thick layer of salt (about ½ inch/1.25 cm) in a small baking dish or other glass container and use the back of a spoon to make 4 hollows in it. Gently place one yolk in each hollow. Cover the yolks completely with more salt, then cover the dish tightly and refrigerate for 1 week.

After a week, the yolks will have firmed up. Remove from the salt, brush off the remaining salt or wipe off with a damp cloth, and wipe the yolks dry.

Lay a large piece of cheesecloth on your work surface. Place the yolks in a row near one edge, leaving about 1 inch/2.5 cm between them. Starting at that edge, roll the yolks up in the cheesecloth. Tie a short piece of string between each egg-lump, to keep them separated, and tie off both ends to seal them.

Hang the lumpy length of cheesecloth in the fridge, or in your basement or another cool place that is less than 50°F/11°C, and leave for a week to 10 days to dry until the yolks are very firm, like hard cheese.

Once they're firm, unwrap the yolks and store them in a tightly sealed container in the fridge for up to 3 weeks.

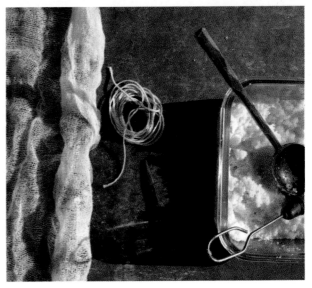

Salt piles beside Lac Rose, in Senegal

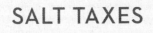

SALT TAXES

Throughout recorded history, governments and rulers that want to raise money—usually to pay for wars and extravagance—have often resorted to taxing salt.

A tax on salt, a daily necessity, is much more onerous for the poor than for the rich. The kings of France started collecting a salt tax, called *gabelle*, in the thirteenth century. The government of Japan began to tax salt in the early 1900s to help raise the money to pay for the Japanese-Russian War of 1905. The British taxed salt at home and in British India. They made it illegal for people in India to gather salt for themselves, and they even built a huge hedge barrier across the country to control the flow of salt; they wanted to centralize and control all salt supplies and all sales of salt.

All these salt taxes had complicated consequences. The gabelle was imposed unequally across France, with different rates in different regions,

all of them high. The tax caused deep discontent and was one of the causes of the French Revolution in 1789. The Japanese tax on salt led to the centralization of the salt supply, and that in turn meant that local salts were no longer sold separately but instead were mixed with salt produced elsewhere, causing many artisanal salt makers to stop production. It was only after the tax was lifted and the government monopoly ended in the late 1990s that consumers had choices and artisanal salt making in Japan revived. The British tax on salt in India led to Gandhi's very effective Salt March in the spring of 1930. That successful defiance of the British helped lead to the country's independence in 1947.

SEAFOOD

IN THIS CHAPTER, YOU'LL FIND STORIES, explanations, and descriptions of a few seafood-based preserved foods, from fish sauce and shrimp paste to salted anchovies, salt cod, and bottarga, along with a couple of recipes.

Seafood is a primary wild-gathered source of protein. Humans have figured out many ways of using salt to preserve these valuable food resources: salting and sun-drying, salt-fermenting, salt-curing, and liquid ferments. The resulting products of that human ingenuity are not simply ingredients for survival, they're also sources of delicious flavor.

As soon as a fish is killed, its cells start to break down. The warmer the temperature and the oilier the fish, the more rapid the breakdown. Before the advent of flash-freezing, salting fish immediately, in dry salt or in brine, was the answer.

In warmer climates, fish can be lightly salted for short-term preservation and then sun-dried. It can then be stored until needed or traded and shipped over long distances. The great fourteenth-century traveler Ibn Battuta (see page 95), when describing the islands we now call the Maldives, wrote, "Each population catches

Salt-preserved shrimp three ways (clockwise from upper right): whole dried shrimp, shrimp paste, and Korean brined shrimp

TOP: *Salt-dried fish, fermented fish paste, shrimp paste, and more, for sale at a market in Karen State, Burma.* ABOVE: *Salted fish drying on racks in the sun, in Saint Louis, Senegal*

the fish of its own island only, which they salt and send to India and China." Where there's not reliable sun to dry fish quickly, salt-preserving fish such as anchovies, cod, and herring requires heavy salting so that enough water is drawn out to prevent the fish from spoiling.

Freshwater and saltwater fish in Southeast Asia, and small ocean fish and squid in Japan and the Philippines, have for centuries been processed into salted fermented fish products, so that nothing goes to waste. The seafood is layered with salt and fermented in sealed containers to produce fish sauce or its coarser-textured cousin, a sort of fish paste. In Japan's Noto Peninsula, fish sauce is made from locally caught seafood that is salt-fermented in a similar way.

For centuries, in the Mediterranean and Black Sea, the roe of tuna, gray mullet, and other species has been salted and dried. Other forms of roe are stored in brine to keep them fresh.

Salt-dried shrimp are a reliable staple in many parts of the world. All over Southeast Asia, and in China and Korea as well, catches of small shrimp are salted and sun-dried, or salted, ground to a paste, and fermented, to preserve them for later. Shrimp preserved in brine (seaujeot) are often used in Korea as a flavoring for kimchi.

SALT-PACKED ANCHOVIES

Anchovies are small oily members of the Engraulidae family, found in temperate to warm waters in many parts of the world. Because their flavor is so forceful, anchovies are often used as an accent in condiments and other preparations, such as Caesar salad dressing, or to make anchovy butter. They are also a wonderful, though often invisible, element in slow-cooked dishes, where they add a generous dose of umami flavor as they melt into the other ingredients; see Slow-Cooked Lamb Shoulder, page 288.

You'll find preserved anchovies in two forms: fillets packed in oil or whole fish packed in salt. The oil-packed fillets are easy to use, with no work needed other than a quick rinse and pat dry. Whole salt-packed anchovies are a bit more work, but their pronounced umami flavor and firmer texture make them ideal as a featured ingredient in a dish such as *pissaladière* (page 316). They are usually packed in a tin layered with salt; the fish will be bathed in some brine, the salt having drawn liquid out of them. Prepare them as you need them, leaving the rest in the tin, or you can process the whole tin when you open it.

Note: The pale vinegared anchovy fillets called *boquerones* from the northern coast of Spain, in Basque Country, are cured using a different process.

Carefully lift out an anchovy from the tin; you may need to scrape away some salt to get at it. Work carefully, as the fish may be stiff and breakable. Rinse off each one, then lay it on a work surface.

Take hold of the tail and lift it gently to carefully peel the top fillet off the bones. Set the fillet aside, skin side down, on an oiled plate, then peel away the spine and bones from the remaining fillet and set it on the plate. Repeat with as many as you wish to prepare. Set aside the bones; they are delicious crisp morsels when lightly fried. If not preparing the whole tin, wrap the tin in plastic and store in the refrigerator.

Trim any fins off the fillets, then feel along each one for stray small bones and remove them. To remove the excess salt, place the fillets in a shallow bowl of water, making sure they are submerged, and let soak for 10 to 20 minutes, turning them over once or twice. The timing will depend on the saltiness of the fish. If they've been sitting a long time in salt, they'll be almost hard. You want them to soak until softened but not so long that they get mushy.

Once they've soaked, lay the fillets out on a cloth or paper towels and pat them dry. They're now ready to be used in a dish.

To store the prepared fillets in oil so they're readily available, make sure the soaked fillets are completely dry. Leave them on the cloth or paper towels until you are satisfied there are no water droplets remaining on them. Pack them into a glass jar, adding extra-virgin olive oil as you go. The olive oil is there to seal them from the air, so add more when you've packed them all in to ensure they are all submerged. Label and store in the refrigerator.

SALT COD

Cod is the name given to a large category of cold-water fish belonging to the genus *Gadus*. Until late in the twentieth century, cod were found in enormous numbers off the Grand Banks near Newfoundland. Salt cod had become a huge cash crop once European fishers discovered Grand Banks cod in the early 1500s. Historians don't agree on who originated the salting of cod, but it seems most likely to have been the Basques, who were already fishing at the mouth of the Saint Lawrence River in 1534, when Jacques Cartier traveled there on his first voyage for the king of France.

What we do know is that when fishers from Portugal, England, Spain, and France who were working off the Grand Banks in the sixteenth century realized that they could bring loads of salt from Europe to Newfoundland to preserve their catch, the salt-cod industry was born. The result was increased food security in Europe.

The cod was often cleaned out at sea, then brought to shore to be salted. For centuries along the coast of Newfoundland, fishing families living in small communities salted the fresh-caught cod and laid the fish on racks to dry in the wind, re-salting it regularly until the salt "struck" (meaning it was salted right through the flesh of the fish). With the collapse of the Grand Banks fishery in the 1990s, most salt cod is now made from fish caught near Iceland and the Faroe Islands or in the North Sea.

Salt cod can be stored indefinitely. Like salt beef, it was a staple on sailing ships, used to feed the crew during the days of the trade in enslaved people from Africa and the trade in sugar and cotton from the Caribbean plantations to Europe and North America. The delicious Jamaican national dish ackee and saltfish (see page 259) has its roots in that terrible trade, for ackee seeds that were brought from West Africa by enslaved people flourished in Jamaica. Enslaved cooks combined the fruit they knew with the salt cod shipped from North America.

Salt cod has been a staple food in historically Catholic countries for centuries because on fasting days people were forbidden to eat meat. Noncoastal populations could not rely on fresh fish, but salt cod was easy to transport and store.

When buying salt cod, look for thick pieces that are not as stiff as a board. Before it is cooked and eaten, salt cod needs a long soaking in several changes of water. Be sure to follow the soaking times indicated in each of the recipes in this book; the salt is tenacious, and undersoaked salt cod is not edible.

SALT HERRING

Herring (the name is applied to various species of the family Clupeidae) is a very rich oily fish that deteriorates quickly after being caught. Salt was the solution to that problem for centuries, until the arrival of flash-freezing. Unlike cod and other whitefish, herring must be salted immediately after being caught, which means either salting on board or returning to shore each day to salt the catch.

The Baltic Sea is historically one of the major sources of herring in Europe. In the twelfth to sixteenth centuries, the salt needed to preserve the herring catch came largely from Lübeck, a German port on the Baltic. The salt was produced in Lüneberg, a city about 60 miles/100 km to the south that lay over a large salt deposit; it had been an important source of salt since before the tenth century. The brine from the salt wells in Lüneberg was boiled over wood fires, denuding the region's forests and resulting in what is known today as Lüneberg Heide, a heathland of scrub and heather. Lübeck grew rich through the sales of salt, but after 1500 the city lost its dominance when lower-priced salt from Brittany and Spain became available to the Dutch and Flemish herring fisheries.

Salted herring is an ingredient in traditional recipes from Scandinavia and northern Europe (see Salt Fish and Potato Casserole, page 264). It needs to be soaked in fresh water and then cleaned. Recipes in old cookbooks assume that you're starting with a salt-hardened whole fish, which might take several days of soaking before you can clean it and cook with it. These days, herring is more available unsalted and flash-frozen than as whole salted fish.

GRAVLAX

In earlier times in Scandinavia, salt was scarce. Instead of salt-curing their catch, people living along the coast would preserve the catch by pressing it between two layers of birchbark and burying it. The term *gravlax* comes from *gravad*, meaning buried, and *lax*, meaning salmon. That long fermentation produced strong-smelling and pungent-tasting fish that is still the epitome of delicious for those who grew up with it.

In North America, what we call gravlax is quite different: salmon that's been briefly cured with salt and sugar and flavored with dill. In the Nordic countries where it originated, it is often served with a mustard sauce.

The idea is elegantly simple: You start with two skin-on salmon fillets, cleaned of any pin bones. Rub a mix of salt and sugar onto the flesh side of each fillet, add some dill, and then sandwich the two fillets together. Press the salmon sandwich lightly with a weight, and refrigerate for 48 hours. The seasoning and herb mixture flavors the fish, and it also cures it and firms its texture by drawing out excess water. Then it's wiped off and the fish is ready to be cut into thin slices and eaten as an appetizer, as part of a smorgasbord spread, on its own or on bread, with or without more fresh dill.

I like making a small amount of gravlax, with about 1½ pounds/675 grams salmon.

NOTE: *Sometimes fish, wild or farmed, can harbor parasites, so when preparing fish that is only lightly cured and not cooked, as in this recipe, the best practice is to start with fish that has previously been frozen.*

Makes about 1½ pounds/
675 grams

About 1½ pounds/675 grams skin-on salmon fillet (1 or 2 fillets); see Note above

2 to 3 tablespoons aquavit or vodka (optional)

About 1 tablespoon/18 grams coarse sea salt

About 2 teaspoons sugar

1 teaspoon freshly ground white pepper, or to taste

About 1 cup/60 grams finely chopped fresh dill

OPTIONAL TOPPINGS

1 tablespoon capers

¼ cup/15 grams chopped fresh dill

1 red onion, thinly sliced

FOR SERVING

1 lemon, cut into small wedges or thin slices

Sliced rye or other whole-grain bread (toasted if not using rye bread)

Good salted butter

You will need a rectangular nonreactive dish (such as a small Pyrex baking dish), a small bowl, a flat surface such as an oval plate to weight the fish, and plastic wrap.

Wipe the salmon dry. Check it for any remaining pin bones, pull them out, and discard them. Place one fillet skin side down in a rectangular glass or other nonreactive container and pour over half the aquavit or vodka, if using. Turn the fish over, place the second fillet on top, skin side down, and pour over the remaining spirits if using. Let stand for 10 minutes if using the spirits, then drain.

Put the salt, sugar, and pepper in a small bowl and mix well. Pat the fish dry and place on your work surface. Spread the seasoning mixture all over the flesh side of both fillets, pressing it on carefully and firmly. Place one fillet in the container skin side down. Spread the chopped dill over the top. Lay the second fillet flesh side down on the dill and press down firmly. Place a flat plate or small cutting board on top of the salmon and top it with a weight (for example, a heavy rock or a full can). Cover with plastic wrap and refrigerate overnight.

The next day, pour off any accumulated liquid. Flip the salmon pair over. Top again with the weight, wrap, and put back in the refrigerator.

The next day, wipe or scrape off the flavoring mixture.

To serve, use a sharp knife held at an angle to slice the fish thinly on the diagonal, leaving the skin behind, and arrange on plates or a platter. If you wish, scatter on some or all of the optional toppings. Serve with the lemon, bread, and plenty of butter.

FISH SAUCE

Fish sauce is a staple condiment in many parts of Southeast Asia, Japan, Korea, and the Philippines—and in my kitchen. Loaded with umami, it gives subtle depth to savory dishes of all kinds.

Fish sauce has a long pedigree. The Greeks and Romans, faced with the wealth of fish in the Mediterranean and the Black Sea, developed various forms of brined fish and fish sauce, starting as early as the fifth century BCE in Greece, or perhaps earlier. Brining and salting preserved the precious food resource so that it didn't go to waste but instead could feed large populations throughout the year.

Scholarly research tells us that there were many forms of fish sauce in ancient times, with various names and made of different ingredients. Some were used as a cooking ingredient (the Greek *garos* and Roman *liquamen*), and others as a table flavoring (the richer, more luxurious *garum*). They are all part of a spectrum of flavorings derived from salting fish and then fermenting it anaerobically (in a sealed container without oxygen). The liquid given off is one product; the paste made from salted fermented fish is another. These ancient fish sauces seem to have been very similar to Southeast Asian fish sauces, and produced in a similar way.

At about the same time as the Roman empire was flourishing, in Cambodia around the Tonle Sap ("great lake"), a similar tradition of brined fermented fish and fish sauce developed. The fish of the Tonle Sap were a vital food source that sustained the great Khmer empires of two thousand and more years ago. The huge harvest of fish from the Tonle Sap every autumn, layered with salt and fermented to create fish sauce and fish paste, could feed the population well throughout the year and enabled the Khmer kingdoms to prosper. The Khmer eventually conquered much of present-day Thailand and the southern part of Vietnam, and in all the areas they conquered, fish sauce took root.

In Southeast Asia fish sauce is an essential source of amino acids (protein) for the rural poor, who for generations subsisted largely on rice, foraged greens, and fish sauce, along with the occasional fish or frogs from local ponds or seafood. The Western world first encountered Thai and Vietnamese fish sauce late in the twentieth century and within a few years, it became a secret—and not-so-secret—ingredient for many chefs and cooks in Europe and North America.

In Laos, a landlocked country, the fish sauce is made from freshwater fish. In the rest of southeast Asia, fish sauce may be made of freshwater or saltwater fish.

Fresh-caught fish are layered with salt in a tightly sealed container to ferment anaerobically for three months to two years. The anaerobic fermentation results in a thin, salty, brownish liquid and fermented solids. The quality of the fish sauce varies, depending on whether it is from the first pressing (the best) or a later soaking of the solids.

In addition, all over Southeast Asia there are fish pastes of various kinds that are more intense versions of fish sauce, sometimes made with rice husks or rice to help with fermentation. Known in Thailand and Laos as *pla raa* or *padaek*, in Vietnam as *mam*, in Khmer as *prahok*, in Indonesia as *trassi*, in Malay as *budu*, and in the Philippines as *bagoong*, the fish pastes are used in cooking and in some composed dishes.

You can add a dash of fish sauce to soups or stews. I also like a little in mashed avocado to bring out its smoky virtues (but without intruding as an identifiable ingredient). At least one Vietnamese fish sauce producer, Red Boat, has started to produce a funky flavored salt infused with the flavor of fish sauce, a salt-on-salt combo. In many dishes, I do part of my seasoning with fish sauce and part with salt.

In Japan, fish sauce is primarily produced on the Noto Peninsula on the west coast of the island of Honshu (some fish sauce is also made on the Akita Peninsula). In Toyama Bay, on the inland coast of the peninsula, fishermen catch squid, called *ma-ika*, in the bay and the squid intestines are fermented with salt for two or three years to produce the fish sauce called *ishiri*. Along the other side of the peninsula, which is washed by the colder and more turbulent waters of the Sea of Japan, fishermen catch sardines and mackerel. That catch is used to make the fish sauce called *ishiru*.

When I stayed on the peninsula, we bought five or six different local fish sauces to do a taste comparison. They tasted more intensely salty than Thai fish sauce and were less pungent than Vietnamese fish sauce. Of those we tried, I preferred the taste of the ishiru to that of the ishiri. The sauces are used subtly in dishes from Noto and by some cooks elsewhere in Japan. It's surprising that they are not better known outside the country.

In Italy, there is a fish sauce known as *colatura di alici*, made in Cantabria from anchovies. To me, it tastes like a rather muted, less complex-tasting version of the fish sauces of Southeast Asia.

SALTED ROE

Of the many kinds of salt-preserved fish roe found around the world, caviar may be the best known. *Caviar* was originally the word for the salted roe of sturgeon from the Caspian Sea or Black Sea, but that catch has been threatened by overfishing and pollution, and sturgeon are now being fished or farmed for caviar in many other parts of the world, including Italy, China, Canada, and Israel. Currently Israel and China are the largest producers.

The roe from many other kinds of fish, from salmon to lumpfish, is processed in a variety of ways around the world. **Lumpfish roe** from fish caught in the North Sea is brined, dyed black or coral pink, and sold in small glass jars. It is the main ingredient in the delicious savory spread *taramasalata*, literally meaning salted roe (see recipe, page 252).

Another premium processed form of roe is **bottarga**, which most commonly comes from mullet these days, but historically also from sturgeon and tuna. The word for bottarga in modern-day Egyptian is *batarekh*, and the tradition of preserving the roe seems to go back millennia there. In modern times, other names for it around the Mediterranean include *botargo*, *buttariga*, *boutargue*, and *poutargue*.

Bottarga is loaded with intense umami and saltiness, rather like Parmesan cheese, and it's rich in good oils. Because its production is labor intensive, bottarga is relatively expensive per pound, but its full flavor means that it can be stretched to serve many people. The sacs of roe are lifted intact, by hand, from the fish and dried before being immersed in brine to soak. The roe is then pressed between boards to squeeze out moisture. Some processors, especially in Greece and Egypt, coat the pressed roe in beeswax; others wrap it in plastic to seal it from the air. Norway is now producing a bottarga-like pressed salted roe from cod roe, and there are related products in Japan and Korea (see Mentaiko, below).

Bottarga keeps almost indefinitely in the refrigerator (best stored tightly wrapped in waxed cloth or plastic to prevent it drying out to hardness); you'll also see it sold frozen. Each sac is encased in a thin transparent membrane called a pellicule, which needs to be peeled off and discarded. Bottarga varies in texture, depending on the way it has been processed and stored, from soft and easy to slice to denser, harder, and easy to grate on a Microplane. It is delicious in small quantities—for example, grated and sprinkled onto scrambled eggs, or very thinly sliced and eaten on good bread or toast, perhaps with a squeeze of lemon and a sprinkling of olive oil.

Combined with olive oil, fresh herbs, and garlic, bottarga makes a delicious sauce for pasta. See Bucatini with Bottarga, page 334.

Mentaiko is the Japanese word for the processed roe of a species of cod known as Alaska pollack, which is popular in Japan and Korea (where it's called *myeongnan*). The roe is rinsed in saltwater, then dry-salted, and left in a basket to cure for three days. In Korea and Japan, it is then coated with a variety of seasonings, including dried red chile pepper. It's often sliced, drizzled with a little sesame oil, and served as a snack with drinks

Mentaiko has also become a flavoring in other dishes. A friend from Japan tells me that she likes it mixed with mayonnaise, which is then used to dress potato salad, a fusion dish known in Japan as *mentai mayo potesala*. The other well-known use for mentaiko in Japan, and now internationally, is in the fusion pasta dish called Spaghetti Mentaiko (see recipe, page 337).

FUGUKO

Near the town of Wajima, on the Noto Peninsula
in the Sea of Japan, is a village of *ama*. Ama are
fisherwomen who dive for abalone and conch, using

only a mask and flippers, no air tanks.
They carry sacks down with them and
stay under for over a minute each time,
collecting their catch. No wonder
that the fish market in Wajima is a
succession of mostly women vendors.

One damp, windy day in mid-April,
I was in Wajima looking for fish sauce,
another product made in the region.
We stopped at the stall of a friend of a
friend to buy some.

After we'd bought several small
bottles of her fish sauce (made from
a mix of sardines and mackerel), she
gave us a taste of something special:

a product that looks and tastes
rather like bottarga (see page 334)
but is much more notorious. Its full
name in Japanese is *nuga fugu noko*,
most often shortened to *fuguko*; it
is the salted and fermented ovaries
of fugu, the infamous (to foreigners
at least) Japanese puffer fish. The
ovaries and the liver of fugu contain
tetrodotoxin, usually referred to as
TTX, a neurotoxin that can paralyze
anyone who eats it. But remarkably,
if the ovaries are salted by soaking in
brine and then fermented in rice bran
or sake lees for three years, the TTX
is eliminated. The resulting product
is safe to eat as well as delicious.
Studies report that it is the salting that
draws out the fats that contain the
poison. Fuguko is now made only by
licensed processors in specific parts of
Ishikawa Prefecture, and reportedly the
government tests each batch before
granting permission to sell it.

The fuguko I tasted in Wajima that
day had an intense salty, rich flavor.
Like bottarga, fuguko is best eaten in
small amounts, in thin slices with plain
rice, for example, or drizzled with a
little sesame oil.

*Friendly fuguko seller at the Wajima market, on
the Noto Peninsula in Japan*

SALTED DRIED SHRIMP

You may have seen packages of dried shrimp in grocery stores, the small shrimp no bigger than your thumbnail and often tinier, ranging in color from pale tan to pink, with a texture that varies from slightly pliable to completely hard and pellet-like.

I first became familiar with dried shrimp as one of the workhorses of Southeast Asian food from Burma to Vietnam, inexpensive and very versatile. They keep well without refrigeration, and so they're a practical source of protein and flavor. But dried shrimp are relied upon in many other cuisines too, from Brazil to Sri Lanka and India, and from Louisiana to Nigeria to Indonesia. They give a slightly sweet and salty flavor to dishes, as well as umami depth. Ground to a powder or pounded into a kind of fluff, they can be simmered in soups or stews; they can be fried until crisp to eat as a snack, or lightly fried to flavor oil.

Dried shrimp are processed in several ways. In the American South, fresh shrimp are boiled in well-salted water until pink and left in the brine to steep. Then they're drained and dried in the sun, the traditional way, or in a dehydrator, until very stiff. At this point, the shells, dried out and brittle, can be pounded away easily. In other places, such as Thailand, the shrimp are not cooked but just soaked in heavily salted water before being dried in the hot sun. Quality varies, but generally larger, brighter-colored, less-dried-out shrimp have more flavor.

Finely ground dried shrimp are used as a topping for *moqueca* (seafood stew) in Brazil and as the essential flavor and source of protein in a dry chutney condiment from the Himalaya (see page 190). Tiny whole dried shrimp are a key ingredient in Brazilian *acarajé*, the famous bean patties of Bahia. They're used in gumbo in Louisiana, to give depth to Malay sambals, and in many dishes and flavorings from Chinese tradition, such as black bean sauce (see recipe, page 189) and flavored oils.

FLUFFY SHRIMP

Fluffy shrimp is my name for dried shrimp powder, a very useful form of dried shrimp that is a common ingredient in Burmese salads. If you have a choice, buy larger and deeper-colored shrimp that still have some flexibility, rather than being rock hard. Here the shrimp are briefly soaked in warm water to soften them a little, then ground in a food processor until they are reduced to a light, fluffy texture. Store shrimp fluff in a well-sealed glass jar as a useful salt-larder flavoring, a quick way of giving a hit of umami to salads, soups, and even sandwiches.

Makes 1 cup/80 grams

1 cup/80 grams best-quality dried shrimp

You will need a small bowl, a food processor or a knife and mortar and pestle, and a glass jar for storage.

Rinse the shrimp and place them in a small bowl with warm water to cover. Let soak for 10 to 15 minutes, until slightly softened.

Drain the shrimp, transfer to a food processor, and process to a slightly unevenly textured fluffy powder. Or coarsely chop the drained shrimp and pound in a stone mortar until reduced to a rough powder.

Transfer to a clean glass jar and cover tightly.

SHRIMP PASTE

Shrimp paste is an essential ingredient in kitchens from Indonesia and the Philippines to Thailand, Vietnam, and Burma. It's a necessary element in most Thai curry pastes and in the thick, pungent dips called *nam prik* in Thai and *ngapi* in Burma/Myanmar, as well as in sambols and salads in Malaysia and Indonesia. Shrimp paste has now become a secret ingredient in some Western chefs' dishes, for a small amount of it gives a depth of flavor, a resonance, without declaring itself.

Shrimp paste is made in coastal regions from tiny shrimp (and sometimes other small sea creatures) that are rinsed, salted, and laid in the sun to dry. They ferment in the sun, disintegrating into a coarse paste, and then are pounded smooth. It can take as much as ten pounds of shrimp to make one pound of paste. The paste is usually a dense mass that is sold in blocks or in small, tightly sealed plastic containers. The paste may be pinkish, mahogany, grayish, or dark brown, depending on where it's made, the color of the local shrimp, and the method of producing it, as well as whether or not other ingredients are added—some places add sugar, coconut milk, or various flavorings. Shrimp paste is available in many Asian grocery stores in Europe and North America. It keeps well at room temperature, but I usually store mine in the refrigerator in a tightly sealed container.

The pungency of raw shrimp paste is a promise of deliciousness to those who love it, but also a reminder that one culture's pleasing food smell is another culture's stench. (Strong cheeses, for example, smell horrible to people from non-cheese-eating cultures.) But we can learn to love other people's salt-fermented foods, and there's adventure to be had in the process.

If shrimp paste is being added to a sauce as a flavoring, it may first be toasted to a crumbled texture which gives it a milder taste. The easiest way to toast it is by wrapping a piece in foil and cooking it on the hot surface of a skillet. (Sealing it before cooking keeps the intense smell of the paste under wraps.)

FISH SAUCE LOVE AFFAIR

I first learned about fish sauce when I was a teenager staying in a pension in Tours, in the Loire Valley, in the late sixties. Two young Chinese brothers from

Cambodia were also part of the household. They pined for the food from home. As we ate Madame J's wonderful meals, they'd talk about the foods and flavors they missed, including fish sauce; there was none in the Loire Valley, for sure. I could only try to imagine it: pungent, salty, and from a place far away.

It's funny how life turns in spirals. Some years later, I traveled to Europe with my then boyfriend, whose aunt was married to a Vietnamese doctor and living in Paris. It was at their table, and in their kitchen, that I finally met fish sauce and got hooked. I heard stories of Vietnamese life that made pictures in my head, complements to the terrible news coming from the ongoing war in Vietnam.

Thanh, the uncle, had grown up in southern Vietnam under French rule. He traveled to France in his late teens to study medicine. When he returned to Vietnam with his wife and young son in the early fifties, the French colonial administration accused him of treating insurgents and told him they could not answer for his safety.

He and the family packed up and moved back to France. It was a terrible story to me, to have been exiled from his homeland to the country that was the colonial oppressor.

Thanh was pleased when I took to fish sauce and to Vietnamese food

with pleasure, bordering on lust. He told me that in Vietnam fish sauce was an essential stimulant to appetite. "If a French person moved to Saigon and didn't eat fish sauce, we knew they wouldn't last. They'd get sick, and end up leaving, often in a coffin," he told me.

I didn't need scary stories to make me love fish sauce. I had a hunger for it, as the essential ingredient in *nuoc cham* (see page 201) and as a seasoning for savory dishes of all kinds. Thanh kept a stock of half a dozen bottles of fish sauce out on the kitchen balcony.

In early 1975, it became clear that Saigon would fall. The end was near. Thanh sent us out to buy up as much fish sauce as we could. "You'll see," he said. "Vietnam will be closed off and we won't be able to get good *nuoc mam*." Others in the Vietnamese community had had the same idea, and stores were limiting customers to a couple of bottles each. We brought back our few bottles to add to the cache on the balcony, and that was that.

Thanh's prediction came true; it was years before Vietnamese fish sauce was again available outside the country, and Thanh, like the other Vietnamese living abroad, had to make do with fish sauce from Thailand.

A small fish sauce maker I visited in Sukhothai, Thailand, presses the salted fish in large ceramic barrels, topped by a weight, to keep out the oxygen.

MEATS

WHEREVER THERE'S A TRADITION OF animal husbandry, there are strategies for preserving meat. The day the animal is slaughtered is a day for feasting on fresh meat, but the animal is butchered to provide food for the family, or the village, for more than one day. As always with a sudden overabundance of food that can spoil, the question is how best to preserve it.

Human ingenuity has resulted in a huge range of possibilities for meat preservation out of relatively few ingredients. In earlier times salting and curing was both an art and the basis of survival. Around the world, versions of salted and preserved meat range from European corned beef, salt pork, and cured sausages to the biltong of southern Africa, and from the charqui of the Andean highlands to the many hams and sausages of China.

Some of these meats are salted and then sun-dried or air-dried until they're almost weightless, while others are salted and then hung in a cool place for long periods to cure and gain flavor. In this chapter, you'll find recipes for a few members of the salted meat family, some dry-salted and air-cured, some brined, that are fun and interesting to make at home.

Small-batch preserving of meat is easy to do and very satisfying both in the kitchen and at the table. As

I researched meat curing and worked on these recipes
I quickly came to appreciate the flexibility of having
salt-cured pork belly on hand that I could use to add
flavor and substance to many dishes, and home-cured
duck breast and basturma that I could slice thinly and
put out as a taste treat for friends and family.

The mesmerizing vertiginous salt terraces outside Maras, Peru, above the Urubamba River far below.
Notice the salt crystals floating on the surface in places.

WHAT HAPPENS WHEN YOU SALT-CURE MEAT?

We don't know when humans realized that drying meat could help preserve it, and we don't know when people figured out that salting meat could prevent spoilage. But until very recently, drying and salting, alone or in combination, were the primary preservation techniques used for meat.

Why do salting and drying work? Food spoils because pathogenic bacteria go to work to break down the cells. Some merely turn the food into something unpalatable, while others make it toxic. Food preservation is about preventing both these things from happening.

Salt draws water out of cells. It's a quick way of drying out tissues, even in damp climates. The resulting reduction of moisture in cells inhibits the growth of pathogenic bacteria. At the same time, helpful lactic acid bacteria (LAB), which can thrive in a mildly salty environment, start reproducing, in the process we call fermentation. So the bad bacteria are discouraged by not having enough moisture to thrive and the good bacteria are encouraged by the salty environment. Those good bacteria multiply, thereby elbowing out the bad.

Meat can be cured with salt in two ways: dry-salting or brining. In dry-salting, the meat is either packed in salt or rubbed with it, triggering the process of osmosis. The two environments—the salt and the meat—interact to achieve equilibrium, an equal proportion of salt and water in both environments. The water in the meat will flow out into the salt and dissolve it to create a brine; that brine is then absorbed back into the meat, salting the interior.

After dry-salting, the meat is placed in a cool, well-ventilated place to air-dry; often it's hung on a hook, so the process of air-drying is often referred to as "hanging" meat. The drying process allows fermentation to continue, which means that the meat gains flavor. Fermentation also increases the acidity, which in turn protects against pathogens. (Some hams are first dry-salted and then brined before being smoked and hung to air-dry.)

In brining, the salt has already been dissolved in water, so when the meat is immersed in the brine, osmosis can begin immediately: the salty brine is quickly absorbed by it. Until the advent of refrigeration, brining was most important as a method of storing meat, especially in northern Europe and in North America. Different cuts of pork and beef were stored in barrels of brine for long sea voyages, or in farmhouse brine crocks or barrels to provide a steady supply of meat throughout the winter. These days, although brining is not necessary for preservation, it is still used for flavor.

DRY-SALTING

For centuries, people with ready access to salt have preserved meat by packing it in salt in a container for days or weeks before hanging it to air-dry. This "salt-box technique" requires a lot of salt and can leave the meat extremely salty. More recently, many people have turned to a method called equilibrium curing, in which

a precise amount of salt is used, an amount in proportion to the weight of the meat, that is just enough to cure the meat. The result is less wasted salt and no need to soak excess salt out of the meat after it has cured to make it palatable.

When I embarked on my exploration of salt-preserved meats, I spent a lot of time with older cookbooks. I wanted to celebrate salt-curing as a remarkable tool that generations of people developed in order to survive food shortages, inhospitable seasons, or long voyages. I began by testing recipes such as salt pork and basturma using the traditional salt-box technique. The meat would sit in a container surrounded by salt on all sides

and pressed down with a weight. Within a few hours, the salt started drawing liquid out of the meat, and eventually that liquid dissolved the salt, so the meat was sitting in a brine. Recipe instructions were to pour off the brine after one or two days and then replace the poured-off salt; I used a lot of salt each time.

The results were delicious but not perfectly consistent, and I worried about their variability. Could I explain the technique to readers in such a way that they could reliably achieve delicious results?

With advice from friends and a wider exploration of readings, I realized that I needed to move into the modern world of "equilibrium curing" so that anyone wanting to try the recipes would have consistent happy results, with no risk of oversalting. The recipes here for salt pork, pancetta, and duck breast prosciutto all use the equilibrium method. I've included one salt-box recipe, for basturma, so that you can see how it works, and because I am so pleased with the results of my basturma experimenting. Perhaps it's appropriate that this preserved meat from an ancient culture is the one with the old-style technique.

My travels in the world of meat curing are a reminder that techniques may change but the time-tested principles remain the same: salt-cure and then air-dry to complete the cure.

BRINE-CURING AND BRINING

In brining, meat is immersed in water mixed with a measured proportion of salt (expressed as a certain percentage salinity), and sometimes other flavorings such as sugar and spices. The brine can be used to preserve the meat (brine-curing), or simply to add flavor and improve texture (brining).

After brine-curing, the cured meat must be soaked or boiled in plain water to draw out excess salt before being cooked and eaten. With brining, after a short immersion in the brine for flavor, the meat is removed, rinsed off, and cooked.

In traditional country kitchens in many parts of northern Europe and North America, there would be one or more crocks or barrels of brine filled with roasts and other large cuts of meat, both beef and pork. This brine-curing kept them safe from spoilage bacteria for long periods, until they were needed. Like many other traditional kitchen methods, maintaining the brine crock required experience and care.

Since the arrival of refrigeration, the brine crock has largely become a tool of the past, with some important exceptions. Corned beef is still cured in brine, both to flavor it and as a way of preserving the meat (brined corned beef keeps very well for at least 2 weeks).

Other traditional brined beef or pork recipes endure because of the wonderful flavor that develops during the process. I've included one recipe, the Brined Roast Pork on page 300, to illustrate brining as part of the cooking process. Although it now seems to be less popular with home cooks and chefs, if done carefully brining turkey and chicken for 24 to 48 hours, or smaller cuts of meat such as pork chops for even just a few hours can—like a salt rub—enhance the flavor and improve the texture of the poultry or meat.

DRY-CURING MEAT

MINDFUL CURING

When I cook at home, I'm fairly casual about measurements, preferring to let my mood and my ingredients guide the way. But when salt-curing meat, you need to be precise. To that end, here are the essential tools and practices you will want to have in mind and in hand:

• A scale, sometimes called a jeweler's scale, that's accurate to 0.1 gram. Inexpensive digital models are available from many online sources. See Taring a Scale, opposite.

• A kitchen scale that can measure up to several pounds or 1 kilogram.

• Clear labels for all projects. I use masking tape and a Sharpie. I wrap the tape all the way around the sealed bag of equilibrium-curing meat so it won't fall off. On it I write the details: date, weight of the meat, etc.

• A place and system for dry-curing and air-curing (see Notes on Air-Curing Meat, page 165).

• Good general kitchen hygiene, with attention paid to the cleanliness of surfaces and tools, from knives to cutting boards to containers to sponges and cloths.

• Particular attention to handling meat and poultry: When raw meat or poultry comes into contact with any surfaces, it can contaminate them with botulism spores or other pathogens. It's important to thoroughly clean such surfaces immediately after you have worked with raw meat or poultry. Food safety experts tell us that all work surfaces should be regularly scrubbed clean with a solution of hot water and bleach (½ cup/120 ml bleach to 1 gallon/4 liters hot water) and then thoroughly rinsed.

CURING SALTS AND FOOD SAFETY

Even when most harmful bacteria have been discouraged by salting, there is one pathogen that is still a risk—botulism (from the Latin word for sausage, *botulus*, so named after being linked to deaths from infected sausages in Europe in the eighteenth and nineteenth centuries).

Botulism is a bacterium (*Clostridium botulinum*) that produces spores. The spores are found in many places in the environment—in soil, for example—and on many common surfaces. Fortunately, the spores themselves are not dangerous as long as they are in the air or in a very dry, cold, acidic, sweet, or salty

A typical digital jeweler's scale

TARING A SCALE

When you weigh an ingredient, you don't usually put it directly onto the surface of the scale itself, but rather into a measuring cup or a ramekin or onto a plate. In order to account for the weight of that container and only weigh the ingredient itself, you "tare" the scale. To tare, first put the empty container on the scale and press the Tare button (if using a non-digital scale, adjust the weight so your scale reads 0). Then add the ingredient to be weighed.

environment, where they will stay inactive. However, under some very specific conditions the spores can germinate and produce toxins, and those toxins are extremely dangerous.

Spores will only produce toxins if they are in anaerobic (low- or no-oxygen) environments that are also moist and warm, with low-acid (pH over 4.6), low-salt, and/or low-sugar levels. The spores won't germinate and produce toxins if frozen. If the toxins already exist on food, they will be destroyed if the food is cooked to 185°F/85°C and held at that temperature for at least 5 minutes.

The main worry about botulism is with sausages and other cured meats such as salami and prosciutto that will be eaten uncooked. Older recipes for salted or brined meat call for small amounts of saltpeter—potassium nitrate—in addition to regular salt to prevent the possibility of botulism poisoning. These days, instead of saltpeter, which didn't produce entirely consistent results, the way to prevent botulism toxins in cured meats is to include measured amounts of similar but more predictable compounds—sodium nitrites and sometimes sodium nitrates—in the salt cure.

These modern preservatives are called by various names, including curing salt, pink salt, Prague powder, and Instacure, and they come in two formulations. Curing salt #1 (and other #1 products), for short-term preserving, is a blend of salt and sodium nitrite. It protects against botulism poisoning, but its effectiveness is time-limited to about 1 month. Curing salt #2 (and other #2 products), a blend of salt, sodium nitrite, and sodium nitrate, is for protecting meats from botulism toxins for more than a month, such as meat that is commercially cured and hung for longer than 30 days and products that will be eaten uncooked after 30 days or longer, such as salami and prosciutto. Curing salt #2 takes a while to act (the nitrates have to react to the local bacteria and convert into nitrites) but is then an effective barrier to botulism toxins for much longer than Curing salt #1.

The recipes here for pancetta, salt pork, and duck breast prosciutto call for Curing salt #1, which will keep things completely safe for up to 30 days. (None of the recipes in this book call for Curing salt #2.) Once that 30-day time period has passed, there is a possibility that botulism spores in the meat could produce toxins. It is a very low probability, but it's there. As a result, to avoid any possibility of botulism poisoning, any cured meat made following the recipes in this book that you want to keep for longer than 30 days should be frozen and/or cooked.

Many home-curing cooks who cure whole muscle meats (as opposed to sausages, which are made of chopped meat stuffed into casings and are at much higher risk of botulism contamination) choose not to use curing salt. I use it for all the equilibrium meat cures here, but you'll notice I chose not to use curing salt for the old-style basturma recipe.

NOTE: *Prague powder/Curing salt #1/etc. should never be substituted for regular salt. Store it, well labeled, in an out-of-the-way place. It is always dyed pink so that it's not mistaken for regular salt.*

NOTES ON AIR-CURING MEAT

When you are dry-salting, once your piece of meat has been salted and rinsed, it needs to air-cure. Air-curing—essentially drying—reduces the water content so that the meat, when cured, will weigh 30 percent less than it did when you salted it. That 30 percent weight loss is the indication that your cure is ready. Air-curing also produces wonderful flavors as the lactic acid bacteria develop.

When I first started exploring salt-cured meats, I was a little intimidated by some of the processes, but I don't want you to feel that way. That's why I'm layering in as much explanation as possible and setting out a number of suggestions about where and how to dry and cure the meat once it's salted. All of these recipes are for small pieces of meat, with none more than 3 pounds/2.25 kg and most around 1 pound/450 grams or less.

Wherever you place the meat to air-cure, you want to minimize the surfaces it touches. The traditional method of air-curing is to hang the meat from a hook in a cool place with good air circulation, a temperature between 40 and 60°F/6 to 15°C, and humidity at 50 to 60 percent. Not many people have such temperature-controlled spaces, but fortunately air-curing in a refrigerator works well for smaller cuts. You can hang it from a hook, suspend it between two tall jars, or—perhaps the simplest method—rest the meat on a mesh rack, with a small tray underneath to catch any drips. If you've placed the meat on a rack, you'll need to turn it over every day to ensure even drying, since airflow will be inhibited by the tray. Wherever you cure the meat, it should be wrapped in cheesecloth to prevent the surface from drying out too quickly, which would create a seal and prevent the interior from drying properly.

The actual humidity and temperature of your curing space will determine the time needed to get to your target of a 30 percent loss in weight, which is why I give a range of curing times.

SALT PORK AND PANCETTA:
Two Takes on Cured Pork Belly

The two versions of cured pork belly set out below are easy to make and very useful larder ingredients. Choose a piece of pork belly no more than 1 inch/ 2.5 cm thick if you will be drying it in a refrigerator. Try to get it with the skin on, or at least with a thick layer of fat on top. I like to use a fine sea salt; pickling salt or kosher salt work well too.

The amounts set out below are based on 1 pound/450 grams of skin-on pork belly. But it's rare that meat comes so precisely weighed, and it is essential that you adjust the amount of salt and curing salt according to the exact weight of the meat you have. That means that you need an accurate scale for weighing your meat and a digital jeweler's scale that can measure small quantities to a 0.1 of a gram (see Mindful Curing, page 162). I'm giving measurements for the curing mixture only in metric because it's easier and more accurate to calculate proportions with metric measures than with pounds and ounces.

Adjust the aromatics according to your meat weight, also, though precision is much less critical there than with the curing mixture. It's the aromatics that distinguish one version of cured pork belly from another; once you've made one of these recipes, you may want to experiment with other aromatics.

I like the simple clean taste of the basic French-style *porc salé* (salted pork). I have freely adapted the recipe from the one in Jane Grigson's classic book *Charcuterie*. In her groundbreaking book *Odd Bits*, chef Jennifer McLagan has a recipe for porc salé that includes the classic French spice mixture *quatre épices*; use ½ teaspoon per 1 pound/450 grams pork belly if you wish.

Pancetta, the delicious Italian equivalent of salt pork, is flavored with garlic and dried thyme. The ingredients for both cures are set out below. Use the same technique for both.

BASIC CURING MIXTURE PROPORTIONS

Here are the proportions for any weight of meat:

Meat. . . . . X grams

Salt . . . . 2.75% (multiply meat weight by 0.0275)

Curing salt #1. . . . . . . 0.25% (multiply meat weight by 0.0025)

Sugar . . . . 1% (multiply meat weight by 0.01)

SAMPLE CALCULATIONS

Here are the amounts for 450 grams pork belly, preferably skin on, and no more than 1 inch/2.5 cm thick:

Pork belly . . . . 450 grams

Salt . . . . 12.4 grams (450 grams x 0.0275)

Curing salt #1. . . . . . . 1.1 grams (450 grams x 0.0025)

Sugar . . . . 4.5 grams (450 grams x 0.01)

Aromatics. . . . . per 450 grams

FOR SALT PORK	FOR PANCETTA
4 juniper berries	**8 juniper berries**
1 teaspoon black peppercorns	**2 teaspoons black peppercorns**
1 bay leaf, coarsely torn	**1 small garlic clove, chopped**
	3 sprigs fresh thyme or ½ teaspoon dried thyme

You will need a kitchen scale, a jeweler's scale, a small bowl, a spice grinder or mortar and pestle, a cutting board, a sealable plastic or silicone bag, a plate or tray, cheesecloth, and kitchen string or a drying rack.

Weigh your meat and set it aside. Calculate the amount of each ingredient you will need for your cure and write them down. Use the jeweler's scale to weigh the ingredients for the cure, putting them in a bowl. Grind your aromatics to a powder and stir them into the cure mixture.

Lay the pork belly on a cutting board and rub the cure evenly over the entire surface. Place the meat and any cure ingredients remaining on the board into a dry sealable plastic bag, pressing out all the air before you seal it. Label the bag with the weight of the meat and the date. Place the pork on a plate or a tray (to catch any liquid that might leak out) and put it in the refrigerator for 5 to 6 days (the general rule is 5 to 7 days per inch of thickness). Because amounts are measured, it won't get oversalted if you leave it for an extra day or two.

Remove the pork from the refrigerator, unwrap it, rinse off the cure, and pat it dry.

continued

Wrap the meat in two layers of cheesecloth (this prevents the surface of the meat from drying out too quickly and hardening), and again label with the weight and the date. I find it helpful to also note the target weight (a loss of 30 percent) on the label. (If you have several cured meat projects on the go, it is vital that you label each so there's no confusion later.) Tie the wrapped pork with kitchen string and make a loop. Hang it in a very cool, airy place, around 50°F/10°C, or hang or place on a rack set over a tray in the refrigerator, and let air-cure until it reaches its target weight, usually around 10 days. If you've placed the pork on a rack, you'll need to turn it over every day to ensure even drying, since the airflow will be inhibited by the tray.

Once the pork has lost 30 percent of its weight, it's ready. You can then store it in the fridge, well wrapped in several layers of clean cheesecloth (to prevent it drying out further). Be sure to label it with the date you finished curing it; consume or freeze it within 30 days.

SALT PORK AND PANCETTA ARE THE COOK'S FRIENDS

To use salt pork or pancetta in quickly prepared dishes: Cut off several thin slices (it's easiest to lay the meat skin side up to slice it). Trim off the skin if you wish (I sometimes leave it on for extra texture), then cut the slices into narrow strips for lardons and fry gently in a cast-iron skillet or other heavy pan until touched with color and crisping. Add to an omelet, or toss into a salad of cooked green beans, or use as an initial flavoring and source of cooking fat when you're stir-frying cabbage or other greens, for extra lusciousness and umami.

To use salt pork or pancetta in a simmered dish, such as beans or lentils: Slice the meat, then trim the skin off the slices. Cut the slices into small bite-sized pieces. Add to beans or lentils as they cook, about ¼ to ⅓ pound/110 to 180 grams salt pork or pancetta to 1 cup/about 200 grams uncooked dried beans or lentils.

Remember that the salt in the meat will do some of the seasoning work in your dish, so you'll need less salt than usual.

DUCK BREAST PROSCIUTTO

Duck breast prosciutto is a real pleasure to make, and to eat. Once it's cured, you can simply slice it thinly and enjoy the transformation, no cooking needed. I also like to use it as I use salt pork and pancetta, to add flavor to stir-fried vegetables or to enrich a soup.

If you can, start with a good-sized boneless duck breast with the skin and a good layer of fat on it—a nice meaty magret works well—weighing at least 3/4 pound (340 grams).

I like to use fine sea salt, but you can also use pickling salt or kosher salt. The breast cures in the fridge with a measured amount of salt, curing salt, and flavoring for 5 or 6 days, and then the cure is wiped off. After that, the breast air-cures wrapped in cheesecloth in a cool place or in the fridge to dry and firm up for about 10 days. (It's the same process as for salt pork and pancetta.)

These measurements are here as a guide; your exact measurements will depend on the weight of your duck breast. I'm listing them in metric because that's the best way to be precise. Start by weighing the duck breast, then make your calculations based on that weight.

BASIC CURING-MIXTURE PROPORTIONS

These are the proportions for any weight of duck:

Duck. . . . . X grams

Salt . . . . 3.0% (multiply meat weight by 0.03)

Curing salt #1 . . . . . . 0.25% (multiply meat weight by 0.0025)

Brown sugar . . . . 1.0% (multiply meat weight by 0.01)

Ground ginger . . . . . . ½ teaspoon per 450 grams meat

These are the amounts for a typical duck breast:

Duck. . . . . 400 grams

Salt . . . . 12 grams (400 grams x 0.03)

Curing salt #1. . . . . . . 1.0 gram (400 grams x 0.0025)

Brown sugar . . . . 4 grams (400 grams x 0.01)

Ground ginger . . . . . . Scant ½ teaspoon (calculated as ½ teaspoon per 450 grams)

You will need a kitchen scale, a jeweler's scale, one or more small bowls, a plate or tray, a sealable plastic bag, a cloth or paper towels, cheesecloth, and kitchen string or a drying rack.

Weigh the duck breast and set aside. Calculate the amounts of cure ingredients you'll need and write them down. Use a small digital scale to weigh the ingredients for your cure. As you measure them out, combine them in a small bowl.

Lay the duck breast on a plate or tray and use your fingers to rub the cure firmly over the entire surface, paying special attention to the skin side. Put the duck into a sealable plastic bag, along with any stray bits of cure that have fallen onto the plate or tray. Press out the air completely and seal. I find it easiest to fold the bag tightly around the duck breast as I press out the air before sealing the bag. Label the bag with the date and the weight.

Place the bagged breast in the fridge and leave to cure for 5 to 7 days, turning it over every day or two. (Because the amounts are measured, if you leave it an extra couple of days, it won't get oversalted.)

Remove the duck breast from the bag; you'll notice that the meat has firmed up a little. Rinse off the salt cure with cold water. Pat the duck dry with a clean cloth or a paper towel, then wrap in two layers of cheesecloth (this prevents the surface of the meat from drying out too quickly and hardening) and label again with the weight and the date. I find it helpful to also note the target weight (a loss of 30 percent) on the label. (If you have several cured meat projects on the go, it is vital that you label each, so there's no confusion later.)

Tie the wrapped duck breast with kitchen string and make a loop. Hang it in a very cool, airy place, around 50°F/10°C, or place it on a rack set over a tray in the refrigerator.

Let the duck air-cure until it has lost 30 percent of its original weight, 8 to 10 days. If you've placed the duck on a rack, you'll need to turn it over every day to ensure even drying, since the airflow will be inhibited by the tray. When ready it will feel very firm to the touch.

Unwrap the duck, slice it thinly, and serve it in any way that you would serve prosciutto. I like it on small pieces of buttered toast, with a squeeze of lemon. It's also a nice addition to a salad of tender greens. Store it wrapped in several layers of fresh cheesecloth in the refrigerator; consume or freeze it within 30 days.

BASTURMA

Basturma, sometimes spelled *pastirma*, is the word used in Armenia, Turkey, and Egypt for pressed, salt-cured beef that is rubbed with a spice paste.

This basturma recipe begins with eye of round or, more expensively, beef fillet. Any visible fat is trimmed off, and then the meat is rubbed with salt to draw out the liquid. After salting, the meat is pressed under a weight to push out most of the remaining liquid. The distinctive part of this curing process is that it doesn't end with salting, pressing, and air-drying. Instead, after the meat has been hung to dry and cure in a cool place for a while, it is coated all over with a paste, called *chaiman*, made of ground fenugreek, paprika, cayenne, salt, pepper, and garlic, and then once again hung to dry and cure. The result is a delicious form of cured beef that is very lean, much like *bresaola*. Basturma should be thinly sliced and eaten as a treat, perhaps as an appetizer, on its own or with lightly toasted bread. Or include bite-sized pieces of the thinly sliced meat in a salad; it's beautiful with frisée. Or use in a sandwich, with salad greens or chopped cooked greens for color and texture.

In the Republic of Armenia, basturma is made with whatever cut of beef people have available, and it is generally quite dried out, better used as an ingredient than eaten on its own. Armenians trust it better when it's very dry, a traditional attitude from hard times, when making sure that meat would last the winter was a matter of survival. In the US, where there is a large Armenian diasporic community, commercial versions of basturma are made with high-quality cuts of meat and dried for less time, so they have a more tender texture. I prefer the North American version, and so that's the recipe here.

Makes about 1½ pounds/ 750 grams

1¾ to 2 pounds/750 to 900 grams fresh (never frozen) boneless fillet of beef or eye of round

Scant 1 cup/225 grams coarse pickling salt

FLAVOR PASTE

¼ cup/50 grams ground fenugreek

¼ cup/30 grams sweet paprika

1 tablespoon freshly ground black pepper

2 teaspoons/10 grams fine sea salt

1 to 2 teaspoons cayenne (for mild to medium heat)

1 teaspoon ground cumin

1 teaspoon ground coriander

2 medium garlic cloves, minced

About ⅔ cup/160 ml water, or as needed to make a smooth, spreadable paste

You will need a rectangular glass or ceramic container that is not much larger than the meat (with a lid or plastic wrap), a small board or plate that fits inside the container, a large can or other weight, kitchen string, cheesecloth, a small bowl, a food processor, a spatula, and a sharp knife.

continued

Trim off any fat or gristle from the beef. Spread a ¼-inch/½ cm layer of coarse salt in the bottom of a glass or ceramic container that will hold the meat fairly snugly and lay the meat on it. Rub the sides of the meat with more salt, then sprinkle a layer of salt on top, reserving a little salt for later.

Cover the container with a lid or plastic wrap and refrigerate for 36 to 40 hours. The salt will draw out moisture. Pour the liquid off after the first 24 hours, turn the meat over, rub the reserved salt on top, and put back in the refrigerator, covered, for another 12 hours or so.

Rinse the meat thoroughly with cold water and dry it well. Wash and dry the container, then place the meat back in it. Top with a small board or plate and top that with a weight (such as a large can of tomatoes). Refrigerate for another 48 hours, checking after 12 hours and pouring off any accumulated liquid. The meat will have firmed up and flattened but still feel a little pliable.

Wrap the meat loosely in two layers of cheesecloth, tie with kitchen string, and make a loop. Hang the meat on a hook to air-cure in a cool, dry, well-ventilated place out of the sun, preferably around 50°F/10°C, for 5 to 7 days; the meat will firm up and stiffen. Alternatively, place on a rack set over a tray in the refrigerator and cure for 10 days, turning the meat every day for even drying.

To prepare the flavor paste, mix all the ingredients except the water together in a bowl. Add a scant ½ cup/110 ml water and stir into a stiff paste. Transfer to a processor or blender and process for about 30 seconds. Add another 1 to 2 tablespoons water and process to a smooth paste. Return the paste to the bowl and add a touch more water if necessary to make a thick, spreadable paste.

Remove the cheesecloth from the meat. You will notice that the meat has become a firmer flattened log. If there are any tough dried-out edges, trim them off. Lay the meat on a baking sheet or tray and use a spatula to spread the paste in an even layer over the entire surface, covering it completely.

Wrap the meat in two layers of clean cheesecloth and tie with string again. Hang it in the cool place or replace it on the rack in the fridge. After a couple of days, the meat will have stiffened and dried further; check the spice paste coating, and if you notice any cracks in it, moisten your finger with water and smooth them closed. Let the meat air-cure for another 5 or 6 days; if the air is humid, leave it for longer.

When it is cured, wrap the basturma well with several layers of fresh cheesecloth and store in the refrigerator; consume or freeze it within 30 days.

To serve, slice the basturma very thin, into shavings. The cut surface of the basturma will be smooth, very dark red-black near the edges and a deep garnet red in the center, with a slight sheen to it. The slices will be rimmed with the dark orange paste.

BRINED CHICKEN

When I am lucky enough to be roasting a fresh chicken from a farmer I know, I focus on letting its good flavor and freshness shine, as in the recipe on page 276. But if I'm dealing with a chicken out of the freezer, or a store-bought bird of uncertain provenance, brining is a way of ensuring a moist-textured bird. Brining is even more effective if you are planning to grill or fry chicken, because the extra moisture enables the heat to travel more quickly through the meat, helping to make certain that the meat will be cooked through.

You can brine the chicken whole, or if you're planning to make grilled chicken, cut the bird into pieces before brining, or buy cut-up chicken.

I usually use a 4 to 5 percent salt solution, plus flavorings, as set out below (about 2½ to 3 tablespoons/45 to 50 grams salt per quart/liter of water). Use some or all of the aromatics suggested for the brine, or instead try a more southeast Asian combination; see the Note.

This amount of chicken will serve 6 when cooked

One 4-pound/1.8 kg whole chicken or 3½ pounds/ 1.5 kg chicken breasts and legs

BRINE

3 quarts/3 liters water, or as needed

½ cup/130 grams coarse pickling salt

⅓ cup/130 grams mild honey or ⅓ cup/75 grams granulated sugar

15 black peppercorns

6 garlic cloves, lightly smashed and peeled

AROMATICS (USE SOME OR ALL OF THESE)

3 sprigs rosemary

3 or 4 sprigs thyme

3 or 4 sprigs flat-leaf parsley

3 bay leaves

You will need a pot that is large enough to hold the chicken and that will fit into your refrigerator (I remove one of my crisper drawers and fit the pot in there) and a kitchen scale.

Place the chicken in a large pot and add the water. It should cover the chicken generously; if you need to add more water, measure the amount you add, then increase the salt in proportion to make a 5 percent brine. (For example, if you add another 2 cups/500 ml, you'll need an additional 1½ tablespoons/25 grams salt.)

Transfer the chicken to a platter and place it back in the refrigerator. Set the pot of water over high heat and bring to a boil. Add the salt, honey or sugar, peppercorns, garlic, and aromatics of your choice and stir until the salt and honey or sugar are completely dissolved. Remove from the heat and set aside to cool completely.

Place the bird in the brine, breast side down. Make sure it is completely submerged; if necessary, add more salted water. Cover and refrigerate for 12 to 18 hours, whatever is convenient.

Remove the chicken from the brine and discard the brine. Wipe the chicken (or pieces) dry. It's ready to be roasted, grilled, or fried.

NOTE: *If you'd like to use Southeast Asian flavorings for the brine: 3 or 4 stalks lemongrass, trimmed of root ends and tough upper parts and smacked with the flat side of a knife or cleaver; 6 to 8 wild lime (makrut) leaves; 8 garlic cloves, lightly smashed and peeled; 15 black peppercorns; 3 or 4 slices of ginger; and, if you like, 10 lightly toasted Sichuan peppercorns.*

Outside Hsipaw, in Burma's Shan State, a man shovels salt produced by boiling down the brine from a salt well.

CORNED BEEF

This is one of those recipes that keeps on giving. Corned beef is usually made with brisket (as is pastrami), the chest muscle of the animal. You can, of course, cook a brisket without salting it, but the corned (brined) version is much more versatile and more delicious.

To make corned beef, which is also called salt beef or salt brisket, the meat is soaked in a brine for 8 days, then gently boiled in water aromatic with spices for 3 to 4 hours. The result is meltingly tender meat that can be sliced and served with potatoes and other vegetables as a hearty feast.

That same tender, pull-apart meat, once cooled overnight in the refrigerator, firms up and becomes a very handy larder resource that keeps for 10 days.

This recipe takes a classic approach, using an array of spices from northern European tradition (including allspice, bay leaf, black pepper, and coriander seed). The spices flavor both the brining liquid and the cooking liquid.

NOTE: *If you are making the corned beef for short-term use (within 5 days), you can omit the curing salt, but your meat will be a dull gray-beige rather than a rosy color. For more detail, see Curing Salts and Food Safety, page 162.*

Makes enough for the Corned Beef Roast (page 297); or use part of it to make Fogo Island Split Pea Soup with Corned Beef and Doughboys (page 222)

One 5- to 5½-pound/about 2½ kg beef brisket (see headnote)

BRINE

3 quarts/3 liters water

1¼ cups/300 grams fine pickling salt

1 teaspoon/5 grams Curing salt #1 (see Note above)

½ cup/125 grams sugar

1 tablespoon black peppercorns

1 teaspoon allspice berries

1 teaspoon juniper berries

1 teaspoon coriander seeds

1 teaspoon black or brown mustard seeds

1 teaspoon ground ginger

A 1- to 2-inch/2.5 to 5 cm cinnamon (cassia) stick

2 bay leaves, crumbled

You will need a large pot, a jeweler's scale to measure the curing salt, a spoon, a very large (4-gallon/16 liter or more) glass or ceramic bowl that can fit in your refrigerator (I take out one of my crisper drawers), a plate or cutting board and something to weight it, and a cotton cloth.

Put 2 quarts/2 liters of the water in a large pot and bring to a boil. Add the salt, curing salt, and sugar and stir to dissolve them completely. Remove from the heat and toss in the remaining spices and the aromatics, add the remaining 4 cups/1 liter water, and let the brine cool completely.

continued

Place the brisket fat side down in a very large (4-gallon/16 liter or more) ceramic or glass bowl or crock that will fit in your refrigerator. Pour in the brine mixture with the spices and aromatics. If you need to add more water to cover the meat, measure the amount you add and then add salt in proportion to maintain a 10 percent brine. (For example, if you need to add 2 cups/500 ml water, add 2 tablespoons plus 2 teaspoons/50 grams salt and stir to dissolve it.) To keep the brisket immersed, place a plate or clean cutting board on top of it and weight it with something (a full can, for example). Cover the bowl loosely with a cotton cloth or plastic bag and refrigerate for 3 days.

Take the bowl or crock out of the refrigerator, remove the weights, and turn the meat over. Replace the weights, cover loosely again, and refrigerate for another 5 days.

Remove the meat from the brine; discard the brine. The beef is now ready to be boiled in water to remove excess salt and then cooked; see pages 222 and 297. You can also freeze the cured corned beef for up to 2 months.

SPICED JERKY from the Shan Hills

I first learned about this jerky from a man in the town of Hsipaw, the capital of one of the former Shan princely states of Burma. I'd asked him what foods were carried by the men who have for decades left their villages to trade or to fight the central government's army. He described strips of spiced dried meat, lightweight and practical, like these.

A couple of years later, I learned how to make the jerky from a Shan man who'd fled across the mountains into northern Thailand in his teens to escape the Burmese army. This recipe is adapted from *Burma: Rivers of Flavor*.

Make this with beef or pork, or with some of each. Traditionally the meat strips are air-dried for several days above a low fire, but you can dry them in a low oven, as described below.

Serves 6 to 8

SPICE PASTE

2 tablespoons coriander seeds

2 teaspoons ground turmeric

2 teaspoons cayenne, or to taste

3 tablespoons minced peeled fresh ginger

6 or 7 large garlic cloves, minced

1 tablespoon/16 grams coarse pickling salt

About 2 pounds/1 kg boneless beef steak, such as flank, flat-iron, or skirt, or boneless pork shoulder or loin

Peanut oil or lard for shallow-frying

You will need a spice grinder or mortar and pestle, a food processor or stone mortar, a knife, a medium bowl, a wire rack, a roasting pan or baking sheet, and a paper bag for storage.

Preheat the oven to 150°F/65°C.

Grind the coriander seed to a powder in a spice grinder or mortar. Then place in a food processor or stone mortar with the rest of the spice paste ingredients and process or pound to a paste.

Cut the meat against the grain at an angle (in order to get the widest slices you can) into ¼-inch-thick/0.5 cm slices. Place the meat in a bowl, add the spice paste, and massage the paste into the strips with your hands.

Lay the the strips on a rack set in a roasting pan or on a baking sheet, so that air can circulate, place in the oven, and prop the door open a little to allow moisture to escape. The strips should be dried out within 2 to 3 hours.

Store the dried strips in the refrigerator in a paper bag, rather than in plastic, for as long as 5 days.

To cook the meat: Cut the strips crosswise into small bite-sized pieces. Fry in about ½ inch/1 cm of hot peanut oil or lard for 3 to 4 minutes, until tender. Serve hot or at room temperature as an appetizer with drinks, or as one of many dishes at a rice meal.

A woman rakes up salt in the salt pans of Khatch, in western Gujarat. In hot season, the salt harvest time, the temperatures are blistering, often above 120°F/50°C.

GUJARAT

The salt pans in Gujarat's Great Rann of Khatch are mesmerizing—flat, gleaming, pale white and blue under a blazing sun. When I was there once in late March, the air was burning hot, yet the women working in the salt ponds were barefoot, standing in a few inches of brine, scraping and raking the salt into low piles. The workers travel back to the area each year. They live in small encampments nearby while they first do the work of preparing the salt pans and then harvest salt during the hot season, from February to May. The working conditions are very tough, and the pay low. What they harvest is the salt many others depend on. I think of salt workers like them often when I pick up a pinch of salt.

PART TWO

FROM LARDER TO TABLE

IN MY KITCHEN, NOT A DAY PASSES without my turning to my "salt larder" for one or more salt-preserved ingredients, either homemade, using the recipes in the preceding chapters, or store-bought. Salted lemons, olives, dried shrimp, kimchi, salt pork, bacalao, and more expand my cooking repertoire, giving it enormous richness. I rub a chicken or a meat roast with salted onions or shio koji to season it before cooking. I flavor a soup or a pot of beans with slices of salt pork, or add a dash of fish sauce or soy sauce, or a spoonful of miso paste, to any number of dishes that need a pop of flavor.

The umami of salt-preserved ingredients adds a valuable intensity and savoriness to vegetarian dishes. And using cured meat as a flavoring rather than putting meat at the center of the plate allows me to eat less of it while enjoying meals that are both wonderfully interesting and sustainable.

This section of the book is designed to give you ideas for the ways you can integrate these wonderful salt-preserved ingredients into your own cooking. The recipes are organized by category of dish, but you'll want to look in the Index too.

CONDIMENTS & SAUCES

Citrus Kosho (center; page 91) and Green Ajika (left; page 92)

BLACK BEAN SAUCE

This larder staple from Chinese tradition is a quick way of giving complexity to stir-fries and slow-cooked dishes alike. The flavors include deep umami from the black beans, lovely pungency from the garlic and ginger, acidity from the wine, and heat from the chile-infused oil.

The recipe takes less than half an hour to put together.

Makes 2½ cups/600 ml

1½ cups/225 grams salted black beans (see page 105)

⅓ cup/25 grams minced shallots or white onion

About 12 dried red chiles

½ cup/125 ml peanut, sunflower, raw (not toasted) sesame, or vegetable oil

½ cup/125 ml Shaoxing wine, dry sherry, or sake

⅓ cup/80 ml soy sauce

3 tablespoons sugar, or to taste

¾ cup/100 grams minced garlic (from 4 medium to large heads)

2 tablespoons minced peeled fresh ginger

Wash two 1-cup/240 ml and one ½-cup/120 ml or five ½-cup/120 ml jars and lids in the dishwasher or in boiling water. Set out on a tray.

Rinse the black beans well in cold water to remove excess salt, drain well, and put in a food processor, along with the minced shallots or onion. Pulse several times, until the beans are broken down to a coarse texture but not to a paste. Set aside.

Break the dried chiles in half and empty out and discard the seeds. Heat the oil in a large heavy skillet over medium heat. When it is hot, toss in the chiles, lower the heat to medium-low, and cook for a minute or two, stirring gently to turn them over and expose all sides to the hot oil, just until the chiles have darkened. (You want their heat to infuse into the oil, but without any scorched bitterness.) Use a slotted spoon or spider to lift the chiles out of the oil, pausing to let excess oil drain off, and set aside for another purpose or discard.

Add the bean and shallot mixture to the pan and stir gently to blend it into the oil. When most of the oil has been absorbed by the beans, after 4 or 5 minutes, add the wine, soy sauce, and sugar and stir them into the mixture. Cook for a few minutes, stirring occasionally, then add the garlic and ginger and cook, stirring frequently, until they have softened and the oil has risen to the surface, about 10 minutes. Remove from the heat and allow to cool for a few minutes.

Spoon the mixture into the prepared jars. Top with the lids, but don't tighten them until the sauce has cooled completely. Label with the date and store in the refrigerator for up to 2 months.

DRIED SHRIMP AND GARLIC CHUTNEY

A delicious condiment from northeast India, called *jinghe achar sukha*, this is more like a crumbled moist flavor powder than a chutney (*achar sukha* means dry chutney). It has medium heat from dried red chiles and pungency from garlic and lightly toasted dried shrimp. A little tomato gives it a balancing touch of acidity. The recipe is adapted from a booklet called *Himalayan Recipes* published in Darjeeling several decades ago.

Most of the people who live in the mountains of India and Nepal subsist on what grows locally: chiles, garlic, potatoes, and rice or another grain, depending on the altitude. Using a valuable ingredient like dried shrimp in a condiment is a way of making the most of it.

Serve at room temperature with any meal. I like sprinkling this on fried eggs, cooked vegetables, or plain rice. It's become one of my favorite condiments.

Makes 2 cups/190 grams

¼ pound/115 grams dried shrimp (see page 151)

Scant 1 ounce/½ cup/20 grams dried red chiles

1 medium head garlic, separated into cloves but not peeled

½ small fleshy tomato (about 1 ounce/30 grams)

½ teaspoon fine sea salt, or to taste

Rinse the dried shrimp in cold water and drain. Place a heavy skillet over medium-high heat, toss in the shrimp, lower the heat to medium, and toast the shrimp, stirring occasionally, until touched with color, about 5 minutes. Remove from the pan and set aside.

Place the skillet back over medium heat and toast the chiles, turning them to expose both sides to the hot pan, until they have softened and started to darken a little; do not let them scorch. Remove from the pan and set aside.

Add the garlic cloves to the skillet and toast, moving them around occasionally to expose all sides to the heat, until softening and lightly scorched. Remove from the pan and set aside.

Add the tomato to the pan and toast it until scorched on the outside and softened (or do this directly over a flame). Set aside.

Discard any chile stems or tough ends, tear the chiles in half, and empty out and discard the seeds. Peel the garlic and coarsely chop. Pull off any really black patches from the tomato and discard.

Place the shrimp in a food processor and grind to a coarse powder, or instead pound to a powder in a stone mortar. Add the chiles and garlic and process or pound. Add the tomato and process or pound to blend it in completely. You want a coarse moist powder, not a paste.

To serve, transfer to a bowl and add the salt, then taste and adjust if you wish.

Store in a clearly labeled tightly covered glass jar in a cool place or in the refrigerator, where it will keep for about 4 months.

LAO SALSA with Anchovies

Jaew is the Lao and Isaan (northeast Thai) word for salsa-like strongly flavored sauces. This one, known as *jaew isaan*, is traditionally made with salted local fish, for which I substitute salted anchovies.

The aromatics are traditionally grilled over an open fire. Here I use a heavy skillet on the stovetop. The technique of scorching the aromatics and chiles gives many jaew dishes their characteristic flavor.

The *galangal* and lemongrass make this a wonderfully aromatic condiment for grilled meat or grilled or steamed vegetables, as well as for sticky rice. The sauce is only mildly hot; for more heat, increase the number of chiles. If you wish, you can include a small tomato in the salsa. Scorch on all sides in a hot skillet, then coarsely chop and stir into the sauce.

Makes about ⅔ cup/175 grams

- 4 medium to large garlic cloves, not peeled
- A 1-inch/2.5 cm piece of galangal, peeled and chopped
- 2 medium shallots, thinly sliced
- 2 dried red chiles
- Pinch of coarse or fine sea salt
- 1 large or 2 small lemongrass stalks, trimmed and minced (see Note)
- 8 salt-packed anchovy fillets, rinsed, patted dry, and finely chopped (see headnote)
- 2 tablespoons fresh lime juice, or to taste
- 1 wild lime (makrut) leaf, torn into small pieces or cut into fine ribbons

Heat a medium heavy skillet over medium-high heat. Add the garlic cloves and toast until well browned, 8 to 10 minutes, moving them around to prevent heavy scorching. Remove and set aside.

Add the galangal and shallots to the skillet and cook over medium-high until the galangal begins to scorch and the shallots have changed color, about 1 minute. Transfer to a food processor or large mortar. Peel the garlic and add to the processor or mortar. Set aside.

Toast the dried chiles in the skillet over medium-high heat until just starting to puff, less than a minute. Don't scorch them. Remove from the heat, discard the stem, then finely chop and transfer, with the seeds, to the processor or mortar.

Add the salt and process or pound the mix to a paste, scraping down the sides as needed. Add the lemongrass and process or pound to a coarse paste, then add the anchovies and process or pound them into the paste.

Transfer the paste to a bowl and stir in the lime juice and lime leaf. Put out as a condiment or as one of many dishes in a sticky rice meal. Leftovers will keep in a sealed jar in the refrigerator for up to 4 days.

CRISPY SHALLOT AND DRIED SHRIMP RELISH

This enticing umami-rich snack and condiment from Burma is called *balachaung* in Burmese. It's loaded with a full range of flavor hits: heat from the red chile, tartness from the tamarind, funky saltiness from the shrimp paste and dried shrimp, and sweetness from the crispy fried onions and garlic. I find it irresistible.

Serve warm or at room temperature with a rice-based meal or, less traditionally, with a meal of grilled meat or grilled vegetables.

Makes about 1 cup/250 ml

About 1 tablespoon tamarind pulp (see Note)

¼ cup/60 ml hot water

6 tablespoons/90 ml peanut or vegetable oil

3 pinches ground turmeric

½ cup/85 grams thinly sliced shallots

15 medium garlic cloves, thinly sliced

¾ cup/65 grams dried shrimp powder (use Fluffy Shrimp, page 152, or store-bought)

1 teaspoon cayenne or other dried red chile powder

1½ teaspoons shrimp paste (see page 153), dissolved in about 1 tablespoon water

½ to 1 teaspoon sugar

¼ teaspoon fine sea salt, or to taste

Put the tamarind pulp in a small bowl with the hot water and mash with a fork to help the pulp dissolve. Set aside to soak for 20 minutes, mashing it occasionally.

Place a small sieve over a small bowl and pour the tamarind liquid through it; use the back of a spoon or a rubber spatula to mash and press the tamarind pulp against the mesh to squeeze out as much flavor as possible. Discard the pulp and set the tamarind liquid (aka tamarind paste) aside.

Place a large heavy skillet or a wok over medium heat. When it is hot, add ¼ cup/60 ml of the oil. Toss in a pinch of turmeric and the shallots, stir, and cook, stirring occasionally, until the shallots start to color, 5 to 10 minutes. Before they start to turn a darker brown, use a slotted spoon to lift them out of the oil, pausing to let excess oil drain off, and set aside in a bowl.

Toss another pinch of turmeric into the hot oil and add the garlic. Give it all a stir and cook briefly, a minute or two, just until the garlic starts to look golden, then lift out, pausing to drain off the excess oil, and add to the shallots.

Add the remaining 2 tablespoons oil to the pan and toss in another pinch of turmeric. Add the shrimp powder and cayenne or red chile powder, stir, and keep stirring as the shrimp powder foams up, absorbs the oil, and then settles into a paste, about a minute. Lower the heat a little, add the tamarind paste, shrimp paste mixture, and sugar, and stir to mix well. Cook until the ingredients have blended into a soft mass, 3 to 4 minutes.

Transfer to a bowl. Add the reserved fried shallots and garlic and toss to mix well. Let cool.

Once completely cooled, the relish can be stored in a glass jar at room temperature for several weeks, longer in the refrigerator.

NOTE: *If you have made tamarind paste from pulp (see page 347) and have some on hand, substitute 1 tablespoon of the paste for the pulp and hot water.*

SALTED SHISO AND SESAME FURIKAKE

If you make Salted Shiso Leaves (page 60), you can dry them and then crumble them to make a flavor powder. In Japanese cooking, these kinds of salted flavorings are called furikake. Commercial furikakes often include dried nori and toasted sesame seeds, among other flavorings.

For this furikake, you'll want to work with at least 25 to 30 dried salted leaves to get a reasonable quantity of furikake; I like making it with even more, say with up to 100 leaves.

Store the powdered furikake in a small jar. It will keep for months. Sprinkle on fish, into creamy soups, or onto plain rice at any meal. The shiso will sparkle in your mouth.

Dried Salted Shiso Leaves (page 60; see headnote)   **Sesame seeds (white or a mix of white and black)**   **Pinch or two of coarse sea salt**

Roughly measure the volume of dried shiso leaves. I use about half of that volume of sesame seeds. Measure out the sesame seeds and then toast them lightly in a heavy skillet over medium heat, stirring frequently to prevent scorching, until aromatic. Remove from the heat and continue stirring for a moment, then set aside to cool.

Place about two-thirds of the sesame seeds, the dried shiso, and salt in a spice grinder. Grind them together briefly, just until you have a coarse powder; pulse the spice grinder so that you stop before you have a very fine powder. (If you're making a large quantity, you may have to work in batches.) Turn out into a bowl and add the remaining sesame seeds. Taste and adjust the salt; you want the mixture to give a clean salty hit, along with the taste of shiso and sesame.

Transfer to a clean dry jar: the easiest way to do this is to curl a sheet of paper into a funnel and pour the mixture through the funnel into the jar. Cover tightly, label, and store at room temperature, out of the sun, with your other spices and flavorings.

VARIATIONS
You can also include dried nori and/or bonito flakes. Toast a nori sheet lightly and tear it up before grinding it in a spice grinder to reduce it to flakes. Use about the same volume of nori flakes as sesame seeds. For bonito flakes, use an amount that is half the volume of the sesame seeds; toast the flakes very lightly in a dry skillet before grinding them.

SEAWEED RELISH

No doubt this useful Japanese condiment, called *shio kombu* (salt-seaweed), originated as a way of using kombu left over from flavoring dashi. I've been making it for years; this is an adaptation of a recipe in *Seductions of Rice*.

Start with dried sheets of kombu from a package, or else with used dashi kombu that you have stockpiled in the freezer.

The seaweed is simmered in acidulated water until it softens completely, then chopped into shreds. The chopped mass is cooked over very low heat in a mix of soy sauce, mirin, and sugar. The resulting dense, nearly black condiment is a delicious salt-tart-sweet umami-rich accent for rice meals, and you may find other uses for it (a good friend loves it with ricotta).

Makes nearly 2 cups/450 grams

About 2 ounces/50 grams wild kombu sheets (about 3 full sheets) or 4 or 5 pre-used sheets

About 1½ cups/360 ml water

1 tablespoon rice vinegar

2 tablespoons mirin

2 tablespoons sake

2 tablespoons Japanese soy sauce (not tamari)

1 tablespoon sugar, or more to taste

2 tablespoons sesame seeds

Wipe off the dry kombu with a damp cloth. Place the kombu in a heavy shallow pan, add the water, and let soak for 10 minutes, or until it is soft enough to cut. (If you're using pre-used sheets, this will take very little time.)

Remove the kombu from the water, cut it into smaller pieces (about 1-inch/3 cm squares) with scissors, and return to the pan of water.

Add the vinegar and bring to a boil. Lower the heat, partially cover, and simmer for 1 to 1½ hours, until the kombu is very tender (if you are working with pre-used kombu, you'll need less simmering time). Stir from time to time, and check as the liquid reduces to make sure it's not running dry; add more if needed. (If your sheets of kombu are very thick and tough, they may need to cook for longer, as much as another hour, until very soft; add more water as needed.)

Lift out the kombu, reserving the remaining liquid (about ¼ cup/60 ml) in the pan. Let the kombu cool for a moment and then chop very finely. You should have about 1¾ cups/400 grams.

Return the kombu to the pan, along with the reserved liquid, and add the mirin, sake, soy sauce, and sugar. Stir and bring to a boil over medium heat, then reduce the heat to very low and simmer for about 15 minutes, uncovered, until most of the liquid has evaporated.

Meanwhile, toast the sesame seeds in a small heavy skillet over medium heat, shaking the skillet occasionally to prevent scorching, just until they start to turn golden and are aromatic. Remove from the heat and continue to shake the skillet for about 30 seconds as it cools.

When the kombu mixture is ready, remove from the heat, add the sesame seeds, and mix well. Transfer to small glass jars.

The relish is best after it has rested for a week or more so the flavors have had time to blend together. It can be stored in the refrigerator for up to 6 months.

MISO VINAIGRETTE

Both white and red miso can add umami depth to salad dressings. The white is milder, the red is best used when the salad is made with stronger flavored vegetables. For example, with cubes of cooked sweet potato or beets or fennel, I use red miso in the dressing with cider vinegar or brown rice vinegar. I use the sweeter white miso in a dressing with fresh lemon juice to balance the lovely bitterness of radicchio or endive.

Makes ¼ cup/60 ml

About 1½ teaspoons Red Miso (page 109, or store-bought) or white miso

1 tablespoon cider vinegar, brown rice vinegar, or fresh lemon juice

3 tablespoons extra-virgin olive oil (or another oil you like)

Pinch of fine sea salt (optional)

Whisk together the miso and vinegar or lemon juice in a small bowl. Add the oil and whisk again. Taste and add salt if needed after dressing a salad.

QUICK ONION-LEMON CHUTNEY

This chutney began as an experiment. I thought salt-preserved lemons would work well with the sweetness of slow-cooked onions, and so they do. There's complexity of flavor from the spice blend, as well as a touch of chile heat. The onions cook in spiced oil and then soften with the addition of a little sugar before the chopped preserved lemon is added late in the cooking. The chutney is beautiful made with red onions, but you can use shallots or regular yellow onions.

Serve at room temperature to accompany hearty main dishes, such as bean stews, roast duck, or grilled or roast lamb or pork (a friend who tested this recipe loved it with smoked salmon).

Makes about 1¼ cups/300 ml

About ⅓ cup/100 grams Salt-Preserved Lemons (page 63, or store-bought)

2 tablespoons extra-virgin olive oil

Generous pinch of ground turmeric

1 teaspoon black mustard seeds

½ teaspoon nigella seeds

¼ teaspoon fennel seeds

1 dried red chile, broken in half, or ¼ to ½ teaspoon cayenne (to taste)

1 medium-large red onion (about 7 ounces/200 grams), finely chopped

¼ teaspoon fine sea salt, or to taste

⅛ teaspoon ground cinnamon (cassia)

About ¼ cup/60 ml hot water

Scant ¼ cup/50 grams sugar, preferably turbinado sugar, such as Sugar in the Raw, or to taste

Chop the lemon, including the pulp, into approximately ¼-inch/0.5 cm dice; set aside in a small bowl.

Place a cast-iron or other heavy skillet over medium heat. Add the oil and turmeric, and when the oil is hot, add the mustard seeds and raise the heat to high. When the mustard seeds start popping, cover the pan and lower the heat to medium. When the seeds finish popping, toss in the nigella and fennel seeds and the chile and stir, then add the onion, stirring to coat with oil. Add the salt and cook, stirring frequently, until the onion has softened, about 7 minutes.

Stir in the cinnamon, add the hot water and sugar and stir, then raise the heat to medium-high and cook until the onion softens further and some of the water has evaporated, about 2 minutes. Stir in the chopped preserved lemon, reduce the heat to medium-low, and cook slowly for several minutes more.

Remove from the heat, transfer to a small bowl, and set aside for several minutes to let the flavors settle. Taste for salt and adjust if necessary, stirring it in well. Transfer to a small serving bowl and let cool.

Refrigerated in a glass jar, the chutney will keep for a month.

VIETNAMESE DIPPING SAUCE

I think it was above all this dipping sauce, called nuoc cham, that introduced foreigners to the pleasures of Southeast Asian fish sauce. The pungency of the nuoc mam (the Vietnamese term for fish sauce) is tamed by its pairing with fresh lime juice and a little vinegar, and their acidity is balanced by a pinch of sugar. Then it's all given some punch with a touch of garlic and chile, becoming a pure example of the dance of hot-sour-salty-sweet.

When I was in Vietnam in 1990 for the first time, the nuoc cham in the south tended to be fairly sweet, while in the north there was more vinegar and less lime. But all these things are a matter of taste, as well as of access to ingredients. The proportions here are a guide; vary them as you please. The small splash of water helps flavors blend, especially if the vinegar or the fish sauce is a little harsh.

Makes about ⅔ cup/160 ml

¼ cup/60 ml Vietnamese or Thai fish sauce

¼ cup/60 ml fresh lime juice

1 tablespoon unseasoned rice vinegar

1 to 2 tablespoons water

1 teaspoon sugar, or more to taste

1 small garlic clove, minced

1 or more bird or other hot fresh chiles, minced

Combine all the ingredients in a bowl and stir. Taste and adjust as you wish. Put out on the table as a condiment, with a small spoon, so that guests can add it to their food as they eat. Or instead give each person a small condiment bowl of the sauce and invite them to serve themselves.

Store leftovers in a well-sealed glass jar in the refrigerator. Flavors will fade after a couple of days; then make a fresh batch.

CLASSIC THAI FISH SAUCE
with Bird Chiles

Wherever you go to eat at a street stall in Thailand, there will be small jars of condiments on the table. If by chance you don't see any *prik nam pla*, as this sauce is called, on the table, you can always request it. It's a go-to for many people because it gives a chile kick and an extra hit of salt and umami to whatever you drizzle it on.

Apart from its usefulness, the other great thing about prik nam pla is how easy it is to make and how well it keeps. Over time, the sauce will mellow as the chiles' heat seeps into the fish sauce.

Makes about 1 cup/240 ml

About ½ cup/50 grams bird chiles (prik ee noo)

About 1 cup/240 ml good-quality Thai fish sauce

Wearing gloves to protect your hands, wash the chiles. Chop off the stems and discard. Finely chop the chiles by hand or by pulsing in a food processor; you want a chop, not a paste.

Transfer to a clean jar, seeds and all. Add the fish sauce, put on the lid tightly, and shake to mix well. The flavor will be very hot to start but will mellow over time.

Serve in individual small bowls, so that guests can drizzle it on their food as they wish. Keep this in a sealed jar in the refrigerator (as I do), or at room temperature, as it's kept in Thailand. Toss when it's over 2 months old and has lost potency, and make another batch.

KIMCHI AIOLI

This kimchi aioli, smooth and rich, has a little chile heat and umami from the kimchi, a garlicky edge, and a subtle hint of sesame oil. It is a little looser than most aioli, more like a sauce. Since kimchis vary in saltiness, check and adjust the seasonings after the aioli is blended.

Ideally, try to make this at least half an hour before serving to give the flavors a chance to blend fully. Use it on beef or pork sandwiches, hamburgers, or freshly grilled vegetables—it's especially good on corn on the cob. Or offer it as a condiment for grilled chicken or shellfish.

Makes about 1½ cups/350 ml

1 cup/150 grams Classic Red Kimchi (page 78, or store-bought), finely chopped, plus 1 tablespoon of the juice

2 medium garlic cloves, chopped

2 large egg yolks

½ teaspoon fine sea salt, or more to taste

¾ cup/180 ml mild extra-virgin olive oil

1 teaspoon unseasoned brown rice vinegar or cider vinegar

1 teaspoon toasted sesame oil

1 teaspoon toasted sesame seeds (optional)

Combine the kimchi, garlic, egg yolks, and salt in a food processor and process until smooth, about 1 minute. Use a rubber spatula to scrape down the spatters on the sides of the bowl. With the machine running, add a thin thread of the olive oil to start and then continue adding the oil slowly until you have added about ½ cup/120 ml. Stop and scrape down the sides again. With the machine running, add the remaining olive oil, followed by the kimchi juice, vinegar, and sesame oil and process for another 15 or 20 seconds.

Transfer the aioli to a bowl, taste for salt, and add more if necessary, in small increments. If you have time, set the aioli aside, covered, in the refrigerator for half an hour or more to give the flavors time to blend. The sauce will thicken a little as it stands.

Sprinkle on a dusting of sesame seeds when you serve the aioli, if you wish. Store leftovers in a clean glass jar in the refrigerator for up to 4 days.

FOLLOWING PAGES: *Sandwich of Slow-Cooked Roast Pork Belly with Crisped Fat (page 302), flavored with Kimchi Aioli and greens*

Grids of fencing in the salt fields outside Kampot, Cambodia, where the fields were full of fresh rainwater and the salt harvest had been abandoned for the season

KAMPOT SALT

Phnom Penh, Cambodia's capital, lies on the banks of the mighty Mekong River. It's a three-hour drive from there to the southern coast and the town of Kampot,

where Cambodian sea salt is harvested. I traveled that route recently in early February. It was dry season, prime salt-harvest time. When I arrived in Kampot, I found a bicycle to rent and pedaled out to the salt fields. They're designed to hold seawater that flows into them from the Gulf of Thailand. The hot sun of the dry season (November to early April) evaporates the water in the large shallow ponds, leaving salt crystals, which are then raked up into piles. But there was no salt to be seen, and few people around. There were no piles of raked salt, and the wooden salt-storage huts were all empty.

People told me that the salt makers had given up for the season because they'd had so much rain in November and December. When it rains during salt-making season, the brine that is slowly concentrating through solar evaporation gets diluted with rainwater, setting back the process by days and sometimes weeks. The fields were wet, but it was with rainwater, not seawater evaporating to make salt.

The solar-evaporation method of salt production relies on predictable weather. It's rare to have rain during the dry season in Southeast Asia. But recent shifts in the weather patterns—due to climate change, experts speculate—mean that salt makers can no longer rely on dry sunny weather. None of the locals I spoke to could say what the future might bring.

SOUPS

SIMPLE VEGETARIAN DASHI

Dashi is the quickly made traditional base for miso soups and for a number of
other Japanese dishes that include broth or liquid. It can be vegetarian, as here,
or can include dried bonito flakes as well.

Makes about 1 quart/1 liter

**1 large piece kombu seaweed,
about 4 by 6 inches/10 by
15 cm, or several smaller ones**

**5 dried shiitake mushrooms,
rinsed (optional)**

About 4 cups/1 liter water

Put the kombu and shiitakes, if using, in a medium saucepan, add the water, and
let stand for 10 or 15 minutes.

Place the pan over medium heat and bring the liquid to just under a boil;
remove the kombu (and set aside for another purpose). Once the broth has come
to a boil, remove from the heat. If using mushrooms, let them soak in the broth for
another 15 minutes or so, then remove and reserve for another purpose.

The dashi is ready. It will keep for up to 5 days in the refrigerator.

VEGETARIAN BROTH

This simple vegetarian broth is very flavorful and only lightly seasoned.

Makes 5 to 6 cups/1.25 to
1.4 liters

2 tablespoons sunflower,
peanut, or extra-virgin olive
oil

1 pound/450 grams soybean
sprouts, washed in cold water
and drained

3 scallions, trimmed and cut
into 1-inch/2.5 cm lengths

9 dried shiitake mushrooms,
rinsed

A 1-inch/2.5 cm piece of fresh
ginger, peeled and thinly
sliced (optional)

2 quarts/2 liters cold water

1 teaspoon fine sea salt or
2 teaspoons light soy sauce

Place a large heavy pot over medium-high heat, add the oil, toss in the sprouts, and stir. Add the scallions, mushrooms, and ginger, if using, and fry, stirring, until the sprouts have started to wilt and become translucent, a couple of minutes. Add the water, raise the heat to high, and bring to a strong boil. Add the salt, lower the heat to medium/medium-low, and simmer, partially covered, for about 2 hours.

Place a strainer or colander over a bowl and pour the broth through it. Discard the solids (or do as I like to, and chop them into an omelet, or eat them with rice, with an egg on top).

Let the broth cool, then store in the refrigerator or freezer in well-sealed containers until needed. It will keep in the fridge for up to 10 days, or frozen for up to 6 months. Taste and adjust the seasoning when you use it.

The well-known salt of Maldon is boiled down from brine piped out of the Blackwater River Estuary, in eastern Essex.

FRAGRANT FISH BROTH

Like Chicken Broth from Scratch (page 214) and Simple Vegetarian Dashi (page 210), fish broth is a very useful source of flavor and pleasure. Serve the broth hot as a simple soup, or pour it over individual bowls of freshly cooked rice noodles or plain rice, or even over leftover rice. Garnish with chopped scallions and chopped fresh coriander (cilantro) or tarragon, if you wish.

This recipe grew out of my travels in Burma/Myanmar, and a version of it appears in *Burma*. Salt-preserved shrimp in two forms gives it satisfying depth: as powdered dried shrimp that flavor the initial oil, and as shrimp paste that is dissolved into the broth. Include lemongrass if you wish, for added fragrance. You can use almost any fish fillets or the more traditional fish heads to make the broth, but avoid salmon and other rich, strong-flavored fish, such as mackerel or black cod, which could be overpowering.

Makes about 5½ cups/1.3 liters

2 tablespoons peanut, untoasted sesame, or vegetable oil

⅛ teaspoon ground turmeric or 2 thin slices fresh turmeric

¼ cup/40 grams minced shallots

2 medium garlic cloves, minced

1 stalk lemongrass, trimmed, smashed flat with the side of a knife or cleaver, and cut crosswise in half (optional)

2 tablespoons Fluffy Shrimp (page 152)

About ½ pound/225 grams fish fillets or fish heads (see headnote), rinsed

About 6 cups/1.5 liters water

Scant 1 teaspoon shrimp paste

1 teaspoon fine sea salt, or to taste

2 scallions, trimmed and finely chopped, or a little chopped fresh coriander (cilantro) or tarragon for garnish (optional)

Heat the oil in a wide heavy pot over medium heat until hot. Add the turmeric, then toss in the shallots, garlic, and lemongrass, if using, and stir. Cook, stirring occasionally, until the shallots are well softened, 4 to 5 minutes. Stir in the fluffy shrimp, which will fizz a little as it hits the oil. Slide in the fish fillets or heads and cook, turning several times, until all sides have been exposed to the hot oil.

Put several spoonfuls of the water in a small bowl, add the shrimp paste, and stir to dissolve it, smearing the lumps into the liquid with the back of a spoon or using a fork to break them up. Add to the pot, along with the remaining water, raise the heat, and bring to a boil. Add the salt, lower the heat to maintain a low boil, and cook, partially covered, for 15 minutes.

Set a colander over a bowl and strain the broth into it. Discard the solids.

If serving as a simple clear soup, garnish with chopped scallions or coriander leaf or tarragon, if you wish.

CHICKEN BROTH FROM SCRATCH

Chicken broth is a versatile larder staple and easy to make. You can start with store-bought chicken backs, necks, and wings or with the remnants of a roast chicken feast. The broth freezes well and is handy to have on hand for making risotto or chicken-rice soup, among many other possibilities.

Whenever I roast a chicken, I save all the chicken "debris"—the carcass and bones, skin, and any remaining pan juices—and refrigerate in a covered container in the refrigerator for a day or two, until I'm ready to make this broth.

If I know I'll be making a Thai or Burmese soup of some kind with the broth, I'll add a bunch of coriander and some lemongrass to it, but for a basic broth for the freezer, I keep things very simple. If I'm using roast chicken remnants for the broth, then it will have a little seasoning from the flavored salt that I rub onto my roast chicken before cooking and I don't add more. If I'm starting with chicken parts, I season the broth very lightly.

Makes about 6 cups/1.5 liters

Carcass from a roast chicken, including the neck and leftover skin, along with any pan drippings (see headnote), or 2 or 3 chicken backs and necks plus 4 to 6 chicken wings

About 2 teaspoons fine sea salt or fine pickling salt or 2 tablespoons fish sauce (optional)

About 2 quarts/2 liters water

1 medium onion, coarsely chopped

3 or 4 slices fresh ginger

About 10 black peppercorns

1 bunch fresh coriander (cilantro), well washed, with roots if possible (optional)

2 or 3 stalks lemongrass, trimmed and smashed with the side of a heavy knife or cleaver (optional)

Combine the chicken "debris" or pieces and salt or fish sauce, if using, in a large pot. Add enough water to barely cover the chicken, then toss in the onion, ginger, peppercorns, and coriander and lemongrass, if using. Bring to a rolling boil, then lower the heat to maintain a low boil and cook, partially covered, for about 2 hours.

Set a colander over a large bowl and strain the broth into it. Discard the solids. Cool the broth, then store, covered, in the refrigerator for up to 3 days, or freeze for up to 3 months.

MISO SOUP

A good miso soup is warming and refreshing at any time of day. It's a great last-minute dish, easy to pull together if you have miso in the fridge.

I like to include a few vegetables or some cubes of tofu; miso soup is an excellent way to flavor tofu's slipperiness.

Serves 4

4 cups/1 liter Simple Vegetarian Dashi (page 210), Vegetarian Broth (page 212), or water

3 to 4 tablespoons/60 to 90 grams Red Miso (page 109, or store-bought)

1 or 2 squares firm or silken tofu, cut into ½-inch/1 cm cubes (optional)

¼ cup/60 grams chopped greens, such as minced scallions, fresh flat-leaf parsley, or mitsuba greens

Bring the broth to a low boil in a medium saucepan. Use a cup to scoop out about ½ cup/120 ml of the liquid. Add 3 tablespoons miso to the cup and stir to dissolve it. Set aside.

If using tofu, add it to the pan and cook for a moment to warm it through. Lower the heat and add the miso mixture. Taste, and if you'd like a more intense flavor, scoop out a little of the liquid and blend in up to another tablespoon or so of miso, then add it back to the pan. Raise the heat and bring the soup to just below a boil, then remove from the heat.

Distribute the greens among four bowls and pour the soup over. Serve immediately.

KIMCHI SOUP

Like Polish kapusniak (see page 220), which is made with sauerkraut, this satisfying Korean meal-in-one soup, called *kimchi jjigae*, originated in frugality and gets its flavor from salt-preserved cabbage. Both soups come from places with harsh winters; both are wonderful comfort food.

Kimchi jjigae gets substance and flavor from a small amount of marinated sliced pork belly. There's satisfying texture from the mix of chopped soybean sprouts and small smooth cubes of tofu. This recipe is freely adapted from Hi Soo Shin Hepinstall's lovely cookbook, *Growing Up in a Korean Kitchen*. You can make a fusion version of the soup by using sliced salt pork or pancetta (page 166) instead of plain pork belly, and omitting the soy sauce in the marinade. Or make a vegetarian version, using vegetable broth instead of chicken, and increasing the quantity of shiitakes and tofu (see the Variation).

Serve as a main course with rice, and perhaps a salad or vegetable stir-fry alongside, or serve as one of many dishes in a larger meal.

Serves 4 as a main, 6 to 8 as one of many dishes in a larger meal

---

¼ pound/110 grams pork belly or about 3 ounces/85 grams skinless salt pork or pancetta (see headnote)

MARINADE

1 teaspoon soy sauce (omit if using salt pork or pancetta)

1 tablespoon rice wine or mirin

1 garlic clove, crushed and peeled

1 scallion, trimmed and minced

1 teaspoon grated fresh ginger

1 teaspoon sugar

1 tablespoon toasted sesame oil

5 dried shiitake mushrooms, soaked in warm water for 20 minutes (see Notes)

1 packed cup/250 grams Classic Red Kimchi (page 78, or store-bought), with some of its juice

About 2 tablespoons peanut or sunflower oil

5 garlic cloves, minced

About ⅓ pound/150 grams soybean sprouts, washed and coarsely chopped

3 or 4 scallions, trimmed and cut on the diagonal into ½-inch/1.25 cm lengths

4 cups/1 liter Chicken Broth from Scratch (page 214, or store-bought) or vegetable broth

½ pound/225 grams firm tofu, cut into ½-inch/1.25 cm cubes

Freshly ground black or white pepper to taste

Fine sea salt if needed

Thinly slice the pork belly, salt pork, or pancetta and cut into bite-sized pieces; set aside.

To make the marinade, combine all the ingredients in a large bowl. Add the pork and stir to coat the meat. Set aside, covered, for 20 minutes.

Drain the shiitakes, reserving the liquid, and cut into fine julienne. Chop the kimchi into small pieces.

Heat the oil in a large heavy pot over medium heat. Add the garlic and shiitakes and cook until slightly softened, a minute or two. Add the pork belly (or salt pork or pancetta) and cook, stirring frequently, until it has all changed color, 2 to 3 minutes.

Add the sprouts, kimchi, and half the scallions and cook for a couple of minutes, until the sprouts are wilting. Add the broth and the reserved shiitake soaking water and bring to a boil, then reduce the heat and cook at a low boil for about 5 minutes. (*You can make the soup to this point up to 3 hours ahead; reheat over medium heat before proceeding.*)

Add the tofu cubes and boil gently for a couple of minutes. Add pepper to taste and adjust the seasoning with salt, if you wish. Toss in the remaining scallions and wait until they turn bright green, then remove from the heat.

Serve the soup in bowls, on its own or poured over rice.

NOTE: *Dried shiitakes are often sold sliced rather than whole; just estimate your 5-shiitake quantity. Fresh shiitakes can be substituted, no soaking needed, but they will need to cook for longer until tender.*

VARIATION

To make a vegetarian version of this soup, omit the pork and use Vegetarian Broth (page 212) instead of chicken broth. Double the amount of tofu (1 pound/ 450 grams), and increase the number of dried shiitakes to about 15; you'll need to increase the amount of soaking water as well.

FOLLOWING PAGES: *Kimchi Soup (left) and Hearty Sauerkraut Soup (page 220)*

HEARTY SAUERKRAUT SOUP

Kapusniak is a Polish soup traditionally made with sauerkraut and potatoes and a little pork. The small amount of meat is there for flavor rather than sustenance, as the sauerkraut and potatoes are the heart of the dish. There are also kosher versions that are made with beef rather than pork, and vegetarian versions; see the Variations below.

I learned about kapusniak from my friend Dina Fayerman, whose parents were born in Poland and survived the Holocaust, coming to Canada in 1950. Although she was raised on her mother's beef kapusniak, she advised me to make it with pork ribs, and to start by softening sliced onions in oil, as her aunt used to do. If you prefer, instead of the ribs, you can use kielbasa, a classic choice here with its smoky flavor, or a pork knuckle or other meaty bone.

The fennel seeds are not traditional, but I like the little hit they give. I take Dina's advice on the potatoes: They need to be floury potatoes, such as russets, and cooked separately. Then they and their cooking water are added shortly before serving, resulting in a thick, delectable soup.

Serve as a meal in one with rye bread. Leftovers are a pleasure.

Serves 4

---

2 tablespoons sunflower oil

2 large onions (about ½ pound/225 grams), thinly sliced

1 teaspoon fennel seeds (optional)

2 cups/500 grams Small-Batch Sauerkraut (page 84, or store-bought), with some of its juices

About 1 pound/450 grams pork ribs or ½ pound/225 grams kielbasa

About 3 cups/720 ml water

1½ teaspoons fine sea salt, or more to taste

About 1½ pounds/675 grams russet potatoes or other nonwaxy potatoes, peeled and cut into ½-inch/1 cm cubes

Freshly ground black pepper (optional)

Place a wide heavy pot over medium-high heat and add the oil. When it is hot, toss in the onions and fennel seeds, if using, lower the heat to medium, and cook, stirring occasionally, until the onions are well softened and starting to brown, about 15 minutes.

Add the sauerkraut, with its liquid, and the pork ribs or kielbasa. Cook, turning the ribs or sausage once, for about 5 minutes on each side, until they have changed color. Add about 1 cup water and bring to a boil, then reduce the heat to medium-low, partially cover, and cook for about 1 hour, or longer if needed, until the meat is very tender. Check occasionally to make sure that nothing is drying out or sticking.

Meanwhile, bring the remaining 2 cups water to a boil in a medium pot. Add the salt and then the potatoes and bring back to a boil. Lower the heat and cook at a medium boil, partially covered, until the potatoes are very tender, about 20 minutes. Remove from the heat.

Lift the meat out of the pot (reduce the heat to low) and cut the ribs apart, or cut the kielbasa into bite-sized lengths, then return to the pot.

Add the potatoes and their cooking water to the soup and stir. Raise the heat to medium. The soup should be thick and lush. If you'd like it more liquid, add a little more water and cook for another 5 minutes. Add pepper, if you wish, taste, and adjust the seasonings if necessary.

Serve in large bowls, with slices of rye bread or other bread.

VARIATIONS

To make a beef version of the soup, substitute a scant 1 pound/about 420 grams oxtails or about ½ pound/225 grams flanken or other well-marbled or fatty boneless beef. Simmer for a good 90 minutes so that the beef becomes very tender.

To make a vegetarian version, increase the oil to 3 tablespoons. Cook the onions and sauerkraut as above until the sauerkraut is very soft, about 25 minutes. Add 1 cup/240 ml Vegetarian Broth (page 212), bring to a simmer, and simmer, partially covered, for 15 minutes or so. Meanwhile, cook the potatoes as directed above, then add them to the pot, with their cooking water. Add pepper, if you like, and adjust the seasoning if necessary. Serve topped with chopped fresh dill or chives and a dollop of sour cream. Put out rye bread with salted butter.

FOGO ISLAND SPLIT PEA SOUP
with Corned Beef and Doughboys

This soup is adapted from a recipe that chefs Tim Charles and Jonathan Gushue of Fogo Island Inn shared at the 2020 Oxford Food Symposium, with the comment: "This is the soup that your nan would make on Saturday, with big salt-beef flavor and a scent that says, 'It's all okay.' Serve this when you are hungry for comfort."

Fogo Island lies off the northern coast of Newfoundland. Corned beef, salt cod, and fresh cod have been the staples of the communities there for centuries. This soup is plain food, spiced only with salt and pepper. It's a frugal (less meat-heavy) version of the corned beef meal known in Newfoundland as Jiggs' Dinner, and, like that classic, it's traditionally served with doughboys, quickly made dumplings.

You can use homemade (page 297) or store-bought corned beef. If you're making this the day you wish to serve it, begin 4 to 5 hours ahead. Put the split peas on to soak when you start cooking the beef and leave plenty of time for the peas to cook through. You can also make this a day or two ahead if you wish, stopping just before you add the vegetables. Refrigerate the soup until an hour or so before you want to serve it, and then reheat it over medium heat.

The recipe makes a generous quantity, a meal-in-one for 10 people.

Serves 10

SOUP

1 pound/450 grams Corned Beef (page 179, or store-bought)

1 pound/2 cups/450 grams dried yellow split peas, soaked in water to cover for about 3 hours

3 tablespoons sunflower or extra-virgin olive oil

2 large onions, coarsely chopped

1 garlic clove, minced

2 cups/160 grams diced peeled carrots

2 cups/160 grams diced peeled turnips or parsnips

2 or 3 medium potatoes, peeled and diced

1 cup/150 grams chopped celery or ¼ cup/10 to 15 grams minced celery leaves or lovage

Freshly ground black pepper

Fine sea salt if needed

DOUGHBOYS

1 cup/120 grams all-purpose flour

1 tablespoon cold butter, chopped into small pieces

1½ teaspoons baking powder

½ teaspoon fine sea salt

¾ cup/180 ml water

Oil for surfaces

Hot or Dijon mustard for serving (optional)

Rinse the corned beef in cold water, place it in a large heavy pot, and add water to cover. Bring to a boil and boil for 1 minute, then remove from the heat and drain. Return the beef to the pot, add water to cover generously, and bring to a boil, then lower the heat and simmer for about 2 hours, or until the meat is very tender.

Drain the split peas, add them to the pot, and bring to a boil. Lower the heat and cook at a low boil until the peas are very tender and starting to disintegrate, about 1 hour. Remove from the heat, transfer the corned beef to a platter or tray, and set aside.

Heat the oil in a large heavy skillet over medium-high heat. Add the onions and cook for a few minutes, then lower the heat to medium, add the garlic, and cook, stirring occasionally, until softened.

Transfer the onions and garlic, with their oil, to the pot of peas. (*You can make the recipe ahead to this point. Bring the pot of peas back to a simmer before continuing.*)

To make the doughboys, mix together the flour, butter, baking powder, and salt in a medium bowl, rubbing the butter between your fingers to blend it into the flour. Add the water and stir to make a sticky, stretchy dough.

Set out a lightly oiled plate and lightly oil two soupspoons. Use one spoon to scoop up a ball of dough (about 1½ inches/3.5 cm across) and then the other to roll it off the spoon onto the lightly oiled plate. Repeat with the remaining dough. Set aside.

Cut the beef into dice about the same as the vegetables and return it to the soup. Add the carrots, turnips or parsnips, potato, and celery or lovage, then add enough water to cover the vegetables completely. Bring to a strong boil, lower the heat, and continue to cook at a low boil, partially covered.

About 10 minutes before the vegetables are cooked through, check the water level. You need a depth of about 2 inches/5 cm to cook the doughboys; add more if needed, and bring back to a boil.

Add the doughboys to the soup, cover (so the tops of the dumplings will steam), and simmer until cooked through, 6 to 7 minutes.

Add pepper to taste, then taste and adjust the seasoning with salt if needed. Serve the soup in large individual bowls. Put out hot mustard or Dijon mustard as a condiment, if you wish.

WARMING BEAN SOUP
with Salt-Preserved Lemon and Miso

This is substantial enough to be served as a one-dish meal with bread, or it can be the soup course in a larger feast. You can make it well ahead, for the flavors only get richer as the soup sits. Although salt-preserved lemon is not usually an ingredient in bean dishes, I love the little zing it gives. The red miso paste adds meaty depth.

Serves 6

1 pound/450 grams dried navy beans, lima beans, or cowpeas, soaked overnight in lightly salted water to cover, or 4 cups/700 grams canned beans, rinsed and drained

¼ cup/60 ml extra-virgin olive oil, plus more for drizzling

1 medium onion, minced or grated

6 or 7 medium garlic cloves, minced

1 tablespoon ground cumin

2 teaspoons fine sea salt

2 teaspoons ground ginger

A 1-inch/2.5 cm cinnamon (cassia) stick

2 teaspoons chile pepper flakes

2 tablespoons tomato paste or 2 medium tomatoes, coarsely chopped

2 bunches flat-leaf parsley or fresh coriander (cilantro), or one of each, trimmed of coarse stems and finely chopped

2 tablespoons Red Miso (page 109, or store-bought)

3 slices Salt-Preserved Lemons (page 63, or store-bought), finely chopped

If starting with soaked dried beans, drain them, place in a large heavy pot, and add water to cover. Bring to a rolling boil, then drain and set the beans aside in a bowl.

Put the pot back over medium-high heat and add the olive oil. When the oil is hot, toss in the onion and cook for several minutes, until starting to soften. Add the garlic and cumin and cook for a minute or so. Add the reserved soaked beans to the pot. Add the salt and water to cover by 1 inch/2.5 cm and bring to a boil. Lower the heat to maintain a steady low boil and cook, partially covered, stirring occasionally and adding extra water as necessary to keep the beans covered by about 1 inch/2.5 cm, for 45 minutes. If using canned beans, simply add them to the onions, garlic, and cumin, along with the salt, and then add enough water to cover them by 1 inch/2.5 cm.

Add the ginger, cinnamon stick, chile flakes, tomato paste or chopped tomatoes, and half the chopped herbs and bring to a boil. Reduce the heat slightly and cook at a low boil, partially covered, until the beans are very soft, about 15 minutes for canned beans, another 20 to 45 minutes for dried, depending on your beans. Add extra water if needed to loosen the texture of the soup.

Scoop about 1 cup/240 ml of the liquid into a small bowl, add the miso, and stir until completely dissolved, then add back to the soup. Add the preserved lemon, bring to a boil, and cook for another 15 minutes at a medium boil. Remove from the heat, cover, and set aside until ready to serve.

About 10 minutes before serving, bring the soup back to a low boil, stirring. Add extra water if you want it less thick, then add the remaining chopped herbs. Taste and adjust the seasoning if needed. Serve in large soup bowls, drizzling about 1½ teaspoons olive oil over each serving.

This is a classic northern Thai landscape: a flat rice-growing valley framed by steep-sided hills (near the town of Tathon with the Nam Mae Kok flowing eastward). It's typical of the complicated terrain that the salt from Bo Kleua has been carried across for centuries.

BO KLEUA

Come February, in northern Thailand, the rice fields in the fertile valleys are a patchwork. It's late in the dry season, so in some fields the rice stubble is tufted rows of pale yellow-beige. In others it's singed with black after being burned off. And in a few places near streams, there is newly transplanted rice, green and hopeful, set out in irrigated paddies bright with sky-reflecting water. The valleys are rimmed by steep limestone hills. The climb out of each valley is a twisting ribbon of road that winds up and around the treed hillsides. It's hard to imagine how people traded across this complicated landscape in the days before roads and motor vehicles, but we know that they did. And one of the trade items was salt, salt from the wells in a tiny corner of Nan Province called Bo Kleua, the name meaning salt well.

Paniers of that salt were carried from Nan on oxen and elephants westward across northern Thailand to Chiang Mai, some eight to ten days' journey away, and also north into China's Yunnan Province. Salt was used as currency in the market in Chiang Mai until the late nineteenth century.

The salt was for preserving and for seasoning. Outsiders tend to assume that all Thai food is seasoned primarily with fish sauce. That's true of the center and the southern part of the country, but until relatively recently, the people of northern Thailand and the Shan States mostly used salt for seasoning—salt from Bo Kleua and other salt wells—and, for umami, they had tua nao, salt-fermented cooked soybeans, often dried into flattened disks (see page 105).

The salt wells of Bo Kleua attract some Thai tourists but are far enough off the beaten path that the village, nestled in a tight valley very close to the Lao border and surrounded by forest, has remained a calm place. Many locals are involved with salt production, and bags of salt are sold on the narrow main street lined with wooden shophouses. The well water that used to be drawn up laboriously by hand, now pumped by a motor, is much saltier than seawater. All during the dry season, families boil it in large, wide wok-shaped vessels over a fire from early morning until the water evaporates in the evening, leaving behind the precious salt (see photo page 371).

SALADS & VEGETABLES

SALTED ONION SALAD

An example of the way salting can transform vegetables, this easy cross between a salad and a palate freshener is very adaptable. I tasted several versions of it in Azerbaijan and Tajikistan.

Thinly sliced onions are salted and left briefly to soften, then rinsed. The softened onions are milder tasting, for salting draws out not just water but also some of the harsher flavor, leaving the onions "salt-transformed" into sweetness. All you need to complete the dish is something tart, most commonly barberries or pomegranate seeds, and a sprinkling of fresh green herbs, such as mint or tarragon or sorrel, or a little dried mint.

Serve alongside hearty meat or bean dishes, or to accompany kebabs of any kind.

Serves 4

2 large white or red onions (nearly ½ pound/225 grams each), thinly sliced

About 1 tablespoon coarse sea salt

About ½ cup/85 grams pomegranate seeds, or more if desired, or ¼ cup/28 grams dried barberries

About 1 tablespoon finely chopped fresh mint, tarragon, or sorrel or 1 teaspoon dried mint

Flake salt or fine sea salt

Scant ½ teaspoon ground sumac (optional)

Place the onions in a bowl, sprinkle on the coarse salt, and toss well. Set aside for about 20 minutes.

In the meantime, if using barberries, place in a bowl and add lukewarm water to cover generously. Let soak for about 15 minutes, or until softened, then drain.

Rinse the onions with cold water, wrap in a cotton cloth, and gently squeeze dry. Place in a bowl. Add the pomegranate seeds or drained barberries and toss to mix. Add the herbs and toss. Sprinkle on a pinch of flake salt or fine sea salt, taste, and add a little more if needed. Toss. Sprinkle on a dusting of sumac, if desired, and serve.

NOTE: *You can also add a dressing, for more intensity: Mix about 1 tablespoon fresh lemon juice with 1 teaspoon pomegranate molasses, add a pinch of cayenne, if you wish, and pour over the rinsed and dried onions. Toss well. Add the pomegranate seeds or barberries, then sprinkle on fresh or dried mint. Omit the sumac. Toss, taste, and sprinkle on a little finishing salt if you wish.*

GREEN OLIVES
in Walnut-Pomegranate Sauce

The received wisdom about olives is that they grow best within a short distance of the Mediterranean or another seacoast. The olives in Iran clearly haven't heard of this rule, for they grow and flourish in the region west of Tehran, cut off from the Caspian Sea by high mountains, and hundreds of miles from the Mediterranean.

This dish, called *zeitoon parvardeh* in Farsi, is a kind of chunky, intensely flavored tapenade that combines salty umami-rich olives with walnuts, garlic, tart-sweet pomegranate molasses, mint, and olive oil.

Make it a day ahead, so the flavors have time to come together. Serve as an appetizer on small pieces of toast, flatbread, or crackers, or put it out in a bowl as a kind of cross between a salad and a condiment. It is a great complement to Persian rice dishes and to grilled meat and vegetables.

Makes about 1 cup/220 grams

1 cup/200 grams large green olives, with pits

¾ cup/75 grams walnut halves or pieces

Scant 2 tablespoons minced garlic

2 tablespoons extra-virgin olive oil

¼ cup/60 ml pomegranate molasses

About ½ cup/15 grams fresh mint leaves, finely chopped, or about 2 teaspoons dried mint

About ½ teaspoon fine sea salt

2 tablespoons pomegranate seeds for garnish (optional)

Cut the olives off their pits in large pieces and transfer to a medium bowl.

Toast the walnuts in a dry skillet over medium heat until just aromatic; they should not change color. Set aside to cool, then transfer to a food processor.

Add the garlic to the food processor and process the walnuts and garlic to a fine texture; transfer to a bowl. (You can also chop the walnuts and garlic very fine with a sharp knife, or pound to a coarse paste in a mortar with a pestle.)

Add the olive oil to the walnut mixture and stir to blend thoroughly, then stir in the pomegranate molasses. Add the mint and mix well.

Pour the dressing over the chopped olives and stir and turn to coat them thoroughly. Cover the bowl and refrigerate at least overnight, or for as long as 2 days. The strong flavors in the dressing take time to come together harmoniously.

Before serving, taste for salt. The amount you need will vary with the olives you use, so season cautiously. Transfer to a serving bowl and sprinkle on the pomegranate seeds, if using.

Leftovers keep very well in the refrigerator for up to 5 days.

ORANGE AND BLACK OLIVE SALAD

Orange salad is a dose of brilliant color and freshness in midwinter, when citrus fruits are in season. I remember my first encounter with it in Morocco, where it was set out on a table of many salads at a busy restaurant in the Atlas Mountains. It's a wonderful example of the way that salt, sweet, and acid can play together on the tongue, becoming greater than the sum of their parts. Serve as an appetizer, or to accompany grilled meat or vegetables, or a hearty winter stew.

The salad is adapted from a recipe in the North Africa chapter of *Flatbreads & Flavors*.

Serves 4 as a side salad or appetizer

5 large, juicy oranges

About ½ cup/100 grams small salt-cured black olives (Moroccan, if you can find them)

½ teaspoon coriander seeds, lightly toasted and ground to a powder

1 garlic clove, minced

¼ teaspoon fine sea salt, or to taste

¼ cup/8 grams finely chopped fresh mint

Generous pinch of chile pepper flakes or hot pimentón (smoked paprika), or to taste

1 tablespoon extra-virgin olive oil

Pinch of sugar (optional)

Peel the oranges and use a knife to remove all the pith. Working on a large plate or rimmed surface to catch the juices, cut the oranges crosswise into ¼-inch/ 0.5 cm slices. Separate the slices into segments, discarding any remaining white pith and connecting tissue. (This may seem finicky, but it's quickly done.) Transfer the cleaned segments to an attractive bowl and add the olives. Set the juice aside in a small bowl.

Combine the coriander, garlic, and salt in a mortar or a bowl and use the pestle or the back of a spoon to pound or press to a paste. Add the mint, chile flakes or pimentón, and olive oil and stir to blend well. Stir in the reserved orange juice. Taste the dressing and add the sugar, if you wish.

Pour the dressing over the oranges and olives, toss lightly to coat, and serve.

CUCUMBER SALAD
with Ginger and Shio Kombu or Shio Koji

This is one of many cucumber dishes that use the heat of ginger to balance the cool of the cucumber. Thin-skinned cucumbers work best here. The seasoning and depth of flavor come from shio kombu (seaweed relish) or shio koji, both of which you can make yourself (see page 198 and pages 100 and 102) or find in Japanese or Korean grocery stores.

Shio kombu is made of shredded kombu seaweed soaked and simmered in soy sauce and mirin with other flavors. Shio koji is a salty fermented rice paste that, like shio kombu, gives great umami depth to the salad. The saltiness of both ingredients helps draw water out of the cucumber slices, softening them and intensifying their flavor.

Serves 3 or 4

About ¾ pound/375 grams thin-skinned cucumber: 1 European cucumber or 2 or 3 Persian cucumbers (see Note)

A 2-inch/5 cm piece of fresh ginger, peeled and cut into matchsticks

2 tablespoons finely chopped Seaweed Relish (page 198, or store-bought) or 1 tablespoon shio koji (page 100 or 102, or store-bought)

1 to 1½ teaspoons toasted sesame oil (to taste)

1 to 2 tablespoons toasted sesame seeds

Sprinkling of togarashi powder or hot pimentón (smoked paprika) (optional)

Fine sea salt if needed

Slice the cucumber crosswise into ¼-inch/0.5 cm slices. Place in a bowl, add the ginger and seaweed relish or shio koji, and use your hands to mix them together. Set aside for 15 minutes. The salt in the seaweed relish or shio koji will draw moisture out of the cucumber and soften the ginger.

Pour off any accumulated liquid from the cucumbers. Add the sesame oil, sesame seeds, and togarashi powder or pimentón, if using, and toss. Taste and add a little salt, if you wish. Serve immediately.

NOTE: *If you have only thicker-skinned cucumbers, peel the cucumber completely. If your cucumber is fat, slice it lengthwise in half or in quarters before slicing crosswise.*

POTATO SALAD
with Anchovies and Herbs

I love potato salad dressed with a heavily herbed vinaigrette. It's so flexible, so fresh. This version includes chopped anchovies as well. (If you don't have any on hand, you could add a little fish sauce to the dressing instead.)

You want firm, waxy potatoes. You can cook them as much as a day ahead, then slide off the peels and assemble the salad about half an hour before you serve it. The radicchio is a nice option if you have a taste for bitter, or you can include a little chopped fennel.

Serves 4 generously

About 1½ pounds/675 grams well-washed unpeeled waxy potatoes

About 1 tablespoon pickling salt or fine sea salt

1 small head radicchio, cored and finely chopped, or 1 cup/ about 150 grams chopped fennel (optional)

DRESSING

About 8 anchovy fillets rinsed, dried, and finely chopped

1 or 2 small shallots, minced

1 to 2 tablespoons fresh lemon juice (to taste)

2 tablespoons brown rice vinegar or cider vinegar, or to taste

1 teaspoon fine sea salt, or more to taste

About 3 tablespoons extra-virgin olive oil

Several bunches of herbs, such as sorrel, basil, mint, tarragon, and/or shiso

Put the potatoes in a pot with water to just cover and bring to a boil. Add the salt, lower the heat to maintain a low boil, and cook until the potatoes are just barely cooked through, 10 to 20 minutes depending on the age and size of your potatoes—a fork should go into the center with a slight resistance. Drain, return the potatoes to the pot, and set aside, covered, to firm up and cool for half an hour.

Slide off the peels and chop the potatoes into small-bite-sized pieces. Transfer to a large bowl. Add the radicchio or fennel, if using.

To make the dressing, whisk the anchovies, shallots, lemon juice, vinegar, salt, and olive oil in a bowl until well blended; set aside for a moment.

Chop the leaves and fine stems of the herbs. Add half the chopped herbs to the dressing and stir, then pour it over the potatoes and toss well to coat. Set aside, loosely covered, for 20 minutes.

Just before serving, add the remaining chopped herbs and toss again. Taste the balance of flavors in the dressing and adjust the salt and acidity if necessary.

CATALAN CHOPPED SALAD
with Bacalao and Olives

This version of the distinctive, refreshing Catalan salad called *esqueixada catalana de bacalao* is made with shredded desalted salt cod tossed with finely chopped onion, bell pepper, and tomato. You need to think ahead, for the cod has to soak for a full 48 hours to ensure that it's completely desalted.

I like to use red or yellow bell peppers for this salad, or a mix, and to include chopped parsley.

Serves 4 to 6 as a side salad or appetizer

½ pound/225 grams salt cod, soaked in 5 or 6 changes of cold water over 48 hours

½ small white onion or 1 shallot, cut into small dice

1 large red or yellow bell pepper, or half of each, cored, seeded, ribs removed, and cut into small dice

2 or 3 medium tomatoes (about ½ pound/225 grams total), cut into small dice

About 1 tablespoon cider vinegar

About 2 tablespoons extra-virgin olive oil

Fine sea salt and freshly ground black pepper (optional)

12 to 15 small black salt-cured olives

Leaves and fine stems from 3 or 4 sprigs flat-leaf parsley, coarsely chopped (optional)

Drain the salt cod. Peel off the skin and discard, then shred the fish, using your fingers, or a knife and your fingers, to pull apart the layers.

Bring about 2 cups/480 ml water to a rapid boil in a saucepan. Put a sieve near your sink. Add the chopped fish to the boiling water, stir briefly, and then immediately drain it in the sieve; with the back of a large spoon, press the fish against the mesh of the sieve in order to squeeze out excess water.

Chop the fish shreds crosswise into short lengths and transfer to a shallow bowl.

Add the diced onion or shallot, bell pepper, and tomatoes to the fish.

Mix together the cider vinegar and olive oil in a small bowl. Pour over the fish mixture and toss. Taste and season lightly with salt and/or black pepper, if you wish. Add the olives and the parsley, if using, and toss again.

Transfer to a platter or serving bowl and serve.

MIXED GREENS with Preserved Lemon

Salt-preserved lemon transforms simple cooked greens into something special.

Start with any leafy greens you like, from spinach to beet greens. Once you've wilted them to tenderness, they are folded into hot olive oil flavored with garlic and spices.

Serve this as a kind of dense salsa, to be scooped up with bread, or as a vegetable side dish. Or use as a hamburger topping.

Makes about 2 cups/300 grams cooked dressed greens; serves 3 as part of a meal

---

About ¾ pound/350 grams greens: chard leaves, spinach, beet greens, or dandelion greens, or a mixture, trimmed of stems, well washed, and coarsely chopped

About 6 tablespoons/90 ml extra-virgin olive oil

About ¼ teaspoon fine sea salt

3 or 4 medium garlic cloves, minced

½ teaspoon nigella seeds

½ teaspoon fennel or cumin seeds

About ¼ cup/10 to 15 grams finely chopped fresh flat-leaf parsley or coriander (cilantro)

About 2 tablespoons finely chopped Salt-Preserved Lemons (page 63, or store-bought)

½ teaspoon hot pimentón (smoked paprika) or Aleppo pepper

1 tablespoon fresh lemon juice, or to taste

½ teaspoon flake salt, or to taste

Rinse the chopped greens again in cold water and drain, leaving some water droplets clinging to them.

Heat a wok or large skillet over high heat. Add about 2 teaspoons of the oil and swirl to coat the pan, then, standing back to avoid oil spatters, toss in the greens. Use a long-handled spatula to turn the greens over and over to expose all sides to the hot pan; sprinkle on the salt after turning them a couple of times. They'll steam-cook to softness in a few minutes (chard, beet greens, and dandelion will take a little longer than spinach). When the greens have just softened, transfer them to a bowl and press out extra liquid; discard the liquid.

When the greens are cool enough to handle, finely chop them.

Place the wok or skillet over medium heat and add 2 tablespoons of the oil, then toss in the garlic, nigella seeds, and fennel or cumin seeds and cook briefly, just until the garlic begins to soften. Add the parsley or coriander, cooked greens, preserved lemon, and pimentón or Aleppo pepper, and stir and turn for a minute to blend the flavors and cook the greens to melting tenderness.

Turn the greens out into a wide shallow bowl. Drizzle on the remaining olive oil (about a scant 2 tablespoons) and the lemon juice and stir, then sprinkle on the salt. Taste and adjust the seasoning if necessary. Serve warm or at room temperature.

GRILLED OR ROASTED VEGETABLES
Three Ways

Here is a trio of seasoning ideas from The Salt Larder that can transform grilled or roasted vegetables into extra-special versions of themselves.

OLIVE OIL AND FISH SAUCE

The basic rule with fish sauce and olive oil as a coating for grilled or oven-roasted vegetables (mushrooms, leafy greens, wedges of cabbage, onions, slices of zucchini, asparagus, cauliflower florets, almost anything) is that you need a light hand. Mix the two together in a bowl in a rough 2:1 proportion, two parts olive oil to one part fish sauce. Just before grilling or roasting, brush onto the vegetables, or drizzle over a platter of the vegetables and toss to coat.

SHIO KOJI

If you have slices of eggplant or zucchini, or kale leaves or onion wedges, or ears of corn, or other vegetables to put on the grill or to roast in the oven, try blending a little oil (olive, vegetable, or toasted sesame) with a tablespoon or more of shio koji (page 100 or 102, or store-bought) in a small bowl and then brushing this lightly on the vegetables 5 to 10 minutes before cooking them. The shio koji will give the vegetables seasoning and wonderful extra umami.

MISO

Another way of giving grilled or roasted vegetables added depth of flavor is to dab on a little miso mixed with oil. Shiro (white) miso works best with most vegetables, as the more intense flavor of darker miso can overpower them. The exceptions are corn on the cob and sweet potatoes, both of which are delicious with the added depth that Red Miso (page 109, or use store-bought) gives. Blending the miso with a little oil makes it easier to brush onto the vegetables.

SPINACH with Sesame

Spinach with gomasio—salt and sesame seeds—is a classic in Japan. Whenever I have a good supply of fresh, bright spinach from the farmers' market, this is my go-to dish, intensely green and delicately seasoned.

I use this cooking method for other greens as well, such as beet or turnip or radish greens, though they take a bit longer to wilt. If you want to make a larger quantity, say double or more, you'll need a very large wok or skillet; or instead do it in two batches.

Serves 2 to 3 as a side

½ pound/225 grams spinach

1 teaspoon olive or vegetable oil

Scant ½ teaspoon kosher salt or coarse pickling salt (a little less if using gomasio)

About 1 tablespoon fresh lemon juice, or to taste

½ teaspoon soy sauce

½ teaspoon toasted sesame oil

1 teaspoon Gomasio (page 38, or store-bought) or ½ teaspoon lightly toasted sesame seeds

Fine sea salt if needed

Wash the spinach thoroughly in two or three changes of water (do this just before cooking, so the leaves still have some water on them). This may sound fussy, but spinach hangs on to the soil it grows in, so it needs meticulous washing. If the stems are large and thick, cut them off and mince them for this dish, or use for another purpose, such as vegetable broth. Coarsely chop the spinach.

Place a large pan or wok over high heat. Add the oil and swirl to coat. Add the spinach stems, if using, and then the spinach leaves, pressing them against the hot pan. Sprinkle on the coarse salt, press again, and use your spatula to turn the mass of spinach over. The leaves will start wilting within a minute. Keep turning them over on themselves and pressing them against the hot pan until all the leaves have wilted and turned bright green and there's some liquid in the bottom of the pan, 3 to 5 minutes.

Remove from the heat and pour off the water. Use the spatula to press the cooked greens firmly and force out even more water; do this several times, discarding the water. Transfer the spinach to a cutting board and slice crosswise in one direction and then the other to chop it thoroughly. Press again to get rid of any remaining water. It will be a compact green mound. Transfer to a shallow bowl.

Mix the lemon juice, soy sauce, and sesame oil in a small bowl. Pour over the spinach and toss gently. Sprinkle on the gomasio or sesame seeds, and, if not using gomasio, a little fine salt. Serve hot or at room temperature.

VEGETABLE SAMBAL

Sambal is the Indonesian and Malay word for dishes of cooked vegetables that are coated with a mixture of intense flavorings, most often including dried shrimp and chiles. In this enticing version, cayenne chiles, dried shrimp, toasted shrimp paste, and lime juice are blended to make a dressing that brings the cooked vegetables to vivid life. Use the sauce for okra, green beans, carrots, or small wedges of cabbage. This recipe is adapted from one in *Penang Nyonya Cooking* by Cecilia Tan (see Resources).

Serve as the vegetable dish in a simple meal for two, or as one of many dishes in a more elaborate meal for four.

Serves 2 to 4

Coarse salt

About ¾ pound/350 grams vegetable: whole carrots, small tender okra, trimmed green beans, or small wedges of cabbage (see headnote)

About ¼ cup/30 grams dried shrimp, soaked in water for 10 minutes, drained, and coarsely chopped

4 green or red cayenne chiles, trimmed of stems, seeds, and membranes

Fine sea salt

1½ teaspoons shrimp paste

¼ cup/60 ml fresh lime juice

About ½ cup/50 grams very thinly sliced shallots or red onion

1 lime, cut into wedges

Bring about 2 inches/5 cm of water to a boil in a saucepan. Salt generously with coarse salt, bring back to a boil, and add the vegetable. Cook just until barely tender, then drain and set aside to cool.

Place the shrimp, chiles, and a pinch of fine salt in a processor or mortar and process or pound to a paste. Set aside.

Place a skillet over medium-high heat. Wrap the shrimp paste in foil, press flat to make a thin package, and heat in the skillet for 3 minutes or so, turning it over halfway through. When you open the package (watch out for hot steam), the paste should have turned pale and be a bit crumbly.

Add to the pounded shrimp mixture and pound or process to blend well. Turn out into a bowl, add the lime juice, and stir to moisten thoroughly, then add the shallots or onion and stir to mix.

Cut the vegetable into bite-sized pieces. Place in a shallow serving bowl or on a platter, add the dressing, and toss. Serve with the lime wedges alongside.

BITTER MELON STIR-FRY
with Black Bean Sauce

Bitter melon is a much-loved vegetable in Asia, but it is usually an acquired taste for those who didn't grow up with it as part of their food culture. You'll find bitter melons in Asian produce stands and food markets. Though it's called a melon, it's shaped more like the cousin of a cucumber. Bitter melons are usually pale green with little bumps along them, like small bubbles in the skin. They can be 5 to 10 inches/12 to 25 cm long but are unexpectedly lightweight; two large ones weigh about 1 pound/450 grams.

Some recipes for bitter melon call for pre-salting it to draw out bitterness, but here the slices are given a short parboiling in well-salted water, which makes the stir-frying very quick. The amount of black bean sauce called for is a range because store-bought sauces vary widely. With the homemade black bean sauce on page 189, I usually use a generous 2 tablespoons.

Serve as a spicy vegetable side.

Serves 4 to 6 as a side

About 1 pound/450 grams bitter melon (2 large or 3 or 4 small)

About 1 tablespoon fine sea salt

1 tablespoon peanut, unroasted sesame, or vegetable oil

2 to 3 tablespoons Black Bean Sauce (page 189, or store-bought), or to taste

Slice the bitter melon lengthwise in half. Use a strong spoon to scrape out the seeds and pith and discard. Cut crosswise on a diagonal into ¼-inch/ 0.5 cm slices.

Bring about 4 inches/10 cm of water to a boil in a large pot and add the salt. Add the bitter melon and boil briefly, 2 to 3 minutes, just until the slices are starting to soften; drain.

Place a wok or a large heavy skillet over high heat. When it is hot, add the oil, lower the heat to medium-high, and add the black bean sauce. Stir it into the oil and cook, stirring, for about 30 seconds. Raise the heat to high, add the parboiled bitter melon slices, and stir to coat them with the sauce, then stir-fry, pressing them against the sides of the wok or the bottom of the pan to expose them to the heat, until softened and cooked through, about 3 minutes. Taste partway through cooking and add a little more sauce if you wish.

Turn the melon out into a shallow bowl and serve.

VARIATIONS

Black bean sauce is also a good companion for broccoli rabe and for dandelion greens. Start with about 1 pound/450 grams of either. Trim off the tough ends.

Blanch the broccoli rabe as above in salted water until barely al dente, then drain and set aside. Once it is cool enough to handle, cut it into 1-inch/2.5 cm lengths. Proceed as above.

Or, if using dandelion greens, wash well and chop into 1- to 2-inch/2.5 to 5 cm lengths. Heat the oil and add the black bean sauce as above. Toss in the dandelion greens and stir-fry for a minute or so. Add about ¼ cup/60 ml hot water, bring to a boil, and cover. Let cook, steaming under the lid, for a minute, then uncover and stir-fry for another minute or so before turning out onto a plate or shallow bowl to serve.

ZUCCHINI in Golden Sand Sauce

I learned of this Shanghainese cooking technique from Carolyn Phillips's book *All Under Heaven*, an exploration of Chinese regional cooking. Golden sand sauce is made from the yolks of brined eggs. It gives an enticing umami depth to any vegetable it coats.

In the course of my sand sauce explorations, I've learned that you really need the full amount of oil (so don't be tempted to cut back), and that the sauce and vegetables must come out of the pan very quickly. If the sauce cooks too long, the egg yolks can separate into clumps (though the flavor will still be delicious).

Serve with plain rice and/or as a side with grilled fish or with roast chicken.

Serves 4 to 6

Vegetable oil

1 pound/450 grams zucchini, cut into ½-inch/1 cm cubes or ¼-inch-wide/0.5 cm wide batons

SAUCE

6 uncooked brined egg yolks (from Brined Eggs, page 127)

¼ cup/60 ml peanut oil, plus more for mashing the yolks

2 garlic cloves, minced

2 scallions, trimmed and minced, or 1 small shallot, minced

2 slices peeled fresh ginger, minced

1 to 2 teaspoons fine sea salt (to taste)

Heat a large skillet with a lid over high heat and add a little oil, barely enough to coat the surface, then toss in the zucchini and stir for a minute or two to expose all surfaces to the hot pan. Add a scant ½ cup/120 ml hot water and immediately put on the lid to hold in the steam. Let cook for a couple of minutes, then check and stir again before placing the lid back on. The vegetable pieces should be tender and cooked through in another few minutes.

Turn the zucchini out into a bowl and let cool for 10 minutes or more before making the sand sauce.

To make the sauce, lightly oil a fork or a small whisk and use it to mash the egg yolks in a small bowl; add a touch of oil to help with breaking them up and whisking them into a smooth texture. Set aside.

Heat a wok or large skillet over medium-high heat and add the oil. When it is hot, toss in the garlic, scallions or shallot, and ginger and stir-fry briefly, then lower the heat to medium. Add the whisked yolks and use your spatula or a long-handled whisk to blend the yolks into the oil. When the sauce starts to foam, in less than a minute, add 1 teaspoon salt and stir, then add the zucchini and stir briefly to coat them with the sauce.

Immediately transfer into a wide shallow bowl and taste; add a little more salt if you wish and stir it in. Serve hot.

FIRM TOFU
in Ginger-Miso Sauce

This takes only 10 minutes to make, but its flavor is as rich and velvety as if it had simmered for a long time. Serve with rice and a cooked vegetable such as Spinach with Sesame (page 240 and pictured opposite).

Serves 2 as a main with rice and a vegetable dish, 4 as a side

SAUCE

1 tablespoon minced peeled fresh ginger

2 tablespoons shiro (white) miso

1 tablespoon light soy sauce

2 tablespoons mirin

¾ cup/180 ml water

1 pound/450 grams firm tofu, cut into slices about ¼ inch/ 0.5 cm thick and 1 inch/ 2.5 cm long

Greens of 1 scallion, minced

To make the sauce, mix together the ginger, miso, soy sauce, and mirin in a medium bowl. Add the water and stir. Pour the sauce into a heavy skillet and bring to a boil over high heat, stirring. Lower the heat to medium and cook for a couple of minutes, until the sauce starts to reduce a little.

Slide the tofu slices into the sauce. Use a spatula to separate them and make sure they're all coated with sauce. Reduce the heat to medium-low and cook for about 5 minutes, shaking the pan a little to make sure the slices are not sticking as the sauce thickens a little.

Turn out into a shallow serving bowl, sprinkle on the scallion greens, and serve.

TELOUET SALT MINE

After you cross the Tiz-n-Tishka Pass on the main Marrakesh-to-Ouarzazate route, there's a small road that turns off along a valley bordered by low pink and

ocher hills. The landscape is bare of people. Beyond the village of Telouet, half an hour farther on, the valley narrows and the road heads steeply downhill between bare cliffs that are tan and charcoal and almost purple, with splotches of white salty soil. Around another bend, you come across a small sign for the salt mine, in French and Arabic.

As I walked up the track that leads to the mine, I was struck by how lovely the place was. But the true wonder is that people have been coming up to this small side valley for centuries, for millennia even, to get salt. Imagining caravans with donkeys, say, maybe camels, arriving to collect loads of salt for distribution up and over the pass to Marrakesh, or down the Ouline River valley in the direction of the desert, I wondered: What did the workers wear? What were they paid?

There was a trickle of water by the path and the ground nearby was white with salt. The cliffs on either side loomed steep and bare. Around a bend, the valley opened out into a kind of small amphitheater. There were low salt-storage sheds and the remnants of small rectangular evaporation ponds rimmed with stones and dirt, now dry and empty. When I peered into one of the sheds, I saw chunks of dark stained salt in a heap. Up ahead was a hole in the cliff face, blocked by a rough wooden door, like the entry to a mysterious cave in a fairy tale. To be in this place that traders had come to for centuries to buy loads of salt sent the hairs on the back of my neck prickling with time-travel wonder.

I learned later from a man in a village farther down the valley that the mine is now worked by only one or two men. He said, "It's for animals, the salt they gather. People now buy salt from the city. But before, our salt was sold all over, from Marrakesh to Ouarzazate, down in the desert."

A salt storage hut and abandoned salt evaporation basin near the Telouet salt mine

FISH

TARAMASALATA

Taramasalata, often colored pink in Greek restaurant and grocery store versions, is a great example of frugality in action, a delicious way of extending a precious ingredient. Salted lumpfish roe (see page 148), with its distinctive flavor, is blended into whatever easy base is available—stale white bread or, as here, cooked potato—and turned into a spreadable sauce with the addition of olive oil and lemon juice. I like to include a touch of garlic. Black roe will yield a grayish dip; red roe results in a pink one.

Serve with pita or other bread or crackers, as a snack or appetizer, or as part of a meal.

Makes about 1 cup/250 grams

1 medium floury potato, such as a russet (about 3 ounces/90 grams), boiled until soft, peeled, cooled, and coarsely chopped

¼ cup/50 grams red or black lumpfish roe

1 medium garlic clove, minced

Scant ½ cup/110 ml extra-virgin olive oil

2 tablespoons fresh lemon juice, or more to taste

¼ teaspoon freshly ground white or black pepper (optional)

Fine sea salt if needed

Put the potato, roe, and garlic in the bowl of a food processor or in a large mortar and pulse or pound until thoroughly blended. If using a processor, drizzle in the oil in a small, steady stream while the machine is running. Alternatively, if using a mortar, pound the mixture as you add the oil in a thin stream.

Pulse or pound the lemon juice into the paste, and then the pepper, if using. Taste, and add a little more lemon juice if you wish. Turn out into a bowl, cover loosely, and refrigerate for half an hour or more, if you have the time, to let the flavors develop.

Taste for salt just before serving (the saltiness of the roe emerges as the dip stands, so it's important not to add salt earlier), and serve. Store leftovers in the fridge for up to 3 days.

SHIO KOJI-MARINATED GRILLED FISH

When I have fish fillets to grill, I often turn to shio koji, smearing some on each fillet about an hour before cooking. The shio koji salts the fish a little, so you need no other salt, and it also gives it extra umami. It's hard to describe that added layer of delicious, but everyone senses it: "What did you do to the fish, what's that extra flavor in each mouthful?" they ask.

I find this method ideal for mild-tasting fish—freshwater fish such as pickerel or lake trout, for example—but use it with any fish you have.

Serves 6

2 pounds/900 grams fish fillets, left whole or cut into portions

A little extra-virgin olive or vegetable oil

About 1 tablespoon shio koji (page 100 or 102, or store-bought)

About 4 pinches fresh tarragon leaves or a sprinkling of ground blue fenugreek (see Glossary) or ground ginger (optional)

Lemon or lime wedges for serving (optional)

About 1½ hours before you want to serve the fish, take it out of the fridge, and put it on a plate or tray. Lightly oil the skin side of the fillets (or the side where the skin was, if using skinless fillets), then turn them flesh side up. With the back of a spoon or your fingers, smear the shio koji paste all over the flesh side. Refrigerate the fish until 15 minutes before you put it on the grill.

Prepare a low fire in a gas or charcoal grill.

Just before grilling, sprinkle the tarragon leaves or ground spice, if using, over the flesh side of the fish. Grill the fish skin side down 5 or 6 inches (12 to 15 centimeters) from the flame, with the lid closed, until the flesh is opaque; a good rule of thumb for timing is 10 minutes for every 1 inch/2.5 cm of thickness.

Transfer the fish to a serving plate or platter and let rest for a minute or two to finish the cooking. Serve with wedges of lemon or lime if you wish.

PANFRIED OPTION: *You'll need one or two large cast-iron or other heavy skillets. Place the pans over medium-high heat, pour a little olive oil or sunflower oil into each pan, and swirl it around with a spatula. When the oil is hot, add the fish skin side down, cover, and cook for 6 to 7 minutes (following the 10-minute rule, above). Flip the fish over just before it's done, cook for about 20 seconds, and then flip it back. Serve as above.*

JAPANESE-STYLE
SALTED SALMON

Serve this simple elegant salmon, *shio jake* in Japanese, as a main with rice or with new potatoes. Accompany it with a side of cooked green vegetables such as Spinach with Sesame (page 240) or Mixed Greens with Preserved Lemon (page 237). In asparagus season, I cook asparagus alongside the salmon, either on the grill or on the same pan under the broiler.

Salting the salmon 24 hours ahead firms up the fish and brings out its flavor. I like to start with a large fillet cut crosswise into thick slices, which then become individual servings.

If you have leftover salmon, remove the skin, break up the flesh, and mix it with a little Kimchi Aioli (page 203) or with homemade mayonnaise flavored with lemon juice and chopped herbs. Serve on toast or with rice.

Serves 3 or 4

About 1½ pounds/675 grams skin-on salmon fillet, cut into 3 or 4 portions

1 to 2 tablespoons mirin or sake

About 1 tablespoon coarse sea salt

Lemon slices for serving

Place the salmon skin side down in a shallow bowl, and pour over the mirin or sake. Set aside to marinate for 15 minutes, turning the slices over partway.

Pour off the liquid and pat the salmon dry. Sprinkle about two-thirds of the salt over the skin side of the pieces. Turn them over and sprinkle on the remaining salt. Lay the salmon in a single layer in a flat glass or other nonreactive container. Cover with a layer of paper towels, top with a lid or foil or plastic wrap, and refrigerate for 24 hours (you can let it go for as long as 48 hours).

About 20 minutes before serving, take the salmon out of the refrigerator. Preheat the broiler or prepare a medium fire in a grill.

If broiling, place an oven rack about 8 inches/20 cm from the broiler element. (You want the salmon to get slightly browned but not crisped.) Pour off any liquid and pat the salmon dry. Place skin side down in a lightly oiled cast-iron skillet or in a parchment-lined baking pan and broil for about 5 minutes or until firmed up and lightly touched with color.

Alternatively, lightly oil the skin side of the pieces and grill, skin side down, about 6 inches/15 cm from the flame, with the lid closed, until just firm, 4 to 6 minutes.

Serve with lemon slices alongside.

THAI SALT-GRILLED FISH
with Lemongrass and Dipping Sauce

The salt-grilled fish of Thailand is a simple affair, unlike the salt-crust–baked fish of European chefs. In northeast Thailand and across the Mekong River in Laos, slender, local freshwater fish are cleaned, pressed into coarse salt, and grilled over charcoal in open-air markets. In Bangkok, the grilled fish sold street-side tend to be larger and to have a stalk of lemongrass perfuming the cavity as they cook. That's the inspiration for this recipe.

In North America, far from the soft air and local markets of Thailand, salt-grilled fish feels like a treat. It cooks quickly on a grill, or under the broiler. Serve it with rice and a salad, as a topping for noodles, or as part of a Thai-style sticky rice meal with leafy greens and a dipping sauce. I suggest using nuoc cham, the Vietnamese dipping sauce, here. It's milder and a bit sweeter than the sauce you'd find in Thailand. Punch it up with a little minced hot chile, if you wish.

Serves 4

4 stalks lemongrass

About ½ cup/140 grams coarse sea salt

Four ½-pound/225 grams or two 1-pound/250 grams trout or pickerel or sea bream, cleaned and scaled

4 or 5 limes, cut into wedges

OPTIONAL ACCOMPANIMENTS

Tender lettuce leaves, such as Bibb

Sprigs of fresh coriander (cilantro) or Vietnamese coriander (rau ram; see Glossary) or Thai basil

Vietnamese Dipping Sauce (page 201) or other hot-sour-salty dipping sauce

Cooked Thai sticky rice or jasmine rice

Prepare a low fire in a charcoal or gas grill, or place a rack about 8 inches/20 cm below the broiler element of your oven and preheat the broiler. If broiling, lightly oil the broiling pan.

Trim off the root ends and dry upper parts of the lemongrass stalks, then smash each with the side of a cleaver or a heavy knife; set aside.

Heap the salt on a small baking sheet or tray.

Rinse the fish inside and out with cold water. Make 2 diagonal slashes in both sides of each fish, then rinse them again quickly. Don't blot dry, as you want the salt to stick to the fish. Press one side of each fish onto the salt, and then the other, and place a lemongrass stalk in the cavity of each one; set aside on a tray.

If grilling, place the salted fish on the grill, cover, and cook for about 5 minutes on the first side, then turn over and grill on the second side for another

5 minutes or so; larger fish will take a little longer. A handy rule of thumb for timing is 10 minutes for every 1 inch/2.5 cm of thickness. When done, the fish will be tender and the flesh opaque; it will flake when tested with a fork. Transfer to a platter. Or, if broiling, place the salted fish on the broiling pan and broil for 8 to 10 minutes, turning the fish over after 4 or 5 minutes.

Serve the fish on a platter or on individual plates, with lime wedges alongside. Show your guests how to peel back the salted skin to expose the flesh (the skin is too salty to eat). Or, if you think your guests will hesitate to deal with a whole fish, before serving, remove the skin, lift each fillet off the bones, and arrange on the platter or plates, either as whole fillets or broken into bite-sized pieces.

If you want, put out a platter or bowl of tender leafy greens, along with sprigs of fresh coriander (cilantro) or Vietnamese coriander or Thai basil. Put out a small bowl of dipping sauce for each guest. Invite them to sprinkle the herbs over their fish and drizzle on a little sauce, then to wrap a piece of fish in a lettuce leaf to eat it, or to use a small clump of sticky rice to pick up a mouthful of it.

NOTE: *To transform the freshly grilled fish, or leftovers, into a Thai salad, mix bite-sized pieces of fish with thinly sliced shallots and chopped fresh Vietnamese coriander or finely chopped fresh mint, dress with the dipping sauce, and toss.*

Salt-dried fish for sale at the daily market in Cachoeira, in Bahia, Brazil

ACKEE AND SALTFISH

I didn't grow up with ackee and salt cod, but in my explorations of salt cod, this has become one of my favorite dishes. Ackee is the fruit of a tree that originated in Africa and now flourishes in Jamaica. In many other places, such as the US, the fruit is available only cooked and canned because the uncooked seeds are poisonous; for more detail, see the Glossary.

Ackee and saltfish is easy to prepare and completely satisfying, from the complex blend of flavors that dance together effortlessly to the soft texture of the ackee. I like it over rice, with sliced avocado on the side. The smooth lushness of the avocado drizzled with a little lime juice complements the dish perfectly.

Unlike other salt cod dishes, there's no need to soak the cod ahead of time. Instead, it is boiled hard in plenty of water for 45 minutes, and that's enough to remove the salt (it's rinsed thoroughly after cooking). Then it's added to an aromatic sofrito of sliced onion, fine-chopped garlic, bell pepper, tomato, and habanero chile, along with the ackee (ackee from a can). The dish and flavors come together in the space of 5 or 10 minutes; total prep and cooking time is just over an hour.

Serve this over plain rice with good bread or toast, or with chapatis if you wish. There will rarely be leftovers.

Serves 3 or 4

½ pound/225 grams salt cod, preferably a thick piece from the middle of the fish that is not stiff as a board

About 2 tablespoons extra-virgin olive oil or vegetable oil

3 or 4 garlic cloves, minced

1 white or yellow onion, thinly sliced

2 or 3 sprigs fresh thyme or 1 teaspoon dried thyme

1 habanero chile, seeded and minced

1 small green bell pepper, cored, seeded, inner ribs cut out, and minced

1 small red or yellow bell pepper, cored, seeded, inner ribs cut out, and minced

1 medium to large tomato, or about 5 cherry tomatoes, cored and coarsely chopped

One 19-ounce/540-gram can ackee (available at Jamaican groceries and online; see Glossary), with its liquid

Greens from 3 scallions, finely chopped

Fine sea salt and freshly ground black pepper (optional)

About 3 cups cooked white rice

OPTIONAL ACCOMPANIMENTS

Fresh bread, soft rolls, or toast

1 large or 2 small avocados, halved, pitted, peeled, and coarsely chopped, drizzled with fresh lime juice

continued

Rinse the cod under cold running water for about a minute, rubbing off the surface salt as you do so. Place it in a pot and add water to cover by about 2 inches/5 cm. Bring to a strong boil and skim off the foam. Lower the heat and cook, partially covered, at a steady low boil for about 45 minutes, until somewhat softened.

Drain the fish and transfer to a large bowl. Add cold water to the bowl to cover the fish by more than an inch, then pour it off. Repeat two more times.

Peel off and discard any skin. Use your fingers to pull the fish apart into shreds; remove and discard any bones or hard bits you come across. Set the fish aside.

Place a wide heavy pot over medium-high heat. Add the oil, and when it is hot, toss in the garlic, onion, and thyme and give them a stir. Add the habanero and bell peppers, stir, reduce the heat to medium, and cook, stirring frequently, until the peppers and onion are very soft, about 10 minutes.

Add the tomato and cook for another 5 minutes or so. (*You can prepare the dish ahead to this point and set it aside for a couple of hours, reheat before proceeding.*)

Add the reserved fish, the ackee and its liquid, and the scallion greens to the pot and stir gently to blend everything together, then simmer for 5 minutes, or until the scallions are very soft.

Taste and add a little salt and/or black pepper, if you wish. Serve hot over rice, with bread and/or chopped avocado alongside, if you wish.

BACALA MANTECATO

This Venetian specialty is like an airy fish pâté, a pleasure to spread on a little bread or toast and eat in great quantity, with perhaps a glass of a nicely acidic white wine. You can also serve it as part of a lunch or light supper, with soup and a salad.

Although it's normally made with stockfish (see Note below), the dish can also be made with bacalao; that version is so delicious that it is the one I'm including here. Traditionally, cooks would beat the cooked fish and olive oil together into a light mousse by hand; this recipe takes the easy route and calls for a food processor. Choose a thick piece of salt cod from the center of the fish; it should be white and a bit flexible rather than extremely stiff.

Makes nearly 2 cups/450 grams

¾ pound/340 grams salt cod, soaked for 48 hours in 3 or 4 changes of water, rinsed, and drained

¾ cup/180 ml milk, or as needed

¾ cup/180 ml water, or as needed

2 garlic cloves, smashed and peeled

2 bay leaves

½ cup/120 ml extra-virgin olive oil

¼ teaspoon freshly ground white pepper, or to taste

Peel the skin off the cod and discard. Chop into several pieces, place in a small pot, and add the milk, water, garlic, and bay leaves. The fish should be just covered by the liquid; add a little extra milk and water if necessary. Bring to a boil, then immediately lower the heat and cook at a low boil, partially covered, for 30 minutes, or until the fish is falling apart.

Lift the fish out of the cooking liquid and place in a bowl; set the liquid aside. Break up the fish with your fingers, discarding any tough pieces or bones. Put the fish and about 1/3 cup/80 ml of the cooking liquid in a food processor. Start the processor and slowly stream in the oil, as if you were making mayonnaise. The fish and liquid will gradually transform into a thick mousse. Add a little more of the cooking liquid as necessary (I usually need a total of about ½ cup/125 ml) to thin the mousse to a light texture.

Turn out into a bowl and stir in the white pepper. Serve at room temperature. Leftovers keep very well in the refrigerator for up to 3 days.

NOTE ON BACALA AND VENICE: *The traditional ingredient for bacala mantecato is called stoccafisso in most of Italy, but in Venetian dialect it's bacala. It comes from Norway. Unlike salt cod, stockfish is not heavily salted, but instead air-dried in the cold.*

SALT FISH AND POTATO CASSEROLE

This variant on scalloped potatoes was inspired by a recipe for salt herring and potatoes in an old book of Swedish recipes called *Smörgåsbord and Scandinavian Cookery* by Florence Brobeck and Monica B. Kjellberg, first published in 1948 (see Resources). The recipe is a reminder that rich fish goes very well with potatoes.

Once a staple in north European and North American markets and kitchens, salt herring can now be difficult to find except online. It's a mark of our modern privilege, because most herring is now flash-frozen as soon as it's caught and so no longer needs to be preserved in salt. But this dish is too delicious and interesting to be passed by. If you can't find salt herring, you can use fresh (flash-frozen and defrosted) herring or another rich fish, such as black cod or mackerel. Another option is to use well-soaked salt cod.

You can make the casserole ahead if you wish and then reheat it, covered, in a low oven. Serve with a fresh side salad, or with pickles.

Serves 4 to 6

About ½ pound/225 grams skin-on salt herring fillets, soaked for 8 hours in several changes of cold water, fresh herring fillets or other fish (see headnote), or salt cod soaked for 48 hours in 4 or 5 changes of water

2 pounds/900 grams Yukon Gold or other medium-waxy potatoes

About 4 teaspoons/24 grams fine sea salt

Butter for greasing the baking dish

1 medium-large onion, thinly sliced

3 large eggs

2 cups/480 ml whole milk

Freshly ground black or white pepper

About ¼ cup/8 grams packed finely chopped fresh flat-leaf parsley

If using salt herring or salt cod, drain, rinse, and pat dry; if using fresh herring or other fresh fish, rinse and pat dry. Cut the fish into small bite-sized pieces and set aside.

Put the potatoes in a pot, add water to just cover, and bring to a vigorous boil. Add about 1 tablespoon salt, cover, lower the heat to maintain a medium boil, and cook until the potatoes are nearly done: a fork inserted into one should find a slight resistance in the center. Remove from the heat, drain, cover, and set aside for 10 minutes, or until cool enough to handle.

Meanwhile, position a rack in the center of the oven and preheat the oven to 375°F/190°C. Butter a 2-quart/2 liter baking dish or baking pan (at least 3 inches/8 cm deep); set aside.

Slide the peels off the potatoes and cut into fairly thin (¼-inch/0.5 cm) slices. Divide into 3 nearly equal piles, with one slightly larger than the other two. Cover the bottom of the buttered dish with a layer of potato slices, using the largest pile. Scatter half the fish and then half the onion slices over the potatoes. Repeat the layers, then top with the remaining potato slices.

Whisk together the eggs and milk thoroughly in a bowl. Add the remaining 1 teaspoon salt, a generous grinding of pepper, and the parsley and stir well.

Carefully pour the egg mixture over the filled dish and place in the oven, uncovered. Bake for about 40 minutes, or until the custard is set at the edges. Remove from the oven, cover with a cotton cloth (to absorb the steam) and then a lid (to hold in the heat), and let stand for 15 to 20 minutes to firm up before serving.

Refrigerate any leftovers. They will set firmly and be delicious the next day, at room temperature or reheated.

Salt-gathering tools beside Lac Rose, with a boat beyond

LAC ROSE

At Lake Retba, better known as Lac Rose, in Senegal, the water is extremely saline, between 30 and 40 percent salt. The lake gets its pink tint from the

microscopic algae that live at the bottom of it. They're halophilic, meaning they thrive in a salt environment (the word comes from the Greek for "salt loving").

In the hot sun, the salt crystallizes on the surface of the water and then sinks to the bottom, forming a thick crust. The men who harvest it work alone, using small narrow wooden boats. They stand waist or chest deep in the water, scraping the salt on the bottom with various implements to loosen it and then scooping it up in woven baskets and dumping it into the boats. It's grueling work, in hot salty water that attacks the skin, so the men wear leggings and socks to protect their legs and coat their bare skin with shea butter.

The salt is tinted pink when it's first harvested, but after it has spent a few days in the sun drying out, the pink disappears and the salt looks white.

When I visited Lac Rose in the nineties (I was doing research for *Seductions of Rice*), there were only a couple of men gathering salt and several women working onshore. The women carried plastic basins of wet salt from the boats to the salt piles nearby, carrying the heavy loads on a padded surface on their heads. They were paid mere pennies for their work, they told me.

In rice-growing countries, children are often told never to waste a single grain of rice. After seeing the painful labor that often goes into local (as opposed to industrial) salt production, I've come to appreciate every grain, as people did when salt was in short supply or very expensive.

EGGS & POULTRY

Grilled Chicken, Southern Thai Style, with Hot-Sweet Dipping Sauce (page 280)

KIMCHI OMELET

Classic red napa kimchi, with its heat and its crunch, makes a delicious and unusual filling for an omelet. It gives it a seductive hit of heat at the end of each mouthful. I like to combine it with some chopped fresh vegetables, such as zucchini or green beans, but that is optional.

This recipe is for a 3-egg omelet, which is a nice size for one hungry person. If you increase it to 5 or 6 eggs (for 2 hungry people, say), then just increase all the other quantities slightly, and make sure your pan is large enough, at least 9 inches/22 cm in diameter. If I have fresh herbs available, I sprinkle finely chopped leaves onto the omelet just before serving.

Serves 1 or 2

3 large or extra-large eggs

½ teaspoon fine sea salt

1 tablespoon mirin

1 tablespoon water

2 tablespoons extra-virgin olive oil or sunflower oil

About ¼ cup/35 grams Classic Red Kimchi (page 78 or store-bought), sliced into thin strips

1 or 2 scallions, trimmed and minced, or 1 small shallot, minced

1 garlic clove, minced

Pinch of ground turmeric (optional)

About ¼ cup/25 grams coarsely chopped zucchini or green beans (optional)

Finely chopped fresh herbs for garnish (optional)

Green Ajika for serving (page 92; optional)

Break the eggs into a medium bowl, add the salt, and whisk well, then add the mirin and water and whisk again. Set aside.

Place a medium (8-inch/20 cm) cast-iron skillet or an omelet pan over medium-high heat. Add 1 tablespoon of the oil and swirl, then toss in the kimchi, scallions or shallot, garlic, and turmeric, if using and stir briefly, then add the zucchini or beans, if using, and cook for about 2 minutes, stirring, until the vegetables are just tender. Empty the pan into a bowl and set aside.

Rinse out the pan, wipe dry, and place over medium heat. Add the remaining 1 tablespoon oil, give the eggs a final whisk, and pour them into the pan. Tilt the pan to distribute the eggs evenly, lower the heat to medium-low, cover, and cook for about 3 minutes, then take a peek. The edges of the omelet should be coming away from the sides of the pan and it should still be wet in the center but starting to firm up. Spread the kimchi-vegetable filling over half the omelet, then fold it over. Let cook for just another minute or so, and slide onto a serving plate.

Sprinkle finely chopped fresh herbs, if using, over the omelet and serve right away, with the ajika, if you wish.

BACALAO TORTILLA

A Spanish tortilla, with its layers of potato bound with egg and cooked in olive oil, is one of those satisfying, reliable foods that the hungry traveler can turn to at any hour in almost any bar in Spain. Even better and more special than the best plain tortilla is the one that includes bacalao, which takes the concept to a whole new level. (So does the vegetarian option of red kimchi; see the Note below.)

As with most bacalao recipes, you need to plan ahead, for the salt cod must be soaked in cold water for 36 to 48 hours.

Because I am not an expert, I find flipping a large tortilla partway through cooking a fraught exercise. So this recipe has two work-arounds: the tortilla is smaller than is typical, made in an 8- or 9-inch/20 to 22 cm skillet, and it is finished under the broiler rather than being flipped over when partly cooked.

Don't be shocked by the amount of oil called for. After it is used to cook the potatoes, it is poured off, giving you a nicely flavored oil that you can set aside in a jar to use later in cooking; I use it for frying vegetables or eggs.

Serve the tortilla at room temperature, cut into wedges, as an appetizer or a main. I find it tastes even better the next day, so don't hesitate to make it ahead. Accompany with a glass of white wine and, if you wish, some chopped tomatoes or a lightly dressed chopped radicchio salad (its bitter edge is a good contrast to the slight sweetness of the eggs).

Serves 3 or 4 as a main, 6 to 8 as an appetizer

¼ pound/110 grams salt cod, soaked in 5 or 6 changes of cold water for 48 hours and drained

½ cup/120 ml milk

½ cup/120 ml water

1 pound/450 grams medium-small waxy potatoes, peeled

1 teaspoon fine sea salt

¾ cup/180 ml extra-virgin olive oil, preferably Spanish

1 medium onion (about 5 ounces/150 grams), thinly sliced

4 large or extra-large eggs

Freshly ground black pepper

Peel the skin off the fish. Tear the flesh into shreds with your fingers, or with a knife and your fingers, removing and discarding any bones you come across. Place in a small saucepan with the milk and water and bring to a boil, then lower the heat, cover, and cook at a simmer for about 10 minutes. Drain, discarding the simmering liquid, and let cool slightly.

Chop the shreds of fish into smaller lengths and pull apart any clumps into flakes. Set aside.

continued

Slice the potatoes into thin rounds, about ¼ inch/0.5 cm thick, and place in a large bowl. Sprinkle on ½ teaspoon of the salt and turn and mix to spread it around.

Heat the olive oil in an 8- or 9-inch/20 to 22 cm cast-iron or other heavy skillet over medium heat. When it is hot, add the potato slices, sliding them in carefully to avoid splashing, and then add the onion. Use your spatula to move things around gently to ensure that all surfaces are covered with oil. Reduce the heat to medium-low and cook until the potatoes are soft, 12 to 15 minutes, stirring carefully or shaking the pan to make sure they cook evenly. If the potatoes start to brown, lower the heat a little more; you want them soft and pale. When they are tender, lift them and the onions carefully out of the skillet, pausing to let excess oil drain off, and place in a large bowl. Set aside.

Pour most of the oil from the skillet into a measuring cup or a jar, leaving just a bare coating (about 1 tablespoon) in the pan, and set the pan aside briefly. Reserve the oil for another purpose.

Break the eggs into a bowl and whisk until foamy, then add the flaked salt cod, the remaining ½ teaspoon salt, and the pepper, and stir. Add the egg and cod mixture to the potatoes and onions and carefully mix them together, without breaking the slices of potato.

Position an oven rack about 6 inches/15 cm from the heating element and preheat the broiler to high.

Place the skillet back over medium heat, and as it heats up, swirl the oil or spread it with a spatula, so that it coats the pan. Gently pour in the egg-potato mixture and then shake the pan to encourage it to settle into an even layer all the way out to the edges (use a spatula to nudge it if you need to). Reduce the heat to low and cook for 10 to 12 minutes, occasionally tilting the pan to help the liquid eggs flow out to the sides of the pan, until the tortilla is starting to look firm on top.

Transfer the tortilla to the broiler and cook very briefly, 1½ to 2 minutes, just until firm. Check for doneness by sticking a fine-bladed knife into the center of the tortilla; if it comes out clean, the tortilla is ready. If not, cook for another half-minute or so.

Remove from the oven and run a knife around the edges of the tortilla to make sure it is not sticking to the sides of the skillet. Place a large plate on top of the skillet and then flip it over so that the tortilla is resting on the plate, bottom side up.

Let stand for at least half an hour to cool to room temperature and firm up before serving, cut into wedges.

KIMCHI TORTILLA

Omit the salt cod and instead add about 1 cup/150 grams finely chopped Classic Red Kimchi (page 78, or store-bought) to the whisked eggs.

CHICKEN ALOO

This home-style dish of chicken cooked with potatoes (*aloo*) from the Shan Hills of Burma/Myanmar is flavored with turmeric, cayenne, and lemongrass. The salt-preserved ingredient traditionally used here is powder made from a dried disk of salt-fermented soybeans (tua nao; see page 105), for which I substitute red miso.

The recipe calls for chicken legs or breasts, or a combination, chopped into smaller pieces. Ask your butcher to do this, or use a sharp cleaver and work on a heavy cutting board.

A Shan cook in exile in northern Thailand taught me how to make chicken aloo years ago; the recipe is adapted from *Burma*. Serve with plain jasmine rice and a simple vegetable side.

Serves 6

About 2 pounds/1 kg chicken legs and/or bone-in breasts, chopped into 1½-inch/4 cm pieces (see headnote)

2 stalks lemongrass

About ¼ pound/110 grams small Asian (red) shallots or larger shallots, cut in half or quartered, depending on size

1 medium to large plum or other fleshy tomato, cut into very thin wedges

2 teaspoons fine sea salt, or more to taste

1 teaspoon ground turmeric

½ teaspoon cayenne

¼ cup/60 ml peanut or vegetable oil

5 cups/1.25 liters water

1 tablespoon Red Miso (page 109, or store-bought), dissolved in ¼ cup/60 ml water

2 pounds/900 grams potatoes, preferably waxy, peeled and chopped into ¾-inch/2 cm cubes

½ cup/25 grams chopped fresh coriander (cilantro) leaves and fine stems

½ cup/40 grams minced scallion greens

Place the chicken in a large heavy casserole. To trim the lemongrass, cut off and discard the tough root ends and the dried upper parts of the stalks, leaving only 2 to 3 inches/5 to 8 cm of aromatic stem. Smash with the side of a cleaver or large heavy knife and add to the chicken. Add the shallots, tomato, salt, turmeric, and cayenne, drizzle on the oil, and place over medium heat. Stir to distribute the oil, then cover and cook for 2 to 3 minutes. Lift off the lid and stir and turn to expose more of the ingredients to the hot surface of the pot, then cover and cook for another few minutes.

Add the water and the dissolved miso paste, raise the heat, and bring to a boil, then lower the heat to maintain a medium boil and cook, covered, for 10 minutes.

Add the potatoes and cook, partially covered, until tender, 10 to 15 minutes. Taste and add salt if needed.

Sprinkle on the chopped coriander and scallion greens, stir, and serve.

ROAST CHICKEN
with Celeriac and Lemon-Apricot Sauce

In this take on roast chicken, the preserved lemon perfumes the bird as it cooks and then, together with chopped dried apricots, makes a delicious little sauce that complements the chicken and celery root beautifully. The only real labor is peeling the celery root (or the alternative potatoes).

If you'd like to brine the chicken, start 24 hours ahead; see the instructions on page 176. Brining will shorten the cooking time by about 25 percent.

One of the happiest results of roasting a chicken, apart from the delicious bird itself, is the carcass and other bits and pieces that remain after the feast, as well as any leftover pan juices. From that debris, you can produce the basis of at least one other meal, perhaps two, if there are leftovers from the chicken. The meat can go into a Thai-style chicken salad (see Note), and the bones, neck, and other remnants can go into a pot with water to simmer into a broth that you can use to make risotto or any number of soups (see Chicken Broth from Scratch, page 214).

Serves 4 or 5 generously

---

2 tablespoons extra-virgin olive oil

1 roasting chicken (3 to 4 pounds/1.3 to 1.8 kg), preferably organic

4 to 5 teaspoons Acadian Salted Scallions (page 46) or 1 tablespoon coarse sea salt

3 tablespoons chopped Salt-Preserved Lemons (page 63, or store-bought)

15 dried apricots, coarsely chopped

2 pounds/1 kg celery root (or substitute waxy potatoes)

Vinegar (any type) or fresh lemon juice

Position a rack in the center of the oven and preheat the oven to 425°F/215°C.

Rub 1 tablespoon of the olive oil all over the chicken. Sprinkle all over with about 1 tablespoon of the salted scallions or 2 teaspoons of the salt and rub the seasoning into the skin. Place the chicken in a lightly oiled roasting pan, breast side down.

Stuff the chicken's cavity with the chopped preserved lemon and apricots. Roast the chicken for about 20 minutes (note the time when you start roasting).

Meanwhile, to prepare the celery root, fill a large bowl with water, add about 1 tablespoon vinegar or lemon juice, and set by your work surface. Peel the celery root and then slice into approximately ¼-inch/0.5 cm slices; cut larger slices in half or quarters. As you work, place the slices in the acidulated water. (If using potatoes, peel and slice the same way, but there's no need to place them in acidulated water.)

When the chicken has cooked for about 15 minutes, place the drained celery root (or potatoes) in a bowl, add the remaining 1 tablespoon olive oil, and toss to coat. Add the remaining 1 to 2 teaspoons salted onions or 1 teaspoon salt and toss again.

Remove the roasting pan from the oven and turn the bird over so that it is breast side up. Add the celery root (or potato) slices to the pan, distributing them evenly around the bird. Lower the heat to 375°F/190°C and roast for another 1 to 1½ hours, or until the chicken is golden brown and the juices run clear. If you have an instant-read thermometer, insert it into the meatiest part of the thigh, not touching the bone; it should read 170°F/77°C.

Take the pan out of the oven and let the bird rest for 10 minutes before carving. Transfer the celery root (or potato) slices to an ovenproof bowl, cover loosely with foil, and place in a warming drawer or back into the turned-off oven, propping the oven door ajar.

Before transferring the bird to a cutting board, scoop the fruit filling out of the cavity and add to the roasting pan. Carve the chicken and arrange on a large platter. Add the celery root (or potatoes) to the platter or serve from a bowl. Stir the pan juices and fruit together in the roasting pan, scrape out of the pan, and transfer to a small bowl; serve with a spoon, so guests can drizzle this on their chicken and vegetables as they wish.

NOTE: *Leftover chicken can be brought to vivid life in a Thai-style salad. Chop or tear the chicken into bite-sized pieces. Combine it with thinly sliced shallots, fresh herbs (Vietnamese coriander, see Glossary; or mint or coriander [cilantro]), and a hot-sour-salty dressing made with fish sauce, lime juice, a minced bird chile, and perhaps a touch of garlic. Use the Vietnamese Dipping Sauce recipe (page 201) as a guide.*

FOLLOWING PAGES: *Roast Chicken, with Quick Onion-Lemon Chutney (page 200) and Mixed Greens with Preserved Lemons (page 237)*

GRILLED CHICKEN, SOUTHERN THAI STYLE

Grilled chicken is hard to beat, especially when it's southern Thai style, flavored with a black pepper–coriander root–fish sauce marinade that is lush with unsweetened coconut milk. Grill over a medium to low flame as they do it in Thailand, to make sure it cooks through without scorching. You can also broil it.

I prefer to start with bone-in legs, but you may prefer breast meat; the recipe is flexible. I like to chop the chicken into smaller pieces to ensure even cooking. You can leave the pieces larger, as they do in Thailand, but then you need to take extra care to cook them slowly.

If you want to use bone-in chicken cut into smaller pieces, ask your butcher to do this, or use a cleaver and a heavy cutting board: separate the legs into drumsticks and thighs and cut the drumsticks into 2 pieces and the thighs into 2 or 3; chop whole breasts in half and then cut each half into 4 pieces. You want lots of surface area for the marinade to coat.

Serve with a dipping sauce (below) or other condiment, and plenty of sticky rice. This is a meal to eat with your hands.

Serves 4 or 5

---

3 pounds/1.3 kg bone-in chicken legs or breasts, or a combination, chopped into 2-inch/5 cm pieces (see headnote)

MARINADE

2 teaspoons black peppercorns or 1½ teaspoons freshly ground black pepper

5 medium garlic cloves, minced

Pinch of coarse or fine sea salt

¼ cup/15 grams coarsely chopped fresh coriander (cilantro) roots and stems (see Note)

3 tablespoons Thai fish sauce

1 cup/240 ml canned coconut milk

Hot-Sweet Dipping Sauce (recipe follows)

Sticky rice for serving

Check the cut surfaces of the chicken and remove any fragments of bone. Put the chicken in a large bowl.

To make the marinade, grind the whole peppercorns, if using, in a spice grinder or mortar. Combine the garlic, salt, pepper, and coriander in a mortar or small food processor and pound or process to a coarse paste. Add the fish sauce and coconut milk and stir or pulse to blend.

Pour the marinade over the chicken pieces and toss to make sure they are all coated. Set aside at room temperature, loosely covered, for about an hour.

Meanwhile, prepare a medium to medium-low fire in a charcoal or gas grill.

Place the chicken pieces on the grill grate, 5 or 6 inches/12 to 15 cm from the flame; reserve the marinade that remains in the bottom of the bowl. Once the bottom of the chicken pieces is starting to brown, 12 to 15 minutes, brush the tops with the marinade and turn them over. Cook on the second side for 10 to 12 minutes, until nicely browned. Insert a knife into a thick piece of meat; the juices should run clear. If the juices are still pink, continue cooking a few more minutes.

Transfer the chicken to a serving plate and serve hot or warm, with the dipping sauce and sticky rice.

NOTE: *Whenever you buy a bunch of fresh coriander (cilantro), be sure to chop off the roots with the lower parts of the stems and store them in a plastic bag in the freezer. Soon you'll accumulate a good stash that you can use in marinades or for making your own curry paste. Rinse them thoroughly before using them.*

HOT-SWEET DIPPING SAUCE

You can't have grilled chicken in Thailand without this lively sauce, called *nam jeem*. It's hot, sour, sweet, and garlicky. It is also good with grilled fish or pork or lamb and with sticky rice. Serve in individual small bowls so each person can dip freely.

Makes 1 cup/240 ml

½ cup/120 ml unseasoned rice vinegar or cider vinegar

½ cup/100 grams sugar

2 garlic cloves, minced

¼ teaspoon fine sea salt

2 teaspoons chile pepper flakes

Bring the vinegar to a boil in a small saucepan over medium-high heat. Add the sugar and stir to dissolve it completely. Reduce the heat to medium-low and simmer for about 5 minutes.

Meanwhile, use a mortar and pestle, or a bowl and the back of a metal spoon, to mash the garlic and salt together into a smooth paste. Add the chile flakes and blend them in.

Remove the vinegar from the heat and stir in the paste. Set aside to cool to room temperature. Serve immediately, or store in a sealed glass jar in the refrigerator for no longer than 2 days.

DUCK BREAST AND BITTER GREENS
with Black Bean Sauce

My testing notes for this recipe say "fabulous." It makes a very special main course yet is easy to prepare for a weeknight dinner. Duck breast needs to be cooked with care, for overcooking makes it tough. I first pan sear the breast briefly in a heavy skillet, to partially cook it and to render some of the fat. Then I slice it and stir-fry it briefly in the rendered fat, along with greens and the black bean sauce.

Serves 3

1 large or 2 small duck breasts (1 pound/450 grams total)

1¼ teaspoons fine sea salt, or to taste

1 tablespoon duck fat, peanut oil, or sunflower oil

About 1 pound/450 grams mizuna greens, dandelion greens, or radicchio, or a mixture

3½ to 4 tablespoons Black Bean Sauce (page 189, or store-bought)

¼ cup/60 ml hot water, or as needed

ACCOMPANIMENTS

Cooked rice

Quick Cucumber Pickles (page 57) or a green salad

Lay the duck breast(s) skin side up on a plate or cutting board and, with a sharp knife held at an angle, cut 3 or 4 parallel diagonal slashes through the skin and fat. Then repeat on the opposite diagonal, to make a crisscross pattern. Rub about 1 teaspoon of the salt into both sides of the breast(s) and set aside on a plate for half an hour.

Heat a cast-iron or other heavy skillet over medium-high heat. When it is hot, add the fat or oil, lower the heat to medium, and use a spatula to spread the oil over the surface of the pan. Place the duck skin side down in the hot pan. Cook for about 3 minutes, then turn over and cook for about 1 minute. Raise the heat to high, turn the duck over onto the skin side again, and cook for another minute or two, until the skin is browned and crisping. Remove the duck from the pan and set aside on a plate or a rimmed cutting board, skin side up, to rest for 10 minutes.

Transfer 3 tablespoons of the rendered fat to a bowl or measuring cup and set by your stovetop; store the rest in the refrigerator to use in later cooking.

While the duck rests, trim any tough ends off the greens, or separate the radicchio leaves, and wash well. Chop into approximately 1-inch/2.5 cm lengths and set aside.

Thinly slice the duck breast crosswise and then cut the slices into large bite-sized pieces. Heat a wok or large heavy skillet over medium-high heat. Add the reserved duck fat and then the bean sauce and stir to break the sauce up as it

cooks in the hot fat for about 1 minute. Raise the heat, toss in the pieces of duck, and stir-fry, pressing the meat against the bottom and sides of the hot pan, for about 3 minutes, or until all the duck slices are touched with color. Transfer the duck to a bowl, leaving most of the sauce and liquid in the pan.

Place the pan back over high heat, add the chopped greens, and stir-fry briefly to coat them with the sauce and fat. Add the hot water and about ¼ teaspoon of the remaining salt and stir-fry for another minute, or until the greens are wilting. Taste and add a little more salt, if you wish. Return the duck to the pan and stir-fry with the greens briefly, for a minute or so.

Turn out into a serving bowl or onto a platter. Serve hot.

SALINAS DE AÑANA

The springs at the Salinas de Añana in Basque
Country, far inland from Spain's Atlantic coast, flow
with saltwater. Until about two thousand years ago,

the original inhabitants of the area
had been boiling that brine over wood
fires to get salt. But using those fires
to evaporate the water meant that
there was ash everywhere and the
hillsides were denuded of trees. After
the arrival of the Romans (around the
time of Julius Caesar), the salt-making
technique shifted to solar evaporation.
Evaporation ponds were built on
terraces down the hillside. The brine
flowed in controlled channels from
the springs, through the evaporating
pools to the lower levels, gradually
concentrating in salinity. Salt making
still goes on that way in Añana.

When I visited the saltworks a
few years ago, the guide there had
already been booked to give a tour
to a Basque-speaking family. Visitors
can't walk around the terraces
unaccompanied, and he told me I'd
need to wait a few hours for an English-
language tour. But I was happy to listen
to Basque. As I walked with them up
and through the terraced works, it was
wonderful to hear the language flow
around me. It felt dreamy somehow.
And by the end of the tour, I'd learned
to recognize a few words in Basque,
including the word for salt: it's *gatza*.

The small town of Añana is right next to the lower levels of the salt-evaporating terraces. The salty spring water flows down through the terraces from its source much higher up the hill.

LAMB, BEEF & PORK

Slow-Cooked Roast Pork Belly with Crisped Fat and Hot-Sweet Sauce (page 302)

SLOW-COOKED LAMB SHOULDER
with Anchovies and Rosemary

I love lamb shoulder this way, slow-cooked to tenderness with layers of Mediterranean flavors: rosemary, garlic, salt-preserved lemon, and chopped anchovies. The anchovies melt into the pan juices.

I like to add chopped vegetables partway through the cooking, as set out below. Serve this with boiled new potatoes or mashed potatoes to help soak up the delicious juices.

Serves 6

A 2½-pound/1.2 kg boneless lamb shoulder roast

1 pound/450 grams red onions, thickly sliced

6 or 7 anchovy fillets, rinsed and minced

1 tablespoon minced fresh rosemary

6 to 8 garlic cloves, minced

3 slices Salt-Preserved Lemons (page 63, or store-bought), or 1 lemon, preferably organic

About 1 tablespoon extra-virgin olive oil

1½ cups/350 ml white wine

1 pound/450 grams small white turnips or carrots, peeled and chopped into 1-inch/3 cm chunks

Preheat the oven to 350°F/175°C.

With the tip of a sharp knife, make shallow cuts all over the fat side of the roast.

Line the bottom of a Dutch oven or other wide heavy ovenproof pot with the onion slices. Place the roast on the onion slices and set aside.

Put the anchovies, rosemary, garlic, and 1 slice of the preserved lemon, if using, in a food processor or mortar and process or pound to a paste. Stir in enough olive oil to make a spreadable paste. If using a regular lemon, zest half the lemon and stir the zest into the paste; cut the lemon in half and set aside.

Rub the paste all over the roast, then turn it fat side up on top of the onion slices. Add the remaining preserved lemon, or the lemon halves, to the pot.

Place the pot in the center of the oven and cook, uncovered, for 15 minutes, then cover and bake for 45 minutes longer.

Take the lamb out of the oven and pour the wine into the pot, then scatter the turnips or carrots around the roast. Cover again, lower the oven temperature to 300°F/150°C, and bake until the lamb is falling-apart tender, another 2 to 2½ hours.

Cut up the lamb and serve hot or warm, with the turnips or carrots, and the pan juices drizzled over.

THAI-STYLE GRILLED BEEF

This is the surest, happiest way I know to grill beef. It's always a success, and the meat can be sliced and served as is, or dressed and transformed into Thai grilled beef salad (see next page; pictured opposite).

Look for grass-fed beef, and if it's local, that's a bonus. I love the flavor of flank, bavette, or flat-iron. The meat is served sliced across the grain, so it is tender.

Marinate the meat for 30 minutes to an hour before you cook it. Serve with plain rice, a simple risotto, or potatoes. Cooked greens and a crisp salad are fine accompaniments too.

Serves 4 or 5

1½ pounds/650 grams boneless beef steak, preferably bavette, flank, or flat-iron

About 3 tablespoons Thai fish sauce

About 2 teaspoons freshly ground black pepper

Lime wedges for serving (optional)

Place the meat on a rimmed plate or in a wide shallow bowl. Pour over the fish sauce and turn the pieces of meat over so both sides are exposed to the liquid. Rub the pepper all over the meat, then set aside loosely covered to marinate for 30 minutes to an hour.

Meanwhile, prepare a medium-hot fire in a charcoal or gas grill.

Grill the meat about 5 or 6 inches from the flame. Timing will depend on the thickness of the steak(s) and on the degree of doneness you prefer. Turn the meat over after the first 3 or 4 minutes. Once you have exposed both sides to the heat, you can test for doneness using your fingertip: If the meat is very soft when you press on the top, it is still very rare. If it is a little firm but still yields easily to your finger, it is medium-rare. If it is firm, it is well-done. Or cut a small slit into the meat to have a look at the color. The meat will continue cooking as it rests after grilling, so err on the side of less cooked when deciding when to take it off the grill.

Once the meat is done as you like it, transfer it to a rimmed cutting board (to catch the juices) or platter and let rest for 10 minutes.

continued

Thinly slice the meat across the grain. Cut the slices crosswise into large bite-sized pieces, if you wish. Put out on a platter and drizzle the meat juices over the slices. Serve with lime wedges, if you like.

NOTE: *If you don't have access to a grill, you can use the broiler. Preheat the broiler, place the meat on the lightly oiled broiler pan, and set it about 5 inches/12 cm below the heating element. Turn the meat over after 3 or 4 minutes. Check for doneness after another 3 minutes.*

THAI GRILLED BEEF SALAD

To use freshly grilled beef—or leftover sliced grilled beef—to make a Thai salad, thinly slice several shallots and place in a small bowl. Add equal quantities of fish sauce and lime juice, then mince 1 or 2 bird chiles and add, seeds and all. Stir and let the shallots absorb the flavors for about 10 minutes.

Put the beef in a bowl, pour the dressing over, and toss well. Add chopped fresh coriander (cilantro), mint, and/or basil and toss again. Taste and adjust the balance of salt and tart flavors if you wish. Serve at room temperature.

KEBABS MARINATED
with Fish Sauce and Pomegranate Molasses

One evening some years ago, when I'd planned to make lamb kebabs marinated Persian style in a mix of pomegranate molasses and ground walnuts, I realized I was out of walnuts. So instead I stirred together a mixture of pomegranate molasses and fish sauce and used that on the cubes of meat before grilling them on skewers over a charcoal flame. They were spectacular.

The marinade works beautifully for both lamb and pork. The tart-sweet of the pomegranate molasses is balanced by the umami saltiness of the fish sauce, and together they bring out the flavor of the meat. Metal skewers help the meat cook evenly.

Serves 6 to 8

¼ cup/60 ml pomegranate molasses

3 tablespoons Thai or Vietnamese fish sauce

3 pounds/1.4 kg boneless pork or lamb shoulder, cut into ¾-inch/2 cm cubes

SUGGESTED ACCOMPANIMENTS

Cooked rice

Flatbreads

Salted Onion Salad (page 230) or chopped salad or Green Olives in Walnut-Pomegranate Sauce (page 231)

Green Ajika (page 92) or White Radish Kimchi (page 74)

Stir together the pomegranate molasses and fish sauce in a large nonreactive bowl. Add the meat and turn and stir it with your hands or a large spoon to coat all sides with the marinade. Cover and let stand at room temperature for an hour, turning several times.

Prepare a medium-hot fire in a gas or charcoal grill.

Wipe off the excess marinade from the meat (this is important, because otherwise the sugars in the pomegranate molasses will scorch in the heat). Thread the cubes onto metal skewers, making sure that they are not jammed together tightly, which would hinder even cooking. Place the skewers on the grill and cook, turning occasionally, until done to your taste.

To serve, slide the meat off the skewers and onto a serving dish. Serve warm or at room temperature, with your choice of accompaniments.

CORNED BEEF ROAST

Many recipes suggest boiling corned beef, but you can also roast it, after a quick initial boil to remove excess saltiness. Here the meat is seasoned with a flavor paste of warming spices and garlic. Start to prepare the roast 6 hours before you wish to serve it; most of that will be unattended time. Serve roasted corn beef with a side of carrot sambal (see page 241; pictured opposite, bottom right).

Serves 8, with ample leftovers

One 5-pound/2.25 kg
 Corned Beef (page 179, or
 store-bought)

FLAVOR PASTE

1 teaspoon coarsely ground
  black pepper

1 teaspoon ground coriander

½ teaspoon ground cloves

½ teaspoon ground allspice

1 tablespoon Dijon mustard

5 garlic cloves, minced

Water as needed

Place the corned beef in a pot of cold water to cover, bring to a boil, and cook for 5 minutes, then drain; this will remove excess saltiness. Place the meat fat side up on a rack set in a roasting pan.

Preheat the oven to 300°F/150°C.

To make the flavor paste, combine the pepper, coriander, cloves, allspice, mustard, and garlic in a mortar or small bowl and pound or mash, adding a little water to make a spreadable paste. Rub onto the fat side of the meat.

Add about 1 cup/240 ml hot water to the roasting pan, then cover the meat and pan tightly with aluminum foil to seal in the steam. Bake for 5 hours, or until very tender. (If you are tempted to check it partway through, you will release steam/moisture, so you'll need to add another ½ cup/120 ml or so of hot water to the pan before covering it tightly again and continuing to cook.)

Remove the foil and roast for another 30 minutes to give the top of the roast some color. Let rest for 20 minutes or more before slicing across the grain.

QUICK CORNED BEEF HASH for Two

I first tasted this classic dish in rural western Pennsylvania while on a road trip from Toronto to West Virginia when my kids were young. We ate it for breakfast, but it can be comfort food for any time of day. The name comes from the French *hâcher*, meaning to chop, because the beef and all the other ingredients are chopped small.

The basics are small cubes of leftover corned beef and chopped waxy potatoes (either freshly cooked or leftover boiled potatoes) cooked with onion in a heavy skillet. If I'm making corned beef hash for a quick supper, I like to include small cubes of carrot and some cabbage, for color and texture. For breakfast, most people will prefer it without the extra vegetables, instead served with fried eggs and maybe fried tomato wedges.

Serves 2

About 2 tablespoons butter or extra-virgin olive oil

1 small onion, chopped

1 garlic clove, chopped

About ½ pound/225 grams leftover cooked Corned Beef (page 179, or store-bought), cut into small bite-sized cubes

3 or 4 medium waxy potatoes, boiled in salted water until barely cooked, drained, peeled, and cut into bite-sized cubes (or use leftover boiled potatoes)

3 or 4 medium carrots, cooked with the potatoes until just tender and cut into bite-sized chunks (optional)

1 or 2 small wedges of red or green cabbage, shredded (optional)

Generous pinch of cayenne or paprika (optional)

OPTIONAL ACCOMPANIMENTS

2 to 4 fried eggs

Fried tomato wedges (from 1 medium tomato)

Heat the butter or oil in a large skillet over medium heat. Toss in the onion and garlic and cook until beginning to soften, 2 to 3 minutes. Add the meat, potatoes, and carrots and/or cabbage and cayenne, if using. Stir to mix well, then press down with a spatula to pack down the ingredients and press them against the hot surface. Reduce the heat slightly and cook for 5 minutes. Add about ¼ cup/60 ml water to the pan, and when it sizzles, cover and cook for a few minutes; the steam will help unite the ingredients.

Remove the lid from the pan and check for color on the bottom of the hash. If it's not browned as much as you want, raise the heat and cook for another minute or two.

Transfer the hash to a small platter, or divide in half and transfer to two heated plates. If you are serving the fried eggs, place them on top of the hash, and serve fried tomatoes on the side, if you like.

BRINED PORK ROAST

In households that kept a brine crock going all winter, some pieces of meat were brined for a long time, while others were cooked after only a week of brining.

This brined roast is a descendant of the brine-crock tradition: the pork is immersed in a flavored brine for 5 days to a week before being cooked in boiling water with a bouquet garni and then finished in the oven. The recipe is adapted from instructions in Jane Grigson's *Charcuterie* for a roast known as *saumure anglaise* in France.

The amount of salt and sugar you'll need for the brine depends on how much water you need, which in turn depends on the size of your roast and the volume of your brining container. It may sound complicated, but it's actually simple; see the method. The basic ratio is 8 percent of the water by volume for both the salt and the sugar; you will need a scale to measure them.

Before making the brine, figure out what bowl or crock you will be using to brine the roast. It needs to be deep enough to hold the meat with at least an inch of liquid on top. And you need a cool place to put it for some days, less than 50°F/10°C. I take out one of the crisper drawers in my refrigerator and put it there.

Serve the pork with roast potatoes and root vegetables, or, for a lighter option, serve it with rice and stir-fried broccoli rabe or another green vegetable.

Serves 6 to 8

One 3- to 4-pound/1.4 to 1.8 kg boneless pork shoulder roast

Fine sea salt or fine pickling salt

Turbinado sugar (such as Sugar in the Raw)

BRINE FLAVORINGS

20 juniper berries

2 bay leaves

1 teaspoon black peppercorns

About ¼ of a whole nutmeg (chipped off or grated)

3 or 4 sprigs thyme

2 or 3 carrots

1 or 2 medium onions

3 whole cloves

A bouquet garni, or about 12 black peppercorns, 1 bay leaf, and several sprigs thyme and/ or rosemary

FLAVOR PASTE

1 tablespoon Dijon mustard

1 tablespoon white or red wine vinegar, apple cider, or cider vinegar

1 tablespoon turbinado sugar (such as Sugar in the Raw)

2 teaspoons ground ginger

Red wine for deglazing the pan

Place the meat in the bowl or crock you have chosen (see headnote). Use a large measuring cup to add enough water to cover the meat by 1 inch/2.5 cm and make a note of the amount, then drain off the water.

It's easiest to use metric measures to calculate the amount of salt and sugar you need for the brine: For example, if you are starting with 2 quarts/2 liters of water (which weighs 2 kg), you will need 8 percent of 2000 grams, which is 160 grams each salt and sugar. With 3 quarts/3 liters, you would need 240 grams each salt and sugar.

Pour the measured amount of water into a pot set over high heat, add the measured amounts of salt and sugar, and stir to dissolve them as you bring the water to a vigorous boil. Boil hard for 2 to 3 minutes, then skim off any foam and remove from the heat.

Add the flavorings—juniper berries, bay leaves, peppercorns, nutmeg, and thyme—to the brine and cover loosely while it cools to room temperature. This will take several hours at least.

Pour the cooled brine through a fine sieve or colander lined with cheesecloth into your bowl or crock; discard the flavorings. Lower the meat into the brine. Put a very clean heavy flat lid on top to keep the meat submerged. Cover loosely with plastic wrap and transfer to the refrigerator or another cool place (less than 50°F/10°C). Let the meat brine for 5 days to a week, turning it every 2 days.

To cook the meat: Drain it (discard the brine), rinse it under cold water, and place it in a deep pot. Add water to cover and bring to a boil, then drain.

Add fresh cold water to cover the meat and bring to a boil. Add the carrots, onions, cloves, and bouquet garni (or alternate seasonings), reduce the heat, and cook at a steady gentle boil, partially covered, for 30 minutes per pound/450 grams (e.g., a 3-pound/1.4 kg roast should cook for 1½ hours, a 4-pound/1.8 kg roast for 2 hours).

In the meantime, put a rack in the upper third of the oven and preheat the oven to 350°F/175°C.

Drain the meat, reserving the cooking liquid; discard the carrot and onion (or eat them as a cook's perk if you like). Place the meat fat side up in a roasting pan and pat dry.

To make the flavor paste, mix the mustard, vinegar, sugar, and ginger together in a small bowl, then spread over the top and sides of the roast. Cook in the upper third of the oven for 25 to 30 minutes until the temperature at the center is at 145°F/63°C. Transfer the meat to a platter or cutting board and let rest for 10 to 20 minutes.

Meanwhile, deglaze the pan by adding some of the reserved cooking liquid and a splash of red wine to make a little sauce.

Slice the meat and serve with the sauce.

SLOW-COOKED ROAST PORK BELLY
with Crisped Fat and Hot-Sweet Sauce

This succulent version of roast pork takes a little advance planning (you need to start 36 hours ahead) but very little work. It depends on a salting technique that I learned from a generous-minded Canadian chef and culinary professor named Michael Olson.

The layer of fat on the meat is rubbed with what Michael calls "skin salt," a mixture of salt and baking powder (in a proportion of 3 parts salt to 1 part baking powder) and then left to sit uncovered in the fridge for about 24 hours to air-dry before being slowly roasted. Accompany it with simple cooked greens.

I follow Michael's recommendation and make a hot-sweet sauce to serve with this; see below.

Serves 4 or 5

1½ pounds/675 grams skinless fresh pork belly, as meaty as possible

1½ teaspoons fine sea salt

½ teaspoon baking powder

1 large onion

HOT-SWEET SAUCE

About ⅓ cup/60 grams minced Hunan-Style Salted Red Chiles (page 52) or Sriracha or other medium-hot chile sauce

About ⅔ cup/200 grams fruit jam or preserve

Place the meat fat side up on a plate. Using a sharp knife, score the fat deeply, but don't cut into the meat. You want a cross-hatching of cuts: Make parallel lines of cuts about ¾ inch/2 cm apart first in one direction and then in the other.

Mix the salt and baking powder in a small bowl and rub it generously all over the fat. Place the meat, uncovered, in the fridge for 24 hours to dry.

About 4 hours before you want to serve the roast, preheat the oven to 300°F/150°C.

Thickly slice the onion crosswise and place the slices in a cast-iron skillet or a roasting pan to make a bed for the meat. Rinse the meat quickly under cold water and pat dry. Place the meat fat side up on the onion slices.

Put the pan in the center of the oven and bake for about 30 minutes. Raise the temperature to 325°F/165°C and continue to bake for another 2 hours, or until the internal temperature of the roast has reached 185°F/85°C.

While the meat is cooking, make the sauce: Combine the chiles or hot sauce and jam or preserve in a food processor or large mortar and process or pound to a paste. Taste and adjust the balance of hot and sweet to your liking. Set aside.

Remove the roast from the oven, pour off the rendered fat into a heatproof container, and set the roast aside to rest, uncovered, for 2 hours.

After the roast has rested for 90 minutes or so, put a rack in the upper third of the oven and preheat the oven to 500°F/260°C.

Place the roast back in the oven and roast until the crust bubbles into crisp crackling, about 10 minutes. Remove from the oven and let stand for 5 minutes.

Slice the meat, arrange on a platter, and drizzle with some of the sauce. Pass the extra sauce at the table.

NOTE ON LEFTOVERS: *Leftover roast pork belly makes spectacular sandwiches. Use a whole-grain bread that can handle the hearty flavors of the meat. Smear some Kimchi Aioli (page 203) or Dijon or hot mustard on the bread, drizzle a little hot-sweet dressing onto the pork slices, and include chopped arugula or other salad greens in the sandwich too. (See photo pages 204–205.)*

SAUERKRAUT with Meat and Potatoes

In France, this dish is called *choucroute garnie* (meaning, literally, adorned sauerkraut), and it is a dream dish for lovers of cabbage and pork. Sauerkraut is not a side here; it's an essential element, along with assorted meats and simple boiled potatoes. Start cooking about 3 hours before you want to serve it.

The recipe calls for a generous proportion of sauerkraut, about ½ pound/225 grams per serving, and an assortment of delicious kinds of pork, including several types of sausages, ribs, and a smoked pork chop. Other versions might include a meaty ham hock, for example, rather than the smoked chop. You want some smoky meat, some pork with fat for flavor, and some sausages that have good bite and firm texture; use whatever sausages you have available. You can include a little salt pork or pancetta too, if you wish.

Most recipes include caraway, but I don't love it, so I use fennel seeds instead. The only other flavorings are juniper berries and some black peppercorns.

Leftover choucroute (reheated with a little more goose or pork fat and a little water) is very satisfying. That's one of the reasons why it's a good idea to make a large quantity. Riesling or another dry white wine is the natural accompaniment to choucroute garnie, or you might try a German or Alsatian beer.

Serves 6

About 9 cups/1.5 kg drained Small-Batch Sauerkraut (page 84, or store-bought)

¼ cup/50 grams goose fat or duck fat or 2 tablespoons each extra-virgin olive oil and butter

1 teaspoon black peppercorns

1 teaspoon fennel seeds

1½ pounds/675 grams pork ribs, in 2 pieces

1 medium onion, coarsely chopped

About 15 juniper berries

¼ pound/110 grams Salt Pork or Pancetta (page 166, or store-bought), trimmed of skin and sliced into thin bite-sized slices (optional)

½ to ¾ pound/225 to 340 grams (1 large or 2 small) smoked pork chops

2 cups/480 ml Riesling, Pinot Gris, or dry hard cider

About 3 pounds/1.3 kg small potatoes

1 tablespoon fine sea salt

About ¾ pound/340 grams bratwurst or knackwurst (3 or 4 sausages)

¾ pound/340 grams kielbasa or Montbeliard or similar sausages, casings removed

¾ to 1 pound/340 to 450 grams frankfurters (3 or 4)

Dijon mustard or other mustard(s) for serving

Place the sauerkraut in a large colander and rinse it thoroughly with cold water. Taste it. I like a little acidity, so one rinse is all I usually do, but you may want to rinse it again. Squeeze out the excess water and set aside.

Preheat the oven to 300°F/150°C.

Place a Dutch oven or other large heavy casserole over medium heat, add the fat, and scatter on the peppercorns and fennel. Add the ribs and brown them on both sides, about 10 minutes. Remove from the pot and slice the ribs apart.

Scatter the chopped onions over the bottom of the pot. Add half the sauerkraut, scatter on the juniper berries, then add the browned ribs, the salt pork or pancetta slices, if using, and the pork chop(s) and top with the rest of the sauerkraut. Add enough wine or cider to just reach the top of the sauerkraut and cook over medium heat just until it comes to a boil, about 10 minutes. Cover the pot tightly with a lid or with foil and place in the oven for 2 hours.

Alternatively, you can finish the dish on the stovetop. Once the liquid in the pot comes to a boil, cover tightly as above, lower the heat to a simmer, and cook for 2 hours.

Shortly before the 2 hours are up, place the potatoes in a pot, add water to just cover, and bring to a boil. Add the salt, cover, reduce the heat to medium-low, and cook until a fork poked into the largest potato goes in with just a little resistance, 15 to 20 minutes. Drain off the water and leave the potatoes in the pot, covered, to cool and firm up.

When the potatoes are cool enough to handle, slide off the peels and, depending on the size of your potatoes, cut them into large chunks, if you'd like. (If you cooked them very early and want to reheat them, melt a little duck or goose fat or lard in a pan, add the potatoes, and fry the potato chunks lightly until warmed through.)

Remove the pot from the oven or stovetop heat, push aside the top layer of sauerkraut, and add all the sausages and frankfurters. Arrange the sauerkraut over them as well as you can, cover the pot tightly again and put back in the oven for another 30 minutes, or until the sausages are heated through. Or cook, covered, over low heat on the stovetop for another 30 minutes or so. Remove from the oven or stovetop heat.

To serve, pull out the smoked pork chop(s) and cut into pieces so there's a taste for everyone. Slice the kielbasa or sausages. Cut the frankfurters and bratwurst in half. If serving on individual plates, mound some sauerkraut on each one and include at least one piece of every type of meat, including the ribs, as well as a generous serving of potatoes. Alternatively, mound the sauerkraut on a platter and arrange the sliced meat and sausages around it and on top. Serve the potatoes in a separate bowl.

Put out Dijon or another favorite mustard and invite guests to help themselves.

OKINAWAN STIR-FRY
with Spam and Bitter Melon

This classic Okinawan stir-fry, called *champuru*, is a delicious and satisfying combination in all its unexpectedness. It may be surprising to think of bitter melon (which we are more likely to associate with India or perhaps southern China) in Japan. I don't know why or how it became such a common vegetable in Okinawa, where it's called *goya* or *karavella*.

At the end of World War II, when the island was occupied by the US army, as in the rest of Japan, there was a real shortage of food. Spam, preserved in salt and shipped in tins, was a valued ingredient after the war, as it was for people in Korea, Samoa, and parts of the Philippines. It was a safe and affordable source of meaty flavor, just as bully beef was for people in postwar England. Canned meats may have started as army rations, but local populations came to depend on them in the postwar period.

I first had this stir-fry at a tiny neighborhood restaurant in Tokyo. The chef-owner was from Okinawa, so I had asked him to make some dishes from there. And, as happens in many small restaurants in Japan, I had the pleasure of watching him make this right in front of me.

It is an ideal dish for one or two people for a quick lunch or easy supper. If you want to make a larger quantity, make it in several batches. You want the wok's heat to cook things quickly, so your wok shouldn't be overfilled.

Serves 1 generously as a complete meal, 2 with rice, 4 as one of many dishes

About 7 ounces/200 grams (2 small blocks) firm tofu

About ⅓ pound/150 grams bitter melon

1¼ teaspoons fine sea salt

2 large eggs

⅛ teaspoon sansho powder (optional; see Glossary)

1 tablespoon toasted sesame oil

¼ pound/110 grams Spam (or substitute ¼ pound/110 grams skinless pork belly or bacon), cut into thin batons about 1 inch/2.5 cm long

1 to 2 teaspoons soy sauce

2 tablespoons sake or white wine

About ⅓ cup/35 grams mung bean sprouts, washed and drained

About 1 tablespoon toasted sesame seeds

Pinch of bonito flakes (optional)

Wrap the tofu in cheesecloth or a cotton cloth and place in a shallow bowl. Put a small plate on top and then a weight, such as large can of tomatoes. Set aside to compress for 30 minutes.

Drain off the water, unwrap the tofu, and use your fingers to break it up into bite-sized pieces. Set aside.

Slice the bitter melon(s) lengthwise in half. Use a spoon to scrape out the seeds and all the spongy soft pulp; discard them. Slice the melon crosswise into very thin half-moons. Place in a bowl, sprinkle on 1 teaspoon of the salt, and toss. Let stand for about 10 minutes, then rinse off the slices and set aside.

Break the eggs into a bowl, sprinkle in the remaining ¼ teaspoon salt and the sansho powder, if using, and whisk briefly.

Place a large wok or large heavy skillet over high heat. Add the sesame oil and swirl to coat. Add the Spam and bitter melon and cook for about 5 minutes, turning and stirring and pressing the meat against the hot surface, until it has changed color and the melon has softened. Add the tofu, soy sauce, and sake or wine and cook, stirring a little to expose the tofu to the heat, for 1 to 2 minutes. Toss in the bean sprouts and stir.

Move the mixture to one side of the wok or pan and lower the heat a little. Briefly whisk the eggs again and pour them onto the cleared space. Stir them a little as they cook, as if you were making creamy scrambled eggs, and then, as they start firming up, fold them into the Spam mixture.

Turn out onto a serving plate and sprinkle on the sesame seeds. Top with bonito flakes, if you wish. Serve hot.

BRUSSELS SPROUTS AND POTATOES
with Salt Pork

This satisfying weeknight supper main is a style of dish that dates back to a more frugal time in Europe, when a small amount of meat was used to give depth of flavor and succulence to whatever vegetables were on hand. You could substitute wedges of cabbage or coarsely chopped bok choy for the Brussels sprouts.

Serves 2 or 3

About 1½ pounds/675 grams waxy potatoes, scrubbed

2 teaspoons fine sea salt

About 6 ounces/175 grams Salt Pork or Pancetta (page 166, or store-bought)

1 tablespoon lard or butter

1 medium shallot, minced

¼ teaspoon fennel seeds

⅛ teaspoon ground cloves

About 15 medium to large Brussels sprouts, trimmed and thinly sliced lengthwise

About ¼ cup/60 ml white wine

Finishing salt of your choice

Freshly ground black pepper

Put the potatoes in a medium pot and add water to just cover. Bring to a boil, add the salt, and cook until just tender, about 20 minutes. Drain and set aside in the pot, covered, to firm up.

Trim the skin off the salt pork or pancetta and cut the meat into small dice. Place a cast-iron or other heavy skillet over medium-low heat, add 4 or 5 of the fattier pieces of meat and cook briefly until the fat has rendered out. Add the remaining meat, raise the heat to medium, and cook until crispy and lightly browned. Remove the pork from the pan and set aside, leaving the fat in the pan.

Place the pan back over medium heat, add the lard or butter, and toss in the shallot, fennel seeds, and cloves. Cook, stirring, for several minutes, until the shallot is translucent, then toss in the sliced Brussels sprouts. Sauté for about 5 minutes, turning them frequently, until starting to soften.

Meanwhile, strip the skin from the potatoes and cut them into bite-sized cubes. Set aside in a wide shallow serving bowl.

Raise the heat under the skillet to medium-high, add about ¼ cup/60 ml water, cover, and cook for 4 to 5 minutes, until the sprouts are barely tender. Add the wine, raise the heat, and boil hard for about a minute, uncovered. Toss in the reserved pork, lower the heat to medium, and cook for a minute or two to allow the flavors to blend. Taste and add salt and/or black pepper if you wish.

Transfer the contents of the pan to the serving bowl and toss to coat the potatoes with the flavored oil. Serve hot.

Men raking and smoothing the salt in their individual plots, part of the Maras salt terraces

MARAS, PERU

The saltworks of Maras, a huge patchwork of shallow evaporation ponds on terraces carved out of steep ocher hillsides, date back to the time of the Incas, or

perhaps even before. The locals have worked them for centuries, laboring for the Incas, and then for the Spanish conquerors, and, after independence in 1821, for big landowners. It was only a few decades ago that the residents of the village of Maras gained control of the saltworks. They work in a communal system to maintain the terraces and to manage the flow of saltwater from the springs at the top of the hill. All local residents are entitled to a pond from which to harvest salt. Some of their salt is sold by the saltworks corporation, which also makes money from entry fees charged to visitors. The rest of the salt is sold at markets in the area.

I spent an exhilarating and scary time exploring the salt terraces one fine September morning. I somehow failed to see the sign by the entrance that said visitors were to stay on the wide track at the top, so I walked down into the steep terraced landscape. There were enticing photo possibilities in every direction. I walked along the narrow clay borders of the ponds, trying to ignore my extreme fear of heights, sometimes inching my way along, stopping to photograph, before moving on. The hillside fell away in all directions. Sometimes I'd reach a dead end and have to turn around and retrace my steps. I'd occasionally pause to change lenses, shoot some

more, and then walk carefully on, picking my way to another promising stopping place. The reflected sky, the water surfaces tinged with white, the complex patterns of the ponds were astonishing and beautiful.

After a while, I headed slowly over toward a couple of men who were working across a stretch of hillside from me. They greeted me with a nod and kept working, smoothing the salt that lay under the red-brown water, while we chatted. When I asked them how things were going, they told me there'd been a problem with rain that year, so their harvest was behind. And when I asked them the best way to get myself up and out of the labyrinth of ponds, they never said a word about the fact that I wasn't supposed to be there; they just pointed me in the right direction with a smile and a wave. After a short steep climb, I scrambled up onto the big wide trail above the terraces with mixed feelings of relief and regret.

A few days later, I had lunch with Tati and Jeremy, who are chefs and guides and live in Maras. When I asked whether the salt terraces were a good business for the people of Maras, the answer was yes. Now they make more money from visitors' entry fees than from salt sales. And no wonder, for the salt terraces are one of the world's most extraordinary landscapes.

GRAINS & PASTA

Summer Soba Noodles with Dipping Sauce (page 329)

PROVENÇALE ONION AND ANCHOVY TART

Long ago in my teens, I learned to make pissaladière, the savory tart of the Niçoise region, from Madame J, who took good care of me when I lived *en pension* with her and her husband in the city of Tours. Madame, generous and warmhearted, was from the Midi, in the south of France, and her husband was from Lyon, so the food she served us was delicious and beautifully judged.

Her version of pissaladière was made with fine pastry and included plenty of cooked-down onions, as well as anchovy strips and small black Niçoise olives.

The word *pissaladière* comes from *pissalat*, the name of a former specialty of the Niçoise region, a salty fermented paste made from immature anchovies and flavored with cloves or nutmeg. Because of declining fish stocks in the Mediterranean over the last few decades, it's now illegal to catch immature fish, and traditional pissalat is no longer made.

This recipe, very like the one I learned from Madame J, calls for masses of onions (don't be shocked; they will melt down to a manageable quantity as they cook), which are flavored with aromatics that reflect the original spices used in pissalat: bay leaf, thyme, and clove. In this version, the crust is made of whole-grain flour, which has wonderful flavor, though you can substitute all-purpose flour. I like the tart best once it has cooled to room temperature, which gives the ingredients time to settle in with one another and the crust time to firm up completely.

You can make the dough up to 2 days ahead.

Serves 6

DOUGH

1¾ cups/210 grams whole wheat pastry flour or another whole-grain flour, preferably freshly milled, or 1½ cups/ 180 grams all-purpose flour, plus more for dusting

¼ teaspoon fine sea salt

11 tablespoons/5½ ounces/ 150 grams very cold unsalted butter

1 large egg, lightly beaten

About 2 tablespoons ice water

FILLING

3 tablespoons extra-virgin olive oil

2 pounds/900 grams onions, thinly sliced

2 sprigs fresh thyme or 1½ teaspoons dried thyme

2 bay leaves

⅛ teaspoon ground cloves

½ teaspoon fine sea salt

About 25 anchovy fillets, rinsed, patted dry, and lightly drizzled with extra-virgin olive oil

About 20 Niçoise olives or other small black olives with pits

Generous grinding of black pepper (optional)

continued

To make the dough, put the flour and salt in a bowl, then grate in the cold butter. Toss to coat the butter. Use a pastry cutter or knife to cut up the butter further, then use your fingers to toss and blend it with the flour so you have soft buttered crumbs. Add the egg and mix it in lightly with a fork or with your fingertips. Add the ice water little by little, tossing and mixing to moisten the flour, just until the dough holds together in a mass when you pull it together.

Turn the dough out, dust with flour, transfer to a heavy plastic bag, and flatten with the heel of your hand into a disk about 6 inches/15 cm across. Seal and refrigerate for at least an hour. (*The dough can be made up to 2 days ahead.*)

To prepare the filling, place two large skillets over medium heat. Add 1½ tablespoons of the oil to each and swirl to coat the bottom of the pans. Divide the onions, as well as the thyme, bay leaves, cloves, and salt, between the two pans and cook, stirring frequently, until the onions wilt and soften, about 5 minutes. Lower the heat slightly and continue to cook until the onions release their liquid, about 10 minutes longer. If the onions start to stick, add a touch of water. When done, they will be very soft and sweet tasting. Remove from the heat, remove and discard the bay leaves and thyme sprigs, and set aside in a medium bowl to cool.

Fresh anchovies "alici" for sale at a market in Venice

Place a rack in the center of the oven and preheat the oven to 375°F/190°C. Lightly oil or butter a 9-by-13-inch/23 by 32 cm tart pan or rimmed baking pan if yours tends to stick; I find I don't need to grease my pan with this dough.

Lightly flour your work surface and turn out the dough. Flatten it by tapping firmly on it with a lightly floured rolling pin or pressing it with your palms, then roll it out to a rectangle a little larger than the pan (about 12 by 16 inches/30 by 40 cm), rolling from the center outward. Be patient as you encourage the dough to relax and extend. Don't worry if it cracks or splits as you roll, just pull or pinch the cracks together; if they won't cooperate now as you're rolling, you'll be able to mend them once the dough is in the pan.

Drape the dough over the rolling pin and transfer it to the tart pan or baking sheet. Gently ease it into the corners and up the sides, without stretching or forcing it. Use a sharp knife to trim off any untidy edges. Use the trimmings to patch any holes or cracks (press down on the edges of the patch to seal it well).

Prick the bottom of the dough all over (about a dozen times) with a fork to prevent it puffing. Lay a sheet of parchment on the dough (large enough to cover the base and come up the sides) and top with pastry weights or dried beans.

Bake for about 10 minutes, until the edges of the dough are firm and just touched with color. Take out of the oven and lift off the parchment and weights.

Spoon the cooked onions onto the center of the dough and spread them out to the edges to completely cover the bottom surface. Lay on the anchovy fillets in a pattern or randomly, as you please, and then do the same with the olives.

Bake for about 15 minutes, until the edges of the crust are lightly brown and pulling away from the sides of the pan. Let cool for at least 20 minutes before slicing and serving; I prefer to let it cool completely.

Top with a grinding of black pepper just before serving, if you like.

KIMCHI PANCAKES
with Dipping Sauce

These small pancakes, made of a batter flavored with chopped cabbage kimchi and a little ground pork and served with a tart dipping sauce, are delectable. They can be served as an appetizer, but I turn to them more often for a light supper, served with soup and/or salad. They pair wonderfully with a light red wine. I also enjoy the leftovers cold the next day, with a little leftover dipping sauce.

The pancakes are traditionally made 7 to 8 inches/17.5 to 20 cm in diameter, then cut into wedges. I find it much easier to make small rounds, because flipping a large round can be tricky. The standard flour for these is all-purpose, but I like them with whole wheat pastry flour. It gives more flavor and a more tender texture too.

For a less-traditional accompaniment, serve with Himalayan achar (see page 190).

Makes 10 to 12 small (2½- to 3-inch/5 to 8 cm) pancakes; serves 4 as an appetizer, 2 or 3 as a main

---

1 cup/150 grams finely chopped Classic Red Kimchi (page 78, or store-bought)

¼ pound/110 grams ground pork

½ cup/45 grams minced scallions (white and tender green parts)

1¼ cups/145 grams whole wheat pastry flour or 1 cup/130 grams unbleached all-purpose flour

½ teaspoon fine sea salt

1 large egg, beaten

1 cup/240 ml cold water

About ¼ cup/60 ml peanut, sunflower, or vegetable oil for cooking the pancakes

Chopped fresh flat-leaf parsley, coriander (cilantro), or mint for garnish (optional)

Tart-Salty Dipping Sauce (recipe follows)

Mix the kimchi, pork, and scallions in a medium bowl, breaking up the lumps in the pork. Add the flour, salt, and egg and blend together until all the flour is moistened. Add the water and stir vigorously. The batter should be thick but pourable; add a touch more water if needed. Set aside for 20 minutes, if you have time, to allow the flavors to blend.

Set out a small measuring cup or a spoon large enough to scoop up 2 tablespoons batter. Place a large cast-iron or other heavy skillet over medium-high heat. When it's hot, add about 1 tablespoon oil and swirl to coat the pan. Lower the heat to medium. Stir the batter, then scoop up about 2 tablespoons of the batter and drop it near one edge of the skillet, smoothing it a little with the back of a spoon to encourage it to spread out. Repeat with 2 or 3 more scoops, only as many as will fit comfortably in your pan. Raise the heat to medium-high to help crisp the pancakes. Cook them on the first side for 2 to 3 minutes, until the bottom is firm, then flip each one over. Add a drizzle of oil to the pan if needed. Cook for another 2 minutes or so, until lightly browned, then flip back over to the first side for another minute. Transfer to a warm plate or platter and cover loosely with a cotton cloth to keep warm. Lower the heat to medium again and repeat with the remaining batter, adding more oil to the pan as needed. Be sure to stir the batter before scooping out each batch so you get the kimchi and pork.

Garnish with chopped herbs, if you wish, and put out small individual bowls of the dipping sauce for drizzling.

TART-SALTY DIPPING SAUCE

This sauce, *cho ganjang* in Korean, is a great pairing with the pancakes, but it also delivers a pleasing hit of bright intense flavor to light vegetable or fish broths, or soups based on them. (If you'd like to make the sauce nonalcoholic, omit the rice wine and increase the vinegar and lemon juice to taste.)

Store any leftover sauce in a sealed glass jar in the refrigerator; it will keep for about a week. I squeeze a little more lemon juice into the leftover sauce to brighten the flavor.

Makes about ½ cup/120 ml

---

2 tablespoons soy sauce

2 tablespoons sake or dry vermouth (optional)

2 tablespoons unseasoned rice vinegar or cider vinegar

1 to 2 tablespoons fresh lemon juice (to taste)

1 tablespoon toasted sesame oil

About 1½ teaspoons toasted sesame seeds or coarsely chopped toasted pine nuts

Pinch each of fine sea salt and freshly ground black pepper

Put the soy sauce, sake or vermouth, vinegar, lemon juice, and sesame oil in a glass jar or a small bowl and shake or stir to blend. Add ½ teaspoon of the sesame seeds and the salt and pepper. Mix well.

To serve, transfer to individual small bowls and sprinkle a pinch of the remaining sesame seeds onto each.

THAI FRIED RICE for One

There are as many versions of Thai fried rice—one of the all-time great one-dish meals—as there are cooks in Thailand. It is always made with cold leftover rice, so make sure your rice has been chilled in the refrigerator for a few hours or longer. If you are using brown rice, it may take a little longer to soften, because it will be firmer and less fragile than the white rice, so cooking times will be slightly longer.

If your wok is large, you can double the recipe, but otherwise, if you have a guest to feed, just quickly make a second serving for yourself. (To double the recipe, double all ingredients except the curry paste and the oil, both of which can just be increased by half again. Fry the eggs separately, one by one, after you've turned the rice out of the pan.)

Ingredients are flexible: You can add a small handful of sliced pork or chicken or a little sliced firm tofu, or just use vegetables and aromatics. And you can use one or more kinds of raw or precooked vegetable as you wish, from leafy greens to corn kernels cut from the cob to green beans chopped into short lengths. Once you think of fried rice as a set of many possibilities, it becomes a fun and creative process.

The recipe includes the option of adding a little Thai curry paste to give an extra hit of flavor to the cooking oil. If you do not use curry paste, you'll need a little more fish sauce to season the rice. The essentials are plenty of garlic, and a light hand so that the rice gets fried but keeps its shape.

I love it with a fried egg on top, *sai kai dao* in Thai.

Serves 1

About 3 tablespoons lard or peanut or vegetable oil

6 small or 3 large garlic cloves, smashed, peeled, and coarsely chopped

1½ teaspoons red or green Thai curry paste (optional)

A small handful (about ¼ cup/30 grams) of thinly sliced boneless pork or chicken or firm tofu (optional)

½ cup packed/about 20 grams chopped leafy greens or finely chopped other vegetables (see headnote)

1½ cups/about 240 grams cold cooked white or brown Thai jasmine rice

About 1 tablespoon fish sauce, or more to taste

3 or 4 sprigs fresh coriander (cilantro)

1 large egg

Fine sea salt

ACCOMPANIMENTS

2 lime wedges

2 or 3 small scallions, trimmed

5 or 6 cucumber slices

About 2 tablespoons Classic Thai Fish Sauce with Bird Chiles (page 202)

continued

Heat a wok or large heavy skillet over high heat. Add half the lard or oil, and when it is hot, toss in the garlic and the curry paste, if using. Stir briefly to prevent the garlic from clumping or burning. Toss in the pork, chicken, or tofu, if using, and stir-fry for about 1 minute, until the meat (if that's what you're using) has all changed color. Add the finely chopped vegetables, if using (not the greens), and stir-fry for a minute or so, until starting to soften. Add the rice, breaking up any clumps, and stir-fry for several minutes, pressing the rice against the sides of the wok or bottom of the skillet, tossing, and then pressing again, to expose all the rice to the hot surface of the pan so that it is heated through, softened, and flavored by the cooking oil. Add the chopped greens, if using, and fish sauce and stir-fry for 30 seconds to a minute, until the greens have wilted. Turn out onto a plate and sprinkle with the coriander. Set aside.

Quickly rinse out the wok or pan, wipe it dry, and place it over medium-high heat. Add the remaining lard or oil, and when it is hot, break the egg into the pan. Lower the heat to medium and cook until the white is opaque. Sprinkle on a little salt, then flip the egg over if you wish and cook briefly, before transferring it onto the mound of rice.

Serve with the lime wedges, scallions, cucumber slices, and a small dish of dipping sauce.

PAD THAI

Pad Thai (*pad* means "fry") is a kind of mash-up of many ingredients that come together in a tart, savory, sweet mass to make a one-dish meal. The essential elements include thin rice noodles, a little sliced pork or chicken (you can skip the meat and increase the amount of tofu), sliced firm tofu, and eggs, along with bean sprouts, salted radish threads, and dried shrimp.

In Thailand, the usual sauces and condiments on the table include red chile powder, and sliced *prik num* (mild green chiles like banana chiles) in mild vinegar.

If you have a large wok, you can make 2 servings at a time, as here, but no more. It's important to cook pad Thai quickly in a very hot wok, so it's better to cook in several batches if necessary than to have an overloaded wok. Get your condiments and extras ready ahead, and all your ingredients, so that the dish can be made quickly and served hot and fresh.

Serves 2

ACCOMPANIMENTS

½ cup/120 ml unseasoned rice vinegar

2 tablespoons sugar

½ banana chile or Hungarian wax chile, thinly sliced

1 English or 2 or 3 Persian cucumbers, thinly sliced

1 lime, cut into wedges

Dried red chile powder or cayenne

PAD THAI

½ pound/225 grams rice sticks (dried rice noodles)

1 heaping tablespoon tamarind pulp, coarsely chopped, or 2 tablespoons homemade tamarind paste (see page 347)

About ¼ cup/60 ml warm water (if using tamarind pulp)

2 large eggs

Pinch of fine sea salt

½ cup/75 grams raw peanuts

1 tablespoon soy sauce

1 tablespoon fish sauce

3 tablespoons peanut oil, vegetable oil, or lard

2 garlic cloves, minced

1 ounce/30 grams boneless pork, cut into small, thin bite-sized pieces

2 ounces/60 grams pressed tofu (see Glossary), thinly sliced

About ¼ pound/110 grams bean sprouts, rinsed and drained

2 scallions, trimmed, smashed with the side of a knife or cleaver, and cut into 1-inch/ 3 cm lengths

6 to 8 dried shrimp (see page 151), soaked in warm water for 10 minutes, drained, and coarsely chopped

1 tablespoon Salt-Dried Daikon Strips (page 87 or store-bought), rinsed and coarsely chopped

Fresh coriander (cilantro) leaves for garnish (optional)

To prepare the chiles for serving, combine the rice vinegar and sugar in a medium bowl, stirring to dissolve the sugar. Add the chiles and set aside.

continued

To make the pad Thai, place the rice noodles in a large bowl, add lukewarm water to cover, and set aside to soak for 10 to 15 minutes, then drain.

If using tamarind pulp, place it in a small bowl, add the lukewarm water, and mash and press with a fork or a spoon so it starts to dissolve. Set aside to soak for a few minutes.

Whisk the eggs with the salt in a small bowl; set aside.

Place a heavy skillet over medium heat, add the peanuts, and toast, shaking the skillet frequently to prevent scorching, until aromatic and touched with color, 4 to 5 minutes. Remove from the heat, coarsely chop, and set aside in a small bowl.

Mash the tamarind pulp, if using, again to try to separate the flesh from the seeds, then press it through a sieve into a small bowl. Discard the pulp and seeds.

Add the soy sauce and fish sauce to the tamarind paste and set this flavoring liquid by your stovetop.

Place all the remaining ingredients by your stovetop, along with a medium plate and a platter or two individual plates or wide bowls for serving.

Place a large wok over high heat and add about 2 tablespoons/30 ml of the oil. When it is hot, toss in the garlic. Stir-fry for a few seconds as it changes color, then add the pork and stir-fry until it changes color, about 1 minute. Add the sliced tofu, press it against the hot wok surface, and then continue tossing and pressing it against the hot wok for just under a minute. Whisk the eggs quickly again and pour in. They will immediately start to cook around the pork and tofu. As they firm up, use your spatula to chop the mass into a few large pieces, then turn it all out onto a plate and set aside.

Place the wok back over high heat, add another tablespoon or so of oil or lard, and toss in the drained noodles. Stir-fry vigorously, tossing them and pressing them against the hot sides of the wok over and over. They will soften, however awkward they feel at the start—just keep at it. After about 1 minute, they will be warm and completely softened.

Push the noodles up the sides of the wok and toss in the bean sprouts and scallions. Stir-fry briefly, then add the dried shrimp and salted daikon strips and toss with the bean sprouts. Pour in the tamarind liquid and stir-fry, incorporating the noodles into the bean sprouts mixture, for about 30 seconds. Add the reserved egg mixture and gently fold into the mass of noodles.

Turn out onto the platter or serve on the individual plates or in the bowls. Arrange the cucumber slices in a row along one edge of the platter or the plates or bowls. Sprinkle on some of the roasted peanuts and set the rest of the peanuts out on the table with the chiles, lime wedges, and chile powder.

Sprinkle coriander leaves over the pad Thai, if you wish, and serve immediately.

SUMMER SOBA NOODLES
with Dipping Sauce

Long ago, just before the turn of the millennium, my ex and I bought a rather neglected farm property two hours north of Toronto, ninety acres that had not been farmed for twenty-five years and had never yielded much. There was a decrepit but beautiful barn and a tiny house that spoke of hard times. We took possession in the spring and spent that first summer giving some loving attention to the house and garden.

We had help, not just from our kids, then turning ten and thirteen, but also from visitors. Friends would come up from the city to lend a hand, and we also had visitors from Japan. Ayako and Yuji had lived in Toronto with their parents and older brother for a few years and gone to early grades of primary school with my kids before they had to return to Japan. Later I stayed with them near Kyoto while I was doing research for *Seductions of Rice*.

The spring we started work on the farm, I'd received a letter from Ayako and Yuji's mother saying she was concerned that they were losing their English. I wrote back to suggest that they come stay with us. And that was how they found themselves tearing out rotten floorboards and hammering new ones into place, running through the fields, exploring the woods, and seeing the Milky Way for what they swore was the first time.

One hot summer day, Ayako suggested that she and Yuji make cold noodles for us all for supper (they'd brought the ingredients with them from Japan). It was our introduction to "summer soba": noodles served in a bath of cold water, dipped into a delectable dipping sauce (*mentsuyu* in Japanese), and eaten with appreciative slurps.

It's a simple concept, requiring only that you take 30 minutes to prepare the dipping sauce before you cook the soba. The sauce is a concentrate flavored with bonito flakes (or, for a vegetarian version, dried mushrooms) that is then diluted with cold water.

Soba noodles made with a little wheat flour as well as buckwheat (usually 20 percent wheat flour) are less brittle and breakable and easier to find than 100 percent buckwheat soba. Allow 1/3 pound/150 grams dried noodles per person if serving as a main dish (as here) and 3 1/2 ounces/100 grams if serving as one of several dishes.

continued

Soba noodles often come tied up in smaller bundles. After you take the noodles out of their package, untie the bundles so the noodles are loose. You want them to cook without sticking to each other. Note that soba noodles are cooked in *unsalted* boiling water.

On a hot day, I like to serve a salad after the noodles, or simply some ripe tomatoes sprinkled with basil leaves and drizzled with olive oil. But if you have a hungry crowd, then you may want to serve a heartier dish such as Thai Grilled Beef Salad (page 292), as we did at the farm that evening with Ayako and Yuji, grilling the beef over a wood fire.

You'll want to provide each guest with a small bowl for dipping sauce and a larger bowl for their noodles, as well as chopsticks.

Serves 4

DIPPING SAUCE

¼ cup/60 ml sake

½ cup/120 ml soy sauce

½ cup/120 ml mirin

1 cup/about 4 grams bonito flakes or 15 dried shiitake mushrooms, rinsed

A 2-inch/5 cm square of kombu

About ¾ cup/180 ml cold water

1 to 1½ pounds/450 to 650 grams dried soba noodles (see headnote)

TOPPINGS AND FLAVORINGS

1 sheet nori, cut into fine strands (see Notes)

Minced greens from 5 or 6 scallions

Wasabi paste (about a generous tablespoon)

To make the dipping sauce, bring the sake to a boil in a small nonreactive saucepan and boil gently for about a minute to evaporate some of the alcohol. Add the soy sauce and mirin, then add the bonito flakes or dried mushrooms and bring back to a boil. Lower the heat, add the kombu, and just before the liquid comes back to a boil, lower the heat even further. Simmer for 1 minute, then remove from the heat.

Let the concentrate stand until completely cool, then strain. (See Notes below.)

Measure out ½ cup/120 ml of the sauce concentrate in a large measuring cup and add the cold water. Taste and adjust, by adding a little more concentrate if you'd like it stronger, or a little more water if you'd like it more mellow. Transfer the sauce to a small jug and put out on the table.

Also put out a plate of the toppings of your choice.

Fill a tall pot with 10 inches/25 cm of water and bring to a boil. Add the noodles in a loose swirl. As they cook, stir them gently from time to time with chopsticks to keep them from sticking together. They should be cooked and supple in 5 to 8 minutes, but check the package instructions.

ON THE LEFT, *Wajima Sea Salt from Hekura Island, 31 miles/50 km offshore from Wajima;* ON THE RIGHT, *Aizu Mountain salt, freshly milled, made in Fukushima Prefecture by boiling down hot salt-spring water*

Put a colander in the sink and put a dozen ice cubes in a large serving bowl. When the noodles are just cooked through, drain them in the colander and run cold water over them to rinse. Shake the colander to remove excess water, then transfer the noodles to the bowl of ice cubes and put it on the table. Use long chopsticks or tongs to serve guests from this central bowl, pausing as you lift each clump of noodles to let excess water drain off.

Invite your guests to sprinkle some nori strands onto their noodles if they want, and to pour some dipping sauce into their small bowls. They can also stir a little chopped scallion and wasabi into their sauce if they wish. Eat by dipping the noodles into the sauce, mouthful by mouthful.

Store leftover sauce concentrate in a labeled glass jar in the refrigerator; it will keep well for a month or more. Use as a seasoning in soups or stews or serve as a condiment, diluted with water to taste, with other noodle dishes or rice dishes.

NOTES: *To make nori strands, it's easiest to roll up the sheet and then cut it finely crosswise.*

If you wish, save your used kombu in the refrigerator or freezer to use for making the Seaweed Relish on page 198.

PASTA ALLA GRICIA

The main ingredient in this delectable pasta sauce is guanciale, the salt-cured pig's cheeks that are one of the brilliant salt-preserved meats of Italy. Whole-grain durum pasta is a great match for the hearty flavors of the sauce.

Serves 4

Coarse salt

About 8 ounces/225 grams trimmed guanciale (buy 9 ounces/270 grams if you will be trimming off the skin yourself)

About ¼ pound/110 grams Pecorino cheese, grated, plus more for the table

1 pound/450 grams dried whole-grain or regular spaghetti, fettuccine, or linguine

About 2 tablespoons extra-virgin olive oil

Freshly ground black pepper

Bring a large pot of water to a boil and salt it generously.

Meanwhile, trim off the skin from the guanciale if necessary. Thinly slice the guanciale and then cut the slices into narrow matchsticks. Finely grate the Pecorino (I use a Microplane to get a light, fluffy texture).

Add the pasta to the boiling water and give it a stir to separate the strands. Cook until the pasta is just barely al dente, 7 to 9 minutes if using regular pasta, almost twice that time if using whole-grain pasta.

Meanwhile, as soon as the pasta is in the hot water, place a large heavy pot that is big enough to hold the cooked pasta over medium heat. Add enough olive oil to coat the bottom of the pot, then toss in the guanciale. Once it starts to yield its fat, raise the heat slightly. The fat portions of the guanciale strips will become translucent in a couple of minutes. Stir frequently to make sure that the guanciale is not sticking to the bottom of the pot. After about 4 minutes, raise the heat to help the meat portion of the guanciale crisp up a little, another minute or two.

When the pasta is ready, scoop out about 1½ cups/360 ml of the cooking water and set aside, then drain the pasta and transfer to a bowl. If the guanciale is not yet ready, add a little of the melted guanciale fat, or else a little olive oil, to the pasta, and toss.

When the guanciale is cooked and crisped, add the pasta to the pot and toss to combine. Reduce the heat to medium-low, add most of the Pecorino and about ¾ cup/180 ml of the reserved pasta cooking water and toss again. Add more of the cooking water as needed to loosen the pasta and create a smooth sauce, tossing and turning well to coat the pasta. Grind black pepper on generously.

Turn the pasta out into a large serving bowl, sprinkle on grated Pecorino, and serve hot.

SPAGHETTI ALLA PUTTANESCA

Serve this intensely warming umami-bomb on a cold evening, or any time you are really hungry. The depth of flavor from the layering of three different salt-cured ingredients—anchovies, olives, and capers—is deeply satisfying.

Serves 4

Coarse salt

3 tablespoons extra-virgin olive oil

3 or 4 garlic cloves, smashed and peeled

One 28-ounce/794-gram can whole tomatoes, with their juices, or 1½ pounds/ 675 grams ripe tomatoes, coarsely chopped, with their juices

6 or 7 anchovy fillets, preferably salt-packed, rinsed and finely chopped

1 pound/450 grams dried whole-grain or regular spaghetti

⅔ cup/120 grams black olives, pitted

2 tablespoons capers, preferably salt-packed

1 tablespoon chile pepper flakes or 2 or 3 dried red cayenne chiles

Freshly ground black pepper

About ½ cup/40 grams finely grated Parmigiano-Reggiano, plus more for the table

Bring a large pot of water to a boil and salt it generously.

Meanwhile, place a wide heavy pot over medium heat. Add the oil, then toss in the garlic cloves and cook for several minutes, until starting to soften. Add the tomatoes, with their juices, the anchovies, and ½ teaspoon salt; reduce the heat to medium-low; and cook, stirring occasionally, until the tomatoes are broken down and the anchovies have dissolved, about 10 minutes if using canned tomatoes, 15 to 20 minutes if using fresh. Stir the olives, capers, chile flakes, and black pepper to taste into the sauce and simmer for 5 minutes to let the flavors blend; keep warm over low heat.

Add the pasta to the boiling water, stir for a moment, and cook until al dente. Just before the pasta is done, scoop out about ¾ to 1 cup/180 to 240 ml of the cooking water and set aside. Drain the pasta and transfer it to a large bowl.

Add the sauce and about ½ cup/120 ml of the reserved cooking water to the pasta and toss gently. Add the grated Parmigiano and toss again, adding a bit more pasta water as needed to create a luscious coating for the pasta.

Serve immediately, putting out more grated cheese and the pepper grinder so guests can serve themselves extra if they wish.

BUCATINI with Bottarga

Puglia, at the heel of the Italian boot, feels close to Greece, both physically and in some ways culturally. This recipe is adapted from a cookbook by Luigi Sada called *La Cucina Pugliese*, where he says that bottarga originated with Greek communities in Puglia long ago. Others trace it back to the Phoenicians.

Here the bottarga is dissolved in hot water and blended with olive oil, garlic, and herbs to make a simple, delicious sauce. The almost al dente pasta is added to the sauce and the two finish cooking together briefly. The whole dish takes less than 20 minutes.

If you can't find bottarga (see page 148) at a market near you, you can order it online. Frozen bottarga thaws very quickly to a soft, dense texture and is easy to chop. If your bottarga is drier and harder, it may be easier to grate it than to chop it.

Serves 4 generously

Coarse salt

1 pound/450 grams dried bucatini or linguine

Scant 1 tablespoon extra-virgin olive oil if needed

SAUCE

3½ ounces/100 grams bottarga (see headnote)

3 garlic cloves, minced

1 teaspoon fine sea salt

⅔ cup/160 ml extra-virgin olive oil

½ cup/about 25 grams finely chopped fresh flat-leaf parsley

½ cup/about 25 grams finely chopped fresh basil

½ cup/40 grams grated Pecorino, plus more for serving

Put a big pot of water on to boil. When it's boiling vigorously, salt it generously, then add the pasta and cook until just barely al dente. Drain. (If the sauce is not ready, transfer the pasta to a large bowl, add the olive oil, toss well, and set aside.)

Meanwhile, make the sauce: Peel the membrane off the bottarga. Slice it and use the knife to mince it, or use your fingers to break it apart into fine granules if that works better. Or, if your bottarga is very hard, use a Microplane or other fine grater to grate it.

Place a wide heavy pot over medium heat. Add 1 cup/240 ml hot water (from the boiling pasta or the tap) and toss in the garlic, then stir in the bottarga and salt. The bottarga will dissolve in the liquid. Add the olive oil and chopped herbs and stir to blend together into a sauce.

Reduce the heat under the sauce slightly and add the cooked pasta. Toss and turn to coat the pasta with the sauce, then add the Pecorino, and toss and stir briefly to blend it in.

Turn the pasta out into to a large bowl and serve. Put out extra grated Pecorino and the pepper grinder.

SPAGHETTI MENTAIKO

It's interesting to compare this dish with the Bucatini with Bottarga on page 334. That one is anchored in local tradition, while mentaiko pasta is a fusion dish that was created in Japan after the Second World War. It uses a salted roe from the Japanese/Korean larder to create a simple uncooked, buttery sauce for spaghetti.

Mentaiko is the Japanese term for salted and seasoned Alaska pollack roe (see page 148). It is usually seasoned with hot chile and sometimes citrus or other flavors. You're likely to find it at Korean and Japanese stores in larger cities, where it is usually sold frozen. If you get the roe without hot chiles, add about ½ teaspoon cayenne per 100 grams of mentaiko.

Spaghetti mentaiko is topped with fine strands of toasted nori rather than grated cheese. Serve as an appetizer or as a light main course.

Serves 2 as a main, 3 or 4 as an appetizer or side

Coarse salt

3 to 4 ounces/100 to 120 grams mentaiko (Japanese-style seasoned fish roe; see headnote)

1 teaspoon hot smoked paprika (pimentón) or ½ teaspoon cayenne if needed (see headnote)

About 3 tablespoons butter, at room temperature

1 tablespoon soy sauce, or more to taste

Freshly ground black pepper

½ pound/225 grams dried spaghetti

1 lightly toasted nori sheet, cut into fine shreds

OPTIONAL GARNISH

5 or 6 fresh shiso leaves or Salted Shiso Leaves (page 60), cut into fine julienne, or about 1 tablespoon Salted Shiso and Sesame Furikake (page 197)

Bring a large pot of water to a boil and salt it generously.

Meanwhile, working over a bowl, cut open the mentaiko, peel back the membrane, and crumble the roe into the bowl. Break it up completely with your fingers or a fork. Add the pimentón or cayenne, if using, and butter and stir until blended into the roe, then add the soy sauce and a generous grinding of black pepper and stir. Transfer to the bowl that you will use for the pasta and set aside.

Add the pasta to the boiling water and cook until al dente. Just before the pasta is done, scoop out about ½ cup/120 ml of the cooking water; stir it into the mentaiko sauce to loosen it.

Drain the pasta and immediately add it to the bowl of sauce. Toss well to coat the pasta; the hot pasta will smooth the sauce as it melts the butter.

Serve in individual bowls or from a serving bowl. Top with the nori shreds and the julienned shiso leaves or furikake.

SALT AND VENICE

A few years ago, I made a trip to Venice during October, when the Biennale was on. I was there to touch base with one of the places whose history is entangled with salt.

The story of the rise of Venice as a sea power and trading giant is partly the story of the way a monopoly of an essential commodity such as salt can lead to riches. The Venetians of the late Middle Ages controlled their lagoon and made salt there. They traded inland up the Po and other rivers. They also extended their power southward down the Adriatic, capturing other salt-making towns and taking control of the salt supply in the region, so they eventually had a monopoly and could demand higher prices. Venetian ships sailing to ports around the Mediterranean for trade were obliged by the government to return home with salt as part of their load. It served as ballast in the ships, and could be stockpiled in Venice.

I found a salt story at the Biennale too. In the main hall of the Arsenale, there was a sculpture made of salt that spoke of both the past and the future. The piece, by Swiss artist Julian Charrière, was called *Future Fossil Spaces* and consisted of pillars of salt reimagined: large bricks of raw salt striped with pinkish-beige and brown layers of sediment were stacked with glass blocks filled with lithium brine to make tall, majestic columns. The title of the piece resonated with me. In an era when edible salt is easily available, lithium has become a valuable salt that we depend on for our modern technology-dependent world: in our cell phones and other devices, in the making of some specialized aluminum and steel, and much more. Both the salt blocks and the lithium brine, metaphors for our past and present dependence on the earth, had been extracted from the huge salt flats in Bolivia, the Salar de Uyuni, the world's most important source of lithium.

Dusk reflections in a quiet canal in Canareggio, in Venice

SWEETS

Miso Cookies with Dark Chocolate Chips (page 358)

CREAMY CANDIED GINGER AND MISO ICE CREAM

This ice cream gets its satiny smooth texture from an egg-rich custard base, sometimes called "French" style. With hits of intensity from the candied ginger pieces, the ice cream has an intriguing suggestion of butterscotch flavor, but it is not very sweet. Remember to put the bowl of your ice cream maker in the freezer at least 12 hours ahead, or whatever the manufacturer recommends. Start making the ice cream at least 4 hours before you want to serve it (or a bit less, if you want soft-serve texture).

Makes 1 quart/950 grams

6 large egg yolks

1 tablespoon Red Miso (page 109, or store-bought)

1 tablespoon shiro (white) miso

1 cup/240 ml whole milk

2 cups/480 ml heavy cream

⅔ cup/140 grams turbinado sugar, such as Sugar in the Raw

About 1 cup/150 grams finely chopped candied ginger

Put a large wide bowl in your freezer along with a tray or bag of ice cubes.

Put the egg yolks in a heatproof medium bowl and whisk briskly until pale and slightly thickened, about 3 minutes. Set aside.

Mix the two miso pastes with about ¼ cup/60 ml of the milk in a small bowl or measuring cup, mashing the miso with a fork or spoon. Pour the mixture through a strainer into another small bowl, smearing the miso against the mesh to extract flavor; discard the solids.

Transfer the miso milk to a heavy pot, add the remaining ¾ cup/180 ml milk, the cream, sugar, and candied ginger, and place over medium heat. Bring to a simmer, whisking to dissolve the sugar. Then continue to whisk or stir occasionally until the liquid starts to steam and you see a little foam around the edges, but do not let it come to a boil. Remove from the heat.

Give the eggs another quick whisk. Whisking constantly, gradually pour the hot cream, in a thin stream, into the eggs. (This technique is called tempering and it prevents the yolks from coagulating on contact with the hot liquid.)

Pour the egg and cream mixture back into the pot, whisk briefly, and place over medium-low heat. Cook, stirring fairly constantly with a silicone spatula, making sure to get into the edges of the pot, until the custard has thickened enough to coat the back of a spoon, 6 to 8 minutes; do not let it boil. The mixture should read 180°F/82°C on an instant-read thermometer.

continued

Immediately pour the custard into a tall clean bowl. Partly fill the wide bowl from the freezer with cold tap water and add some ice cubes. Place the bowl of custard in this ice bath, taking care that water doesn't slosh into the custard. Cover loosely and let cool for half an hour, then discard the ice bath.

Cover the bowl of custard with plastic wrap and place in the refrigerator to chill for 2 hours, or as long as overnight.

Give the cooled custard mixture a stir, then pour through a coarse strainer into your ice cream maker. Transfer the ginger pieces to a small bowl and set aside in the refrigerator.

Churn the ice cream according to the manufacturer's instructions. When it is almost ready, add the reserved ginger pieces and let the machine churn a few seconds longer to distribute them evenly. You can serve the ice cream now at this soft-serve texture or transfer it to a freezer container, scraping it all out with a spatula. Smooth the top, cover with a lid, and place in the freezer. It will be solid in an hour or so, and it can be kept frozen for several weeks.

SALT AND ICE CREAM

Before the arrival of modern ice cream makers, salt was an essential tool for making ice cream. An ice cream base needs to be chilled to below freezing to get it to set. Surrounding the container of creamy mixture with ordinary ice does not take it to a cold enough temperature; the ice melts before the cream gets sufficiently chilled. But when salt is added to the ice, the water on the surface of the ice becomes saltwater, which has a much lower freezing point (28°F/-2°C) than fresh water (and the saltier the water, the lower the freezing point (from 28 to 21°F/-2 to -6°C). The resulting slush of salted ice water chills the cream enough so that it sets. It all seems very counterintuitive, I know!

In traditional ice cream makers, the cream and sugar mixture go into a mixing chamber that is on a spindle so that its paddle can be turned with a handle. The salt and ice mixture in the outer container surrounds the inner chamber and chills the cream mixture as it's cranked round and round, for even chilling, until it becomes ice cream.

With modern ice cream makers, you simply combine all the ingredients and whisk or blend them together, chill them, and then pour the mixture into the prechilled bowl of the machine and let it do the work. The result is ice cream with a "soft serve" texture. For firm ice cream, transfer it to a container and put in the freezer for an hour or more.

EASY TAMARIND-MISO ICE CREAM
with Chocolate Chips

This recipe skips the eggs found in French-style ice cream yet still has a luscious consistency. Make the tamarind paste before you start making the ice cream, if you don't have it on hand. Remember to put the bowl of your ice cream maker in the freezer at least 12 hours ahead, or whatever the manufacturer recommends. Start making the ice cream at least 3 hours before you want to serve it (or a bit less, if you want soft-serve texture).

Makes 3½ cups/850 grams

1 teaspoon Red Miso (page 109, or store-bought)

2 teaspoons shiro (white) miso

1 cup/240 ml whole milk

2 cups/480 ml heavy cream

⅔ cup/140 grams turbinado sugar, such as Sugar in the Raw

3 tablespoons Tamarind Paste (page 347)

3 to 3½ ounces/80 to 100 grams semisweet or bittersweet chocolate, chopped into small chips

Mix both miso pastes with about ¼ cup/60 ml of the milk in a small bowl or a measuring cup, mashing the miso with a fork or spoon. Pour the mixture through a strainer into another small bowl, mashing the miso against the mesh to extract flavor; discard the solids.

Transfer the miso milk to a heavy pot, add the remaining ¾ cup/180 ml milk, the cream, and sugar, and place over medium heat. Bring to a simmer, whisking to dissolve the sugar. Scoop out about ½ cup/120 ml of the mixture and stir the tamarind into it to blend completely. Pour back into the pot and stir to blend. Heat the mixture, stirring occasionally, until the liquid starts to steam and you see a little foam around the edges; do not let it come to a boil. Remove from the heat.

Pour into a clean bowl, cover loosely with a cotton cloth and set aside to cool until lukewarm or cooler. Cover with plastic wrap and place in the refrigerator to chill for at least 2 hours, or as long as overnight if more convenient.

Give the cream mixture a stir and pour into the ice cream maker. Churn the mixture according to the manufacturer's instructions. When the ice cream is almost ready, add the chocolate pieces and let the machine churn a few seconds to distribute them evenly. Serve the ice cream now if you want a soft-serve texture, or transfer it to a freezer container, scraping it all out with a spatula. Smooth the top, cover with a lid, and place in the freezer. It will be fairly solid in an hour or so, and it can be kept frozen for several weeks.

continued

TAMARIND PASTE

You can use store-bought tamarind paste, but the flavor is better if you buy a block of tamarind pulp (tamarind flesh and seeds in a dense, dark brown block) and soak it to extract the paste. I like to make a batch of this thick paste and store it in the fridge, where it will keep for up to 2 weeks.

Makes 1 cup/240 ml

½ pound/225 grams tamarind pulp (see Glossary)

1 cup/240 ml hot water

Cut the block of tamarind pulp into chunks and place in a bowl. Add the hot water, mash the pulp a little, and set aside to soak for 5 to 10 minutes.

Mash the tamarind pulp with a fork or a strong spoon to break it up, then continue mashing until it has softened enough that you can press it through a small sieve (I use a metal tea strainer) into another bowl, mashing and pressing it to extract flavor. Use a spatula to wipe off the puree that has accumulated on the underside of the sieve and add it to the paste. Discard the pulp.

Store the paste in a glass jar in the refrigerator for up to 2 weeks.

Easy Tamarind-Miso Ice Cream with Chocolate Chips (top); Creamy Candied Ginger and Miso Ice Cream (bottom; page 342)

MISO-ESPRESSO CARAMEL CUSTARD

I love crème caramel, and that's why I decided to use miso to flavor the custard part of a rich crème caramel, rather than the caramel itself. Make it in a loaf pan, as here, or instead in ramekins (see the Note below).

After the custard has cooked in its water bath and chilled overnight, you have the pleasure of inverting it onto a serving platter and lifting off the loaf pan. The custard emerges with a gleaming top surface of red-brown caramel. Serve it in slices, drizzled with any extra caramel. I've freely adapted this method from David Lebovitz's recipe for a loaf-shaped flan.

The custard (made with milk and cream and plenty of eggs) is flavored with both miso and espresso. The salt in the miso mellows the bitter edge of the coffee. Use a red miso such as the one on page 109, or a store-bought miso. The miso-espresso custard tastes like a rich café au lait with a hint of mocha salt. The caramel adds sweetness and a pleasing touch of bitter.

Make this the day before you want to serve it. It will keep in the refrigerator for up to 4 days. Allow just under 2 hours for preparation plus cooking time the first time you make it.

Serves 6 to 8

Butter for greasing the loaf pan

CARAMEL

1 cup/200 grams granulated sugar

¼ cup/60 ml water

5 or 6 drops fresh lemon juice

CUSTARD

2 tablespoons Red Miso (page 109, or store-bought)

1½ cups/360 ml whole milk

¾ cup/180 ml strong espresso, at room temperature

1 cup/240 ml heavy cream

8 large eggs, at room temperature

¾ cup/150 grams granulated sugar

Lightly butter a 9-by-5-inch (23 by 13 cm) loaf pan and place it by your stovetop. For the water bath, set a pan (such as a roasting pan) that the loaf pan fits into easily and that is at least 3 inches/7.5 cm deep onto a baking sheet.

To make the caramel, put the sugar in a heavy medium pot or large skillet and spread it out evenly. Add the water and lemon juice and set the pot over medium-high heat. As the sugar heats and melts, gently swirl the pot just enough to ensure that the water moistens all the sugar and that it is heating evenly. It will start to bubble and to turn a light brown and then very quickly progress to a medium brown (don't walk away). Watch carefully, and as soon as you see a wisp of smoke, remove the pot from the heat and quickly and very carefully pour the caramel

into the buttered pan. It should flow and coat the bottom surface; tilt the pan gently back and forth if necessary.

Place the loaf pan in the larger pan on the baking sheet, making sure it's level so that your caramel layer sets level, and set aside to cool.

Place a rack in the lower third of the oven, preheat the oven to 300°F/150°C, and put a kettle on to boil.

To make the custard, put the miso in a medium bowl, add about ½ cup/ 120 ml of the milk, and whisk until the miso is completely dissolved. Strain through a sieve set over a bowl, pressing the miso against the mesh to extract flavor; discard any solids. Transfer back to the medium bowl, add the rest of the milk, the espresso, and cream, and whisk again.

Break the eggs into a medium bowl, add the sugar, and whisk vigorously for several minutes, until foamy. Continue whisking as you slowly add the milk mixture. Give it a final whisk and then pour it into the caramel-lined loaf pan.

Carefully put the baking sheet with the two pans into the oven. Then carefully pour hot water from the kettle into the larger pan until it comes to just past halfway up the sides of the custard pan.

Bake for 40 to 45 minutes. The custard is done when the top surface is set and, if you gently shake the pan, it undulates. If you have an instant-read thermometer, the internal temperature should be 175°F/82°C. Or insert a paring knife into the center of the custard; it should come out clean.

Remove the baking sheet from the oven and leave the custard in the water bath for 30 minutes to cool and firm up, then lift the custard pan out and let it cool to room temperature on a cooling rack or on the counter.

Cover loosely and refrigerate for at least 4 hours or, preferably, overnight.

To serve the loaf, run a fine-bladed knife around all sides. Place a long platter or plate on top and flip the pan over to turn the flan out. The top will have a lovely rich sheen from the caramel. Cut into slices and serve immediately. (There may be extra caramel in the pan, which you can tip or scrape out onto the slices of custard.)

NOTE: *If you'd like to use individual ramekins, lightly grease eight 6-ounce/180 ml ramekins with butter. Set them in a large roasting pan that holds them comfortably and set it on a baking sheet. Divide the hot caramel evenly among the ramekins and set aside while you make the custard. Transfer the custard mixture to a jug or large measuring cup to make it easier to pour it into the ramekins. Put the baking sheet into the oven and add enough hot water to the roasting pan so it comes slightly more than halfway up the sides of the ramekins. They should be done in about 20 minutes; use a thermometer or the tests for doneness described above.*

MISO CARAMEL SAUCE

Salted caramel is delicious, so why not salted caramel with miso to give it extra umami? This sauce is very flexible, a helpful larder item for easy last-minute desserts: use as a topping for ice cream or plain cake, drizzle it over pineapple slices, or spoon over grilled or panfried bananas with a squeeze of lime juice for some balancing acidity.

Or, if you are making homemade ice cream, once it has churned and is at the soft-serve stage, transfer it to a freezer container and swirl some caramel sauce into it. Put it into the freezer to harden to the consistency you wish.

Makes about 1 cup/250 ml

2 tablespoons shiro (white) miso

¼ cup/60 ml plus 2 tablespoons water

¾ cup/180 ml heavy cream

¾ cup/150 grams granulated sugar

5 or 6 drops fresh lemon juice

Place the miso in a small bowl, add the ¼ cup/60 ml water, and stir to blend. If it seems at all lumpy, strain through a sieve, discarding any solids; set aside.

Place the cream in a measuring cup or jug and set aside while you make the caramel.

Before you start making the caramel, please read through the recipe carefully, so that you can anticipate the steps.

Put the sugar in a medium saucepan and shake the pan to spread it out, then add the remaining 2 tablespoons water and the lemon juice and set over medium-high heat. Shake the pan a little until the sugar is entirely moistened. Then watch, without shaking the pan, as the mixture develops pale bubbles. The process goes surprisingly quickly, so don't look away. When the bubbles have turned a rich golden brown and the caramel is just barely starting to smoke, remove from the heat.

Work quickly yet carefully: Hold a long-handled spoon in one hand and the cup of cream in the other and stand back a little, because when the cream is added to the hot caramel, it will bubble and can spatter. Carefully pour a little of the cream into the caramel, stirring constantly as you do; some of the caramel may harden, but don't worry, it will melt again. Add the rest of the cream little by little, stirring constantly, then add the miso liquid and whisk briskly to blend it in completely.

Transfer the sauce to a nonreactive container and let cool. Store in the refrigerator, covered, for up to 2 weeks. The sauce will thicken when cold; soften it with a quick zap in the microwave or heat gently on the stovetop.

YOGURT CAKE
with Ground Salted Nuts and Preserved Lemon

This cake is very forgiving. It's baked in a loaf pan and looks like a pound cake, but the crumb is less dense and more tender. Serve at any time of day, say a slice with morning coffee, or as a dessert topped with ice cream or fresh fruit. I usually leave it in the pan, but you can turn it out once it has cooled.

I've flavored it with two ingredients from my salt larder: brine-soaked salted nuts and salt-preserved lemons (although you can just use a fresh lemon if you don't have any preserved lemons on hand). If you don't already have the salted nuts on hand, you'll need to prepare them a day ahead.

Serves 8

Oil for greasing the loaf pan

1 cup/130 grams flour (see Note)

1 cup/200 grams turbinado sugar, such as Sugar in the Raw

½ cup/50 grams ground Salted Walnuts or Salted Almonds (page 71; see Notes)

2 teaspoons baking powder

Pinch of fine sea salt

½ cup plain whole-milk yogurt

3 large eggs

2 tablespoons finely chopped Salt-Preserved Lemons (page 63, or store-bought)

½ cup/120 ml extra-virgin olive oil

Place a rack in the center of the oven and preheat the oven to 350°F/175°C. Grease an 8-by-4-inch/20 x 10 cm loaf pan lightly with oil and line the bottom with parchment paper.

Whisk the flour, sugar, ground nuts, baking powder, and salt together thoroughly in a medium bowl; set aside.

Put the yogurt and eggs in another bowl and whisk to blend completely. Stir in the lemon.

Pour the wet ingredients into the dry ingredients and use a rubber spatula to stir and fold them in until fully mixed. Add the olive oil and fold and stir until the oil is completely blended in; the first time you do this, it may seem unlikely, but don't worry, it will eventually be incorporated.

Pour the batter into the parchment-lined pan. (Place the pan on a baking sheet for easy transport, if you like.) Place it in the oven and bake for 50 to 55 minutes. To test for doneness, insert a skewer or a fine-bladed knife into the center of the cake; it should come out clean.

Remove the cake from the oven and let cool completely before slicing.

NOTE ON FLOUR: *I prefer whole-grain flour for this cake. I like a combination of ½ cup/60 grams whole wheat pastry flour and ½ cup/70 grams spelt flour, Red Fife, or another single-varietal wheat flour. But you can use 1 cup/130 grams all-purpose flour if that's what you have.*

NOTE ON GRINDING THE NUTS: *The best tool for this is a food processor. Add a little spoonful of the sugar called for in the recipe to the nuts and pulse them until you have medium to fine crumbs; you don't want a paste.*

BRETON SALTED-BUTTER CAKE

Brittany, windswept and stony, was for a long time a world apart. Breton is a Celtic language and the region had strong ties to Celtic communities in Cornwall and Wales across the Channel, as well as to those in Asturias and Galicia in northwestern Spain. Apart from its distinctive music and language, and its people's reputation for thrift and hardiness, Brittany is known for salt from the Guérande, north of the mouth of the Loire River. The nearby city of Nantes was the principal port for ships bringing sugar back to France from plantations in the French colonies in the Caribbean. This combination of plentiful supplies of salt and sugar is in the taste of *kouign-amann*.

The cake feels like a creative example of the frugal practicality of people in Brittany. It starts with a proofed bread dough, originally a piece left over after the rest of the dough was used for loaves of bread. The dough is flattened and folded over salted butter and sugar several times, to make a simple enriched layered dough. Shaped into a boule and pierced through, so that the butter and sugar melt down to make a caramelized bottom crust, the dough is transformed into a brilliant rustic cake (*kouign* means cake in the Breton language and *amann* means butter).

Serves 8 to 10

Flour for dusting

About 1½ pounds/675 grams whole-grain or part-whole-grain well-risen bread dough, at room temperature

⅓ pound/150 grams ice-cold salted butter, plus about 2 tablespoons butter, melted

About ¾ cup/150 grams granulated sugar

Lightly flour your work surface and your hands, and gently flatten the dough into a rectangle about 12 inches/30 cm long and 5 to 6 inches/12 to 15 cm wide. Thinly slice the cold butter and divide into 3 equal portions. Place one portion, in pieces, evenly over two-thirds of the length of the dough. Sprinkle over about ¼ cup/50 grams of the sugar. Fold the bare top third of the dough over the center, then fold the other flap over, as if you were folding a letter. Rotate the dough 90 degrees, flatten it out again to a rectangle, and repeat with another third of the butter and a little more than half the remaining sugar. Turn and flatten once more, then repeat with the last third of butter only. The dough will feel soft and weak and the butter may be breaking through a little. Don't worry.

Lightly grease a 9-inch/22 cm cast-iron or other heavy ovenproof skillet with butter. Place the dough in the skillet and flatten it gently, pressing it lightly out

continued

with your fingertips toward the edges of the pan to form a round. With a sharp knife, make 6 or 7 cuts (each about 2 inches/5 cm long) right down through the bottom of the dough in a starburst pattern radiating out from near the center, but not meeting there.

Cover the dough loosely with a cotton cloth or plastic wrap and let rise for 45 minutes to an hour at cool room temperature (a little over 68°F/20°C). The dough will rise a little, but it will not double in volume because it is so weighed down with butter.

Meanwhile, place an oven rack in the center of the oven and set a baking stone or pizza stone on it, if you have one, or use a baking sheet. Preheat the oven to 450°F/230°C.

Just before baking, brush the melted butter generously over the cake and sprinkle on the remaining 2 to 3 tablespoons of sugar. Bake for 20 to 25 minutes, until very golden brown. Remove from the oven.

Both the top and bottom of the cake will have a caramelized surface. Remove it from the pan, decide whether you want it top or bottom side up, and place on a rack accordingly to cool for at least 30 minutes. Serve warm, cut into wedges.

MISO COOKIES
with Dark Chocolate Chips

These shortbread-like whole-grain cookies are lush with butter and richly flavored with dark chocolate and miso, all of which bring out the taste of the flour. If you have a favorite whole-grain wheat or spelt flour, use it combined with whole wheat pastry flour in a 50:50 ratio as set out below. If you don't yet have a favorite whole-grain flour, use this as an opportunity to look for freshly milled whole-grain flour, preferably from a single varietal of wheat. If your whole-grain flour is very coarsely ground, start by sifting out the coarsest bran from 10 ounces/300 grams of flour, then measure out the flour you need for the recipe.

I use organic cane sugar, but you can use whatever you have. As for the miso, you want a good shiro (white) miso; if you have only red miso, use it but reduce the quantity to 2½ teaspoons.

I mix the dough in a stand mixer. If you don't have one, you can make it by hand or in a food processor.

The cookies are brushed with a miso-flavored milk wash just before they go into the oven. (Again, if using red miso, reduce the amount, to ³/₄ teaspoon.) Make them the day before you wish to serve them, if possible. They come into full flavor and texture once they've had an overnight rest.

These instructions are adapted from a recipe developed by my friend Dawn Woodward, aka dawnthebaker, of Evelyn's Crackers, a dedicated professional whole-grain baker.

Makes about 40 cookies

DOUGH

2½ cups/250 grams whole-grain Red Fife flour or your favorite whole-grain flour (see headnote)

2 cups/250 grams whole wheat pastry flour

¾ pound/3 sticks/360 grams cold unsalted butter (preferably cultured butter), coarsely chopped

¾ cup/160 grams granulated sugar

½ teaspoon fine sea salt

4 teaspoons shiro (white) miso (see headnote)

2½ ounces/75 grams dark chocolate (70% cacao), finely chopped, or small chocolate chips

MILK WASH

1 teaspoon shiro (white) miso (see headnote)

1 tablespoon milk

To make the dough, combine the two flours, butter, sugar, salt, and miso in the bowl of a stand mixer fitted with the paddle attachment and mix on low speed until a dough starts to form, scraping down the bowl as needed. Add the chocolate and mix for another 30 seconds or so.

Turn the dough out onto a very lightly floured surface and pull it together into a firm shape. Cut into 4 equal pieces and roll each one under your hands into a cylinder about 6 inches/15 cm long and 1½ inches/4 cm in diameter. Wrap each one in plastic wrap, wax paper, or foil and refrigerate for at least 1 hour, and as long as overnight, whatever is most convenient.

Place the racks in the upper and lower thirds of the oven and preheat the oven to 350°F/175°C. Line two baking sheets with parchment paper.

For the wash, dissolve the miso in the milk in a small bowl, whisking to blend well. Put out a pastry brush.

Cut the dough cylinders crosswise into approximately ½-inch/1 cm thick pieces and lay the cookies on the parchment-lined baking sheets, leaving 2 inches/5 cm between them. Brush the wash onto the tops of the cookies.

Bake for about 18 minutes, or until the edges of the undersides are lightly touched with color; use a spatula to carefully lift one or two cookies to check. The cookies are very soft when they come out of the oven, so leave them on the baking sheets for 30 minutes to firm up a little before transferring them to a rack to cool and firm up completely.

If you can, wait a day, or at least overnight, before serving the cookies, for their flavor develops further after they cool.

SALTED ALMOND CHOCOLATE BRITTLE

An airy version of nut brittle, with savory overtones from soy sauce, this treat is made of toasted almonds topped with a skim of dark chocolate and, if you'd like, fleur de sel or another flake salt. I'm grateful to my friend Cassandra Kobayashi for developing the recipe.

Make the basic version first and then play with additional flavors if you wish: you could include a pinch of ground cayenne in the syrup, use peanuts or toasted sesame seeds with or instead of the almonds, and on top, instead of flake salt try a pepper-salt mixture such as Sichuan Pepper Salt or Chile Salt (page 37).

Prepare all your ingredients in advance and please read through the recipe before starting. You'll need a digital candy thermometer to show you when the syrup has reached the "hard crack" stage, 300°F/150°C. Monitor the temperature closely as the syrup heats, because just a few seconds can make the difference between perfect and burnt.

Makes two 9-by-7-inch/23 by 18 cm rectangles (to break into pieces)

1 cup/140 grams raw whole almonds or Salted Almonds (page 71)

1 teaspoon baking soda

2 ounces/60 grams dark chocolate, chopped into ¼-inch/0.5 cm pieces

1 cup/200 grams granulated sugar

2 tablespoons corn syrup

1 tablespoon molasses (dark or blackstrap)

4 tablespoons/60 grams salted butter

2 tablespoons water

1 tablespoon soy sauce, such as regular Kikkoman

About 1 teaspoon fleur de sel or other flake salt (optional)

If using raw almonds, preheat the oven to 325°F/165°C, or set a dry heavy skillet over medium heat.

Spread the almonds on a small baking sheet and roast them in the oven for 10 to 12 minutes, until aromatic and touched with color. Or toast them in the skillet, shaking the pan, for just a few minutes. Set the nuts aside to cool.

Or, if using the salted almonds, roast them in the oven or toast them in the skillet, but reduce the cooking times by at least half; since they are already roasted, you just want to crisp them up a bit. Set aside to cool.

Coarsely chop the nuts; set aside.

Lightly oil two sheets of parchment paper. Arrange one-third of the nut pieces to make a 9-by-6-inch/22 by 15 cm rectangle on each sheet; reserve the remaining nuts to use as a topping.

continued

Place the baking soda and chopped chocolate near your stovetop. Have an oiled silicone spatula and your thermometer nearby too.

Combine the sugar, corn syrup, molasses, butter, water, and soy sauce in a heavy pot and bring to a boil over medium-low heat, stirring with the oiled spatula just until the sugar is dissolved. (Having the pot on a burner that is no bigger than the bottom of the pan will help with even heating.) Let the mixture come to a boil, without stirring it again; if it seems to be heating unevenly, swirl the pan gently. Bring the syrup to 300°F/150°C, the hard crack stage. As the water boils off, the mixture will darken and the uniform bubble pattern will change to a "tufted" look, with some areas pulled down between puffed-up sections of bubbles. Once the syrup reaches 300°F/150°C, the hard crack stage, immediately remove the pot from the heat (if the syrup turns a shade darker beyond this, it can quickly burn). Immediately add the baking soda and stir vigorously with the oiled spatula to incorporate. The mixture will bubble up and lighten in color. (Be careful not to touch the pot or syrup, which will be extremely hot.)

Pour and scrape the syrup onto the rectangles of chopped almonds on the parchment and use the oiled spatula to spread the syrup out. Let cool for 30 seconds, then sprinkle with the chopped chocolate. As the chocolate melts, use the spatula to spread it over the brittle. Sprinkle on a little salt if you'd like, and then the remaining chopped almonds. Press lightly on the almonds to help them stick.

Let cool completely. (If it's a hot day, finish cooling the brittle in the refrigerator.) Break into chunks once cool and store in a well-sealed bag or container at room temperature.

SALTED DRINKS

We're accustomed to salting our food, but many drinks can also benefit from salt. Salt is an essential ingredient in hot-season drinks in different parts of India, most often black salt, or kala namak (see page 23), which is used to flavor cooling green mango juice. The mangoes are cooked, often grilled or roasted, then peeled and blended with water, cumin, black pepper, black salt, sugar, and sometimes mint leaves to make a very refreshing tart-sweet-salty drink.

Also on the subcontinent, lassi, made from yogurt and water, is usually a salted savory drink, although in the West, people most often make sweet versions (banana or mango lassi being the go-tos). In Iran, Iraq, and Afghanistan, similar yogurt drinks (called *ayran* in Farsi and *doogh* in Arabic) made with water or soda water are salted, and sometimes flavored with a pinch of cumin or with mint.

A little salt added to lemonade will enhance the sweetness and enliven the citrus while neutralizing any bitterness. And salted tart fruits such as umeboshi plums make a delicious drink when used to flavor soda water.

Salt tea with butter, almost a meal in itself, is the staple traditional drink of Tibetans, and also of Mongolian people. Butter tea is made in a kind of churn, a tall narrow wooden cylinder with a pole set into it. The steeped tea is put into the cylinder, butter and salt are added, and then churned and blended. Perhaps because of salt in the groundwater, the clear tea of the Uyghurs of Xinjiang in northwest China is also salty.

In Ethiopia, some people add salt to their coffee instead of sugar. And salt is a classic ingredient in campfire coffee to lessen bitterness. That may also be part of its role in the harsh-tasting brick tea of the Tibetans and Mongols, along with providing electrolytes.

On the alcoholic drinks front, we're used to the rim of salt on a margarita glass, which adds sparkle to the lime juice. In times past, cold sake was salted, and that has now returned. Salt can have a role with other cocktails beyond margaritas. Because it dampens the intensity of bitter, a light touch of salt can bring sweetness forward and make citrus flavors dance. Added in the form of a mild brine, salt releases aromatic molecules into the drink, enhancing that first sip. Brine is an important tool for bartenders, sometimes hidden, sometimes celebrated, as it is in dirty martinis, which use the brine from olives. I was surprised when I realized how often it contributes to mixed drinks.

Salt as a complement to drinks is as familiar as beer and salted snacks. But in Oaxaca, home of mescal, there's another kind of salt complement. Crisp fruit such as jicama or pineapple is a side snack eaten with mescal, but first it's sprinkled with *sal de gusano* (see Glossary). You can also sprinkle your bar snacks with one of the pepper salts in this book (page 37) or another flavored salt.

LEFT TO RIGHT: *Umeboshi plums with soda water; mango lassi; aryan (tart yogurt drink); martini with olives and a little brine; mescal (with sal de gusano and orange slices alongside); classic margarita with chile salt on the rim*

SOME SALT CHEMISTRY

THE SALT WE EAT IS SODIUM CHLORIDE, NaCl. THE SODIUM IS WHAT GIVES IT the taste of salt. (The only other salt that tastes "salty" is lithium salt, a pairing of lithium with chloride. Potassium salt and calcium salt both have a bitter taste.)

A salt molecule is 40 percent sodium by weight and 60 percent chlorine. A teaspoon of fine table salt (which is denser than most other salts) weighs slightly over 6 grams and contains just over 2 grams of sodium, sodium being the element that's most significant in nutritional health.

Seawater is about 3.5 percent salt by weight. That means that 1 quart (about 1 liter) contains about 2 tablespoons (about 35 grams) of salt, mostly sodium chloride, with traces of other salts. When saltwater evaporates, salt precipitates out.

Harvesting salt that is dissolved in water requires energy to evaporate the water, converting the water into a gas. To evaporate 1 gram of water, you need about 540 calories of energy—traditionally from the sun or from a wood, gas, or coal fire. You can imagine the effort and ingenuity traditional people had to put into making salt from seawater or other liquid salt sources.

If you would like to harvest salt yourself, and you live near a source of unpolluted seawater, pour some of it through a fine strainer (say, a fine cloth or fine filter) to strain out dirt particles, put it in a pot, and boil it down until you are left with salt.

The food writer and oyster fisher Tamar Haspel has written that she keeps a pot of seawater on her woodstove in winter to help humidify the house. The result is sea salt, for as the water evaporates, the salt precipitates out.

ANTI-CAKING ADDITIVES

In high humidity, a thin layer of moisture coats each salt granule or crystal. It's not pure water, but is actually brine: it has a little salt dissolved in it. When the air gets drier, the salt in the brine recrystallizes, and these crystals connect and bind the salt together, caking it. The old home remedy against caking was to keep a little rice in the saltcellar. The rice absorbed moisture and helped break up clumps.

The modern commercial remedy is to add an anti-caking agent, which works either by absorbing moisture or by coating the crystals so that those on the surface don't dissolve.

Most table salt contains about 2 percent anti-caking agent; some kosher and refined sea salts also contain anti-caking agents. You may see yellow prussiate of soda (which is an old and less scary term for sodium ferrocyanide) or potassium ferrocyanide, sodium aluminosilicate, calcium carbonate, magnesium carbonate, monocalcium phosphate, tricalcium phosphate, or silicon dioxide listed on the label. I generally choose additive-free salts, but if you live in a very humid climate, you might want salt with an anti-caking additive.

WHY IS SALT IODIZED?

Iodine is an important mineral that helps control thyroid function and related activities. As our bodies don't make it, we need to get it from other sources. Iodine deficiency causes goiter (an enlarged thyroid) and other health problems. In earlier times, when everyone mostly ate locally, people living near the sea had access to iodine-rich foods such as seaweed and ocean fish, and the soil nearer the sea tends to be more iodine-rich as well, so crops grown in it contain some iodine. Sea salt contains a small amount of iodine, though not enough to provide an adequate supply on its own.

The soils in mountain regions and in some river valleys are iodine-poor, though, and people living in those areas and eating only foods produced there have historically been iodine-deficient.

Public health authorities around the world realized about a century ago that salt is an extremely practical way of distributing iodine as a nutritional supplement; the US and Switzerland were the first countries to make iodized salt a priority. The goal of ensuring that everyone in the world has adequate iodine in their diet has thus become the goal of iodizing regular table salt in every country. This effort is paying off. Recent World Health Organization reports show that in most of the world, iodized salt is the norm, and the incidence of goiter and other iodine-deficiency conditions has fallen dramatically.

Iodized salt, particularly industrially processed iodized salt in the more prosperous countries, often contains anti-caking agents in addition to iodine. The salt has usually been cleaned of every other trace mineral, so it has no aroma except that of iodine. In North America, iodized salt sometimes contains a little added sugar, because the form of iodine used there to iodize salt is potassium iodide (instead of the potassium iodate used in the rest of the world). Because potassium iodide is less stable in moist or hot environments, dextrose (a sugar) is added to help stabilize it.

The campaigns to iodize salt have also worked hard to persuade citizens that iodized salt is cleaner and better. The result is that in Thailand, for example, despite the existence of good-tasting local salt, I was told by a chef there that most people think of non-iodized local salt as unclean. It's often difficult now to find anything but iodized salt in local markets in Thailand and in other countries as well.

But many cooks today in affluent societies prefer not to use iodized salt, knowing that we can get enough iodine from other sources. Iodized salt has a distinctive, not particularly pleasant taste and smell. Note that not all table salt is iodized.

Regardless of your feelings about iodized salt, it's important to avoid using it for pickling, because the iodine can cause discoloration in your vegetables. That is one of the reasons pickling salt contains no additives at all.

SALT AND OUR BODIES

Salt is critical for humans (and animals) because it controls fluid balance and facilitates nerve and muscle function. We regulate our salt amounts mostly through our kidneys, preserving the amount we need and excreting any excess. We also lose salt when we sweat, so we need to replenish it.

Salt accounts for about 0.4 percent of our body weight. Our blood is particularly salty, about 9 percent salt. When we seriously lack salt, our saliva changes. It becomes less salty, and we become more sensitive to the taste of salt. Perhaps this is a question of survival: once humans became sensitive to the taste, they were more able to detect even faint traces of salt and to seek it out successfully. Hunting cultures get enough salt from meat (remember that salty blood), but once humans began to depend more heavily on grains and plants, they needed extra salt. Similarly, in the animal world, herbivores need more salt than carnivores.

We don't generally consciously consume salt to maintain our 0.4 percent balance; we use salt because we like the flavor. In the industrial world, that can mean that we're eating more salt than we should. Overconsumption of salt is linked to high blood pressure, kidney disease, heart disease, and stroke. Doctors believe that we should consume less than 3 grams per day, or about 1/2 teaspoon of table salt, but the average consumption in developed countries is closer to 1 1/2 teaspoons (9 grams). The greatest source of salt in most people's diet is processed food that contains large quantities of salt.

Salt-encrusted wall at the Salinas de Añana

SALT GEOGRAPHY & HARVESTING TECHNIQUES

THE STORY OF HUMANS AND SALT IS A COMPLEX ONE. OVER THE COURSE OF human history, humans have developed a number of ingenious ways of producing salt. Some of these have been deduced by archaeologists from remnants and ruins, some were recorded, and, of course, some, both industrial and artisanal, are still used today.

Historically, the way that a particular salt was produced depended on where it was located, and in what form, and on the technology available at the time.

Unless the salt is waiting out in the open to be gathered, as crystals by the side of a salt lake or the seashore, it is necessary to put energy into producing it. If it's rock salt (halite) underground, it needs to be mined. If it's dissolved in water, either in the ocean or in a saltwater well inland, that water needs to be collected and evaporated, by the sun or else by boiling, which requires valuable fuel. In prehistoric times, boiling saltwater only happened once people had figured out how to make crude containers (out of dried or baked clay) that could be placed on some kind of tripod over a fire without breaking or leaking.

Below are the basic ways salt is found in the environment and some of the harvesting methods and technologies that humans have invented to extract it.

GATHERED

There are many places this still happens. Salt is gathered from the Wood Buffalo Salt Plains in northern Alberta, Canada, and from Tuz Golu in Turkey. It is cut by hand from salt pans in Ethiopia's Danakil. For many centuries, salt has been cut from salt pans and shallow deposits near the Sahara Desert. Because the water of, for example, Lac Rose in Senegal and the Dead Sea, between Jordan and Israel, is supersaturated, salt can be gathered from underneath the water (see page 267). The Salar de Uyuni, a huge salt flat and salt deposit in Bolivia, has salt lying on the surface that has traditionally been gathered by local people. (There are also huge quantities of brine under the surface that are pumped out and evaporated.)

Salt deposits are relatively soft, for a rock, and so sometimes get squeezed out of the rock layers where they are found, appearing on the surface. The result is what people call "salt glaciers," which occur in dry desert places such as Xinjiang, in western China, and Iran.

In Bo Kleua (see page 227) the brine from the salt well is boiled in large wok-like pans set into a kind of stove over a wood fire, until the salt floats up and can be skimmed off. Here baskets of harvested salt hang, draining off the last of their bittern (see nigari in Glossary), while more brine boils beneath them.

MINED

The first salt place I ever visited was a salt mine near Salzberg. There was an underground lake, caverns carved out of the rock, and history going back thousands of years. There's a cathedral in the salt mine of Zipaquira in Colombia. And there are similar rock salt mines in Poland, Germany, Pakistan (in Khewra, home of pink salt), and northeastern England.

Nowadays rock salt may be mined with dynamite, as in other hard-rock mining, or it may be dug out with machinery. At many salt mines, the salt is now "mined" with water and then evaporated out.

EVAPORATED

If salt is dissolved in water, as it is in the oceans and in salt wells and salt springs, harvesting it requires energy to evaporate the water. One possible source of energy is the sun, or a combination of sun and wind. Another is fire or another heat source that can be used to boil the brine. (Brine from the sea is on average 3.5 percent salt; brine from salt wells varies in salinity.)

Here's a glimpse of various salt-harvest evaporation methods and some of the places past and present where they have been used.

EVAPORATED BY THE SUN AND WIND

Seawater is solar-evaporated in salterns (basins) in places where there's plenty of wind and sunshine, including Guérande and Ile de Ré on the Atlantic coast of France; Trapani, in Sicily; Messolonghi, in Greece; Gozo, Malta; Kampot, Cambodia; southern Thailand; Pangasinen, in the Philippines; Sinan County, South Korea (where the highly prized cheonilyeom salt is produced); Khatch in the Gujarat region of India; Hawaii; San Francisco Bay; Amagansett, on Long Island; and many more locations.

In Maras, Peru (near Cusco), the brine from the salt spring flows downhill onto evaporation terraces built of terra-cotta/clay on steep hillsides, and the salt is then raked up from there (see page 313). Salt production in Añana, Spain (in Basque Country), uses a similar technique, in which the brine flows downhill through a succession of evaporation terraces (previously clay-based and now largely cement-lined), finally concentrating for harvest at the bottom of the hill (see page 284).

Tools of the trade at the Salinas de Añana: paddles for skimming salt and baskets for collecting it, with the salt evaporation ponds behind, and on the hillside, storage places underneath the structures that support the terraces

EVAPORATED BY BOILING

Seawater is boiled over a fire—originally fueled by wood, peat, dried branches, or coal, and now usually fired with natural gas—in many places, including Maldon in Essex and Gweek in Cornwall; Vancouver Island and Saltspring Island, British Columbia; Newfoundland; any prefecture in Japan that has a seacoast; Oregon; and Achill Island and Beara Peninsula, in Ireland.

Most of the brine that is hauled or pumped up from salt wells has historically been boiled over a fire to produce salt. The outstanding example of this technique is found at the huge saltworks in Sichuan, the first place where deep salt-well technology was developed and used, beginning more than two thousand years ago. At least as early as the fifteenth century, local natural gas was used to power the pumping of brine to the surface and to boil the brine. Other historically notable places include the salt wells near Liverpool, in Droitwich and other "wiches," and Avery Island, Louisiana, where a huge salt dome was exploited in pre-Columbian times by aboriginal peoples, and more recently by various commercial interests. And there has been small-village salt making for centuries in many places in Europe, and in Southeast Asia, some of it still active (see Bo Kleua, page 227).

Seawater is boiled using geothermal energy by a producer called Saltverk in Reykjanes in western Iceland. Geothermal springs heat the seawater, first to concentrate the brine, and then to do the final evaporation to create salt crystals.

CONCENTRATING BRINE BEFORE BOILING

The higher the salt content of the brine, the less time or fuel is required. In places where fuel is in short supply, and sunshine is scarce, people long ago figured out various ingenious ways of concentrating the brine, sometimes letting nature do the work, before doing the final heating for evaporation.

On the Noto Peninsula of Japan, salt producers use *enden* methods, spraying or tossing seawater onto finely raked sand over and over, to leave a salty residue, then rinsing the sand with seawater strained through a filter to produce a more concentrated brine, before boiling it down. A similar method is to spray seawater onto bamboo screens over and over, then rinse the screens with seawater. The resulting brine, which has a higher salt concentration, is then boiled down.

In Senegal and elsewhere, at low tide (if it hasn't rained), the soil of the banks of tidal rivers has extra salt. Small salt makers gather the soil, rinse it off through a filter, using incoming tidal seawater, and then boil down the brine.

In northern Russia, the Pomors, who are a Russian population living in Karelia along the coast of the White Sea, traditionally concentrated seawater by freezing. The area is like a bay of the Arctic Ocean, a subregion with its own history and culture. We're used to thinking of salt making as a product of heat and evaporation, but in earlier times, the Pomors used cold as the first step: in winter, they froze barrels of seawater. A layer of freshwater ice (because fresh water freezes at a higher temperature than saltwater and is less dense) would rise to the surface and could be discarded. Repeated several times, this left a more concentrated brine in the barrel, which could then be boiled down to produce salt.

In Kwa Zulu in South Africa, there are salt deposits around the salt spring called Baleni. It's a sacred place that women visit every year in the dry season in order to gather salt. They collect the salty mud at the edge of the swamp by the spring, then rinse it through a filter to get a clean brine, which they then boil down. People in other places in Africa and elsewhere with no access to salt springs or salt deposits developed similar techniques of scraping salty mud, cleaning it through filters, and then boiling the brine over a fire.

MODERN MINING AND EVAPORATION METHODS

Most large salt deposits are now exploited using salt-well technology: Water is pumped underground to dissolve the salt. The brine is then pumped to the surface, evaporated, and processed using the modern methods described below.

Today commercial processing of salt from brine, whether seawater or land-based brine, is done by vacuum evaporation rather than in open pans. The salt is then refined in various ways to eliminate impurities, such as magnesium and calcium salts and any dirt or organic matter, and to create crystals of specific shapes and sizes, from those of kosher salt to fine or coarse pickling salt, along with a range of sizes of refined sea salt.

SALT ARCHAEOLOGY

Salt archaeology is a growing field. Early settlements in China, in Romania, in England, at Ban Chang in Thailand, and in many other places are being analyzed via the remnants and debris of the salt-making technologies that these early peoples used. In the Neolithic and Bronze Ages, people figured out various methods of evaporating water in coarse clay basins set on tripods or supports above fires. The broken remnants of these "beakers" and the legs or stubs of crudely fired clay that supported them above the fires are evidence of early salt-making technology. Sometimes the salt-making place was part of a settlement, sometimes those locations seem to have been used only seasonally. These archaeologists have also found other remnants, smaller containers that these early peoples used to store or transport salt. When those pots or bowls are found in locations farther away from the original settlement, they may indicate trade.

The research into early salt-making has also looked at other uses of salt in prehistoric times. Those include strengthening ceramics, tanning hides, cheese-making, separating gold from silver, and more. The conclusion the specialists draw is that availability of salt was a major factor in the location of early settlements, not just for food and food preservation reasons, but also for all kinds of trade and manufacturing reasons.

BREATH AND SALT

Several years ago, Elvira Santamaria, a conceptual artist from Mexico City, staged a mesmerizing performance piece called "Salt Cartographies" at Sur Gallery in Toronto.

Over a number of days, she worked to sculpt a salt landscape on the floor of the gallery, using only her breath. This was breath as a direct tool for creating art, rather than as a means for talking or for making music. Her deliberateness was memorable, as was the concentration it took to move waves of fine salt with only her breath. I sat entranced for several hours, taking the occasional photograph, listening to the soft sound of her breath, watching her get up from the ground to move to another spot on the edge of the landscape, where she'd lie back down, look carefully at the area she was intending to work on, and blow again. Sometimes she blew in short, sharp gusts, other times in long, slow sweeps, making the fine grains drift and tremble into new shapes.

I had been thinking about this book project for more than a year by then. Her work was an inspiring reminder that there are many ways of honoring our essentials.

Conceptual artist Elvira Santamaria creates a salt landscape, breath by breath, in "Salt Cartographies," her 2018 performance at the Sur Gallery in Toronto.

GLOSSARY

ACKEE: The fruit of *Blighia sapida*, an evergreen tree native to tropical West Africa, ackee is, like the lychee and the longan, a member of the Sapindaceae (soapberry) family. Seeds were brought to the Americas by enslaved people and traders in the late eighteenth century. The trees flourished in Jamaica, where the national dish is ackee and saltfish (see page 259). The fruits are pear-shaped and red. The fruit pulp can be eaten only once it is fully ripe. The seeds of the unripe fruit are poisonous, which is why it is illegal to import raw ackee into some countries, including the US. In North America, ackee is mostly available canned. The fruit pulp is a creamy white when raw, and turns a strong yellow when cooked.

ALEPPO PEPPER: Ground dried red chiles that turn a deep burgundy red when ripe, Aleppo pepper has a fruity taste and mild to medium heat. Because a little salt is used in the drying process, the pepper has a slight saltiness. It's a delicious table condiment as well as an ingredient in dishes from the eastern Mediterranean. Peppers grown and processed in southern Turkey, such as Urfa from Sanliurfa and Antep from Gaziantep, can be substituted.

ALLSPICE: The fruit of a tree, *Pimenta dioica*, that is native to the Americas, allspice has a warming flavor and an aroma reminiscent of a blend of cinnamon, clove, and nutmeg. It is also known as Jamaica pepper or myrtle pepper. The fruits are picked green and then sun-dried. They look like large smooth peppercorns, a little smaller than juniper berries, and are medium brown in color. Allspice is used in meat dishes and desserts.

AMCHOOR POWDER: A tart flavoring made from green mangoes that are dried and ground to a powder. The aroma is slightly sweet, but the taste is pleasingly tart. Because the mangoes are peeled and sliced before being sun-dried, the flesh turns pale brown, and the powder is a tan color. It keeps well and is a useful source of tart mango intensity when the fruit is out of season.

ASAFOETIDA: A seasoning derived from the root of a plant in the Umbelliferae family, asafoetida substitutes for the pungency of onion and garlic in strict Hindu cooking, and as a flavor enhancer in other South Asian cooking. The root of the plant is cut and the resin that is exuded is scraped off and dried, then ground into a powder. When raw, the powder smells strongly of sulfur, but when cooked in a dish, the sulfurous element dissipates.

BARBERRIES: The fruit of the shrub *Berberis vulgaris*, which grows wild in parts of Asia and Europe, these are small, bright-to-dark red, tart, and loaded with vitamin C. They are widely used, both fresh and dried, in Persian cooking, added to rice dishes, for example, to give a tart flavor. Because barberry bushes can host wheat rust, many parts of North America ban the commercial growing of barberries. Consequently, most of the barberries sold in North America are imported in dried form.

BEAN SPROUTS, MUNG AND SOY: Bean sprouts are hypocotyls, the tender stems that beans send out when they germinate. The most commonly available in grocery stores are those of mung beans (*Vigna radiata*). Mung bean sprouts are fine, tender filaments that are best lightly cooked, although some people do eat them raw. Store them in the refrigerator and wash well before cooking. Soybean sprouts, from soybeans (*Glycine max*), are thicker and stronger-textured than mung bean sprouts. They are most often found in Chinese and other Asian grocery stores. Sometimes they come with the remnant bean seed attached, but often it has been picked off, because it is a little tough and takes longer to cook than the sprout.

BIRD CHILES: Also known by their Thai name, *prik ee noo*, bird chiles are small, pointed, and quite hot; they may be green or red. Unlike most other chiles, bird chiles come from a perennial variety of capsicum. Bird chiles are sold in Southeast Asian grocery stores and in larger well-stocked groceries.

BLUE FENUGREEK: Called *utsko suneli* in the Republic of Georgia, blue fenugreek (*Trigonella caerulea*) is used widely in Georgian dishes. It is a native of West Asia and Europe, is related to regular fenugreek, but it has a sweeter, more herbal flavor. The plant is harvested as it finishes blooming and both the dried leaves

---

and fine stems and the seedpods are used for flavor. When crushed, it has some of the maple-syrup aroma of regular fenugreek. Dried fenugreek leaves can be substituted. Blue fenugreek imported from Georgia has recently become more available in the West, and some is now being grown in North America.

BONITO FLAKES: *See* Katsuobushi

CASSIA: *See* Cinnamon/cassia

CAYENNE CHILES: Cayenne chiles are medium-hot, long, pointed, slightly fleshy, and either green or red. I think of them as the workhorse chile of Asia. They're sold in many Asian groceries. Dried red cayenne chiles are called for in many South Asian recipes. When ground to a powder, dried red cayenne chiles are the spice called cayenne.

CELERY LEAVES: The leaves of celery (*Apium graveolens*) are coarser than coriander (cilantro) leaves, with a strong celery aroma and taste. Sold in East and Southeast Asian groceries.

CHEONILYEOM: A Korean sea salt that is somewhat coarse-textured and prized for pickling and making kimchi, this is produced by solar evaporation; the name translates as solar salt. Coarse pickling salt or sea salt can be substituted. Sinan County, Korea, is the area best known for producing it.

CINNAMON/CASSIA: The spice labeled "cinnamon" in many markets is often cassia (*Cinnamonum cassia*),

from a tree related to the cinnamon tree (*Cinnamonum verum*). Both cinnamon and cassia are harvested as "quills," which are curved dried pieces of the aromatic bark. Cinnamon quills are pale tan, easy to break, and have a complex floral aroma; cassia quills have a tougher texture. The flavor of ground cassia is more intense and less nuanced than that of true cinnamon. You can use the two interchangeably in recipes.

CONGEE (ALSO KANJEE, KHAO TOM, JOK): A soothing rice soup or rice porridge, most often eaten for breakfast or a late-night snack, congee is made of plain rice cooked in plenty of water until the grains are softened or even broken into a smooth mass (depending on the culture and the cook). Congee can be topped with many kinds of savory flavorings; many of these toppings come from the salt larder, from brined pickles in Japan to hardcooked brined eggs in China.

DRIED MANGO POWDER: *See* Amchoor powder

FENUGREEK SEEDS, FENUGREEK LEAVES: Fenugreek is a leguminous plant (*Trigonella foenum graecum* L.) that has triangular brown-gold seeds. Both the seeds and the leaves are used, the seeds as a spice and the leaves as an herb and a vegetable. Fenugreek seeds are used as a spice in South Asian cooking and in Ethiopia. Ground fenugreek seeds are the essential ingredient in the paste that coats basturma (see page 172). *See also* Blue fenugreek.

GALANGAL: A relative of ginger, galangal is a rhizome, *Alpinia galanga*, widely used in Thai cooking. It has a warming resiny flavor without the hot bite of ginger. The rhizomes are fine-skinned and pale yellow-white in color, with regular parallel fine dark lines around them, often with a pinkish tinge at the growing end. You can find galangal in many Asian grocery stores. Look for plump, firm rhizomes. Dried galangal has little flavor.

GLUTINOUS RICE FLOUR: The flour ground from raw sticky rice, also known as glutinous rice, and sold in Asian groceries. Regular rice flour and glutinous rice flour are not interchangeable, so please read the labels carefully.

GOCHUGARU: Korean chile powder made from ground dried red Korean chiles, which are mildly hot, gochugaru is used in kimchi and chile oil, and it is also put out as a table condiment. It's available at Korean grocery stores; look for coarsely ground chile powder that is labeled sun-dried (*taek-yung* or *taek-yang* in Korean), which is more expensive but has a more interesting flavor. It's a bit sweet, smoky, and fruity. Store in a glass jar out of the sun.

GOCHUJANG: Gochujang is a Korean chile paste that is sweet and hot. The sweet comes from glutinous rice and malted barley powder and the heat from fine Korean chile powder. It is used to add depth and a little heat to bean dishes, meat stews, and many other dishes.

ALBANIAN: kripë • **AMHARIC:** chewi • **ARABIC:** milh • **ARMENIAN:** agh •

GREEN MANGO: There are two categories of green mango—those that are very tart and green even when ripe, and those that are green because they are unripe. The green mango called for in this book is the unripe one. The season for green mangoes (from India or Southeast Asia) is March until May; they are sold in many Asian grocery stores. If left at room temperature, they will ripen and sweeten and gradually turn a golden yellow. *See also* Amchoor powder.

HALITE: *Halite* is the technical term for the mineral we call salt, NaCl, or sodium chloride, when it has been mined from the earth rather than evaporated from saltwater. A chunk of halite is called rock salt. See page 10.

JUJUBES: *Ziziphus jujube* is a small tree that bears reddish fruits known variously as jujubes, red dates, or Chinese dates. The fruit is used to flavor tea and healing soups in China and as a sweet ingredient in kimchi and soups in Korea. The fruits are meaty like dates and date-shaped with a long narrow pit, but they're not as sugary sweet as dates. Look for them in Asian groceries.

JUNIPER BERRIES: Although they look like berries, these fruits of various species of *Juniperus* (small evergreen trees) are actually small, smooth coniferous cones. They are usually the size of coriander seeds or a little larger, round, and firm. Fresh juniper berries are green (the stage at which they are used to flavor gin), but they slowly ripen and age into a dull blue-black. They need to be slightly crushed or cooked in liquid to release their flavor, for their outer layer is not aromatic.

KAHM YEAST: An aerobic yeast that appears as a fine white or creamy white film on the top of low-salt ferments once the pH has dropped, kahm yeast is not harmful, and it is NOT a mold. If it forms during fermentation, just skim it off. Once refrigerated, kahm will grow much more slowly.

KATSUOBUSHI: Often referred to in the West as bonito flakes, katsuoboshi flakes are made from tuna that is cooked, smoked, and fermented, not salt-preserved. They give dashi broth its umami depth and are also used as a garnish on cooked dishes.

KOMBU: There are many varieties of edible kelp, and *kombu* is the word used for many of them. The sheets of dried kombu used in Japan for making dashi are sold in clear cellophane packaging. Seek out wild kombu if possible. The sheets are tough and thick but will soften in warm water. Kombu should be heated in hot water but not boiled.

LEMONGRASS: Lemongrass is an aromatic widely used in Southeast Asian cooking. Choose firm, heavy stalks, a sign of freshness. To use, trim off the tough root ends, then very thinly slice the bottom 2 inches/5 cm or so of the stalks (the upper part is not aromatic) or smash the stalks with the flat side of a cleaver or a heavy knife to use whole as an aromatic in liquids. Lemongrass grows well in a sunny location in relatively sandy soil.

LOVAGE: This tall perennial herb, *Levisticum officinale*, is strong tasting and vigorous, both in the garden and on the tongue. It has a sharp, intense celery flavor. The flowers are yellow

and the leaves are a medium green and matte-textured, with lobes and indents reminiscent of leaf celery.

MAKRUT (WILD LIME): The fruit and leaves of a tree, *Citrus histrix*, that produces bumpy green limes with aromatic zest and double-lobed perfumed leaves. Both the zest and leaves are used in Thai cooking, especially in the center and south of the country, but the fruit itself has little or no juice. The leaves are used whole as aromatics in Thai curries.

MARIGOLD PETALS, DRIED MARIGOLD: The dried petals of the marigold *Tagetes patula* are used as an herb in the Republic of Georgia and in some regions of Turkey. They are sold in Turkish and some other Eastern Mediterranean grocery stores. They add a yellow color and an earthy flavor as well as a slightly acid spiciness.

MIRIN: Mirin is a naturally sweet rice wine, about 14 percent alcohol, that is an important flavoring in the Japanese kitchen, giving dishes a fermented depth and a hint of sweetness. The alcohol is most often boiled off during cooking. Mirin can be found in many large grocery stores, as well as in Japanese and Korean markets. It can be replaced by sake sweetened with a little sugar.

MITSUBA: A parsley-like herb, mitsuba (*Cryptotaenia japonica*) is sold in Japanese and Korean grocery stores. It has a crisp freshness with a hint of celery, but without the intensity of celery leaf or lovage.

MUSTARD GREENS: The greens of *Brassica juncea*, which have a slightly hot taste, are delicious eaten raw when young, or blanched, stir-fried,

---

AZERI: duz • **BASQUE:** gatza • **BENGALI:** labana • **BURMESE:** sarr • **CATALAN:** sal •

or salt-pickled (see Quick Salt-Preserved Mustard Greens, page 66). They may be green or green tinged with a little dark red. Other varieties of mustard green, such as the spicy, lacy-edged brighter green leaf known as mizuna, may have a spicy edge but without a strong identifiable mustard flavor.

MUSTARD OIL: The oil extracted from the seeds of *Brassica juncea* and *Brassica nigra* (*see* Mustard seeds). Mustard oil, distinctive tasting and pungent, is an important ingredient in Bengali, Nepali, and various north Indian cuisines, giving a warming edge to dishes. Look for "first pressing" oil.

MUSTARD SEEDS/BLACK MUSTARD SEEDS, MUSTARD: The mustard seeds called for in the recipes this book are the seeds used in South Asian cooking, which are dark reddish brown to black. The seeds are usually dropped into hot oil early in the cooking process to pop, exposing the inner flavorful part of the seed to the oil. Mustard seeds are the source of mustard oil (see above). All mustards are brassicas; the two commonly used in South Asian cooking and for oil are *Brassica juncea* and *Brassica nigra*. Mustard seeds are ground to produce hot mustard (sometimes known as English-style mustard) and mustard powder; most other mustards are a blend of mustard paste, vinegar, and spices.

NAPA/NAPPA CABBAGE: Also known as Chinese cabbage or Chinese lettuce (and in Australia, as wombok), this brassica, *Brassica rapa* ssp. *pekinensis*, has become widely available; it is now grown not only in China, Korea, and Japan but also in North America and Europe. Its long, slightly stiff white leaves with pale-green frilled edges, attached at the root end, form a tight nested bundle. They are crisp and have a high water content. You can pull off the leaves one by one or cut the whole bundle crosswise, depending on how you wish to use it. Napa is the best known ingredient in classic kimchi.

NIGARI: Also called bittern, this is the magnesium-rich liquid that drains off sea salt as it is drying. Nigari is used in the production of tofu as a coagulant, much as rennet is used in cheese-making.

NIGELLA: These small black seeds, also known as kalonji or black onion seeds, among other names, come from the annual plant *Nigella sativa*, which has blue or white flowers. Nigella is native to West Asia but is now widely grown in Europe and North America. The seeds have a slight oniony taste and are rich in oils. They are sometimes sprinkled on flatbreads in West and South Asia, have a pleasant nutty taste when heated in oil, and are used to flavor curries and other simmered dishes; they are also one of the spices in the Bengali mix of whole spices known as *panch phoran*.

NORI: Nori is a processed seaweed widely used in Japan, most notably as a wrapper for the sushi rolls called *futomaki*. It is made by drying, shredding, and pressing various edible seaweeds into flat papery sheets. Nori is sold in packages of sheets, sometimes whole, sometimes pre-cut into strips. It is best toasted lightly before use. Some nori is sold pre-toasted, in which case its deep green has darkened to a blackish green color.

ONIGIRI: Japanese rice balls that are actually usually triangular in shape. They may be plain, but most often cooked rice is wrapped around a flavoring such as umeboshi plum and then smoothed and shaped into a thick triangle and wrapped in a strip of nori. Onigiri are classic snacks that are widely sold in Japanese and Korean groceries.

PERILLA: *See* Shiso

PIMENTÓN, SMOKED PAPRIKA: A specialty of Spain, made from ground, smoked red chiles, this spice has a seductive aroma and flavor. Smoked paprika can be sweet (*dulce*) or hot (*picante*). Smoked paprika has become more popular in North America recently and is now available in many grocery stores as well as spice shops and Mediterranean groceries.

POMEGRANATES, POMEGRANATE SEEDS: Pomegranates are the fruit of a low tree or shrub, *Punica granatum*, that is native to the eastern Mediterranean. They are in season from about late September until late April. Look for firm, heavy fruits. There are several methods of extracting the seeds. I like to cut a triangle in the skin, making a shallow cut that does not reach the seeds, and then lift it off. This gives access to the interior. You can then pull off sections of skin and lift the seeds off and into a bowl, discarding the pith that separates the batches of seeds.

POMEGRANATE MOLASSES: A thick tart-sweet flavoring that is made and widely used in Turkey, Iran, and the Caucasus, pomegranate molasses (also known as pomegranate sauce) is made of the juice of tart

---

CAMBODIAN/KHMER: ambel · **ESTONIAN:** sool · **FARSI:** namak · **FILIPINO:** asin ·

pomegranates cooked down into a thick liquid. Pomegranate molasses can be found widely. Buy several kinds if you have the opportunity, in order to taste and compare. My favorites are predominantly tart with a slightly sweet edge.

POMELO: The fruit of the tree *Citrus maxima*, pomelo is the largest and heaviest of the citrus fruits, and one of the ancestors of grapefruit. The flesh is protected by a relatively thin, tough yellow or yellow-green skin and a very thick layer of pith, and is less juicy than grapefruit flesh, with a milder, sweeter flavor, without bitterness. Pomelo is native to Southeast Asia, but the trees are now also grown in South Asia and the Caribbean. Because of their thick skin, pomelos keep well. Look for them in Asian grocery stores and specialty markets.

RICE NOODLES, RICE STICKS: The dried shelf-stable versions of fresh rice noodles, these are widely available in large supermarkets and Asian groceries. To use, rehydrate them by dropping them briefly into hot water just until softened, or moisten them slightly and then stir-fry.

SAEUJEOT: A form of Korean brined shrimp consisting of small fine shrimp and shrimp pieces stored in brine, found in most Korean grocery stores. Once opened, store in a sealed container in the refrigerator.

SAL DE GUSANO: Gusano are roasted and eaten in Mexico's Oaxaca. They look like worms but are actually the larvae of a moth, *Comadia redtenbacheri*. They eat the interior flesh of the maguey plants

that are used for making mescal. The worms are toasted on a clay comal, which gives them a nutty flavor and a crisp texture. Sal de gusano is made by grinding toasted worms with dried red chiles and salt. The blend has a pleasantly earthy taste with a little heat. If you are not in Oaxaca, you can buy jars of sal de gusano by mail-order and at some specialty shops.

SANSHO POWDER: Related to Sichuan pepper, sansho is the fruit of a variety of prickly ash, *Zanthoxylum piperitum*, that is native to Japan and the Korean peninsula. It is sometimes called Japanese prickly ash. In Korea, a closely related variety is called *sancho*. Like Sichuan pepper, but less intense, sansho powder numbs the tongue. It is usually a pale green to beige in color. Sansho is one of the aromatics in the Japanese spice combination shichimi togarashi. Look for sansho powder in Japanese and Korean grocery stores.

SESAME OIL, TOASTED SESAME OIL, SESAME SEEDS: Sesame seeds, from the fruit of the *Sesamum indicum* bush, are grown commercially in many parts of the world, especially Burma, Sudan, Nigeria, China, and India, and the seeds and oil pressed from them are relied upon by cooks in many places, from Japan to the Eastern Mediterranean. The plant grows well even in drought conditions and poor soil. Sesame oil is thought to be humankind's oldest cooking oil. Plain (raw) sesame oil is pale gold. A very important cooking oil in parts of India and in Burma/Myanmar, it is excellent for frying because it has a relatively high smoke point and a neutral flavor. European and North American cooks may be more familiar

with toasted sesame oil, the aromatic oil made from roasted sesame seeds that is used primarily as a flavoring in Japan and parts of China. Toasted sesame oil is a reddish brown. Look for oils marked "product of Japan."

The seeds are used as a flavoring in both sweet and savory baked goods and in savory dishes but are most valuable as a source of oil. They are also the main ingredient in tahini. Because of their high oil content, sesame seeds should be stored in the refrigerator, and, like nuts, should be tasted before you use them to make sure they have not become rancid. The seeds come hulled or with hulls on. Their flavor is best when they are lightly toasted.

SHICHIMI, SHICHIMI TOGARASHI: A spice blend used in Japan as a seasoning for noodles, eggs, vegetables, and many other dishes, shichimi is a combination of coarsely ground dried red chiles (*togarashi*) and six other spices. The classic mix includes sansho, dried orange peel, black and white sesame seeds, and two of the following: ground ginger, powdered nori, poppy seeds, or hemp seeds. Sometimes different citrus, such as yuzu, is included.

SHISO: An herb related to mint and native to Japan and Korea, *Perilla frutescens* is sometimes known as beefsteak plant or perilla, after its Latin name. In some varieties the leaves are fine and green; in others they are burgundy, sometimes tinged with green. For more information, see the recipe for Salted Shiso Leaves on page 60.

SICHUAN PEPPER: Known as *hua jiao* ("flower pepper") in Mandarin

---

FINNISH: suolaa　·　**FRENCH:** sel　·　**GAELIC (SCOTS):** salainn　·　**GEORGIAN:** marili　·

and *makwen* in northern Thai, Sichuan pepper is the fruit of a kind of prickly ash, *Zanthoxylum bungeanum*. The peppercorns contain a shiny black seed that is discarded, leaving the tingle-and-numbness-inducing dried husks, reddish black and aromatic. The Japanese spice sansho (usually sold as a powder) is a close relative; *see* Sansho powder. Peppercorns from varieties of prickly ash are used widely from Nepal to Indonesia.

SOBA NOODLES: Made from finely milled buckwheat flour or a combination of buckwheat and wheat flours, soba noodles are sold dried in small bundles. They may be relatively short (8 inches/ 20 cm long) or longer, like spaghetti (up to 12 inches/30 cm). Because buckwheat contains no gluten (the protein that gives wheat pastas their structure), cooking soba requires careful timing and attention to prevent the noodles from becoming mushy. Put them into boiling unsalted water only when everything else for your dish is ready. Swirl them when you drop them into the water to prevent them from sticking together, and then boil just until supple (check the package instructions). Immediately empty them into a colander and rinse with cold water, then turn out into a bowl of cold water to keep them from sticking together. See the recipe on page 329.

SORREL: Sorrel is a temperate-climate tender-leafed perennial herb with a distinctive lemony acid taste. It's used in European cooking (for example, in French sorrel soup) and is also used fresh in salads or as a garnishing herb. Note that *sorrel*

is the word used in Jamaica and elsewhere for hibiscus flowers, which make a delightfully acidic red-tinted tea or cold drink.

SOYBEAN SPROUTS: *See* Bean sprouts

SUMMER SAVORY: An annual that is very popular in Provence, as well as in Quebec and Atlantic Canada, summer savory (*Satureja hortensis*) is used, both fresh and dried, to flavor poultry and meat dishes and sausages. It is also an important element in the classic version of Québécois salted herbs, herbes salées (see page 49), and it is one of the herbs in classic herbes de Provence.

SUNFLOWER OIL: The mild-tasting yellow oil pressed from sunflower seeds (specifically *Helianthus annuus*) is widely used as a cooking oil in the Caucasus and in Iran, as well as in Eastern Europe. Russia and Ukraine produce more than half the world's supply. Sunflower oil is high in both linoleic and oleic acid. It should be stored in the refrigerator or a cool, dark place. As with any seed oils, look for cold-pressed oil to avoid oil produced using chemical solvents.

SURIBACHI: This traditional Japanese mortar is ceramic and has parallel ridges in the bowl, running from the rim to the bottom. You use a wooden pestle to mash and press the food you are grinding against the ridges to soften or pulverize it. (You'll need a brush to clean out the ridges when you're finished.) It's an ideal tool for some kinds of grating, when you want a broken-up texture, rather than a pounded texture, and it's beautiful as well.

TAMARIND PULP, TAMARIND PASTE: *Tamarindus indica* is a large hardwood tree (it is, in fact, a legume) that bears long pods filled with pulp and seeds. Tamarind pulp is used as a flavoring in many foods and drinks to give a tart-sweet edge. The young leaves and growing tips of the branches and the flowers are also edible. Tamarind trees grow in many places, from Southeast Asia and India to tropical and subtropical areas in the Caribbean and even Florida.

Tamarind pulp comes in dark pressed blocks wrapped in clear cellophane, usually from Thailand or Vietnam. Smaller blocks weigh ½ pound/250 grams, larger blocks are twice that size. Most of the seeds have been removed, but some remain. The pulp needs to be chopped, mashed with warm water, and pressed through a sieve to produce tamarind paste. (You can also buy tamarind paste, either in a tube or a tin, but it often has a metallic taste.) I recommend buying the pulp and processing it as you need it. Store any leftover paste in a clean glass jar in the refrigerator, available for adding as a souring agent to curries and also to sweets (see Easy Tamarind-Miso Ice Cream, page 345).

TOFU: Tofu is made from soybeans. The beans are cooked until soft, then mashed and pressed or squeezed. The liquid they give off is "soy milk." A coagulant is added to the soy milk, traditionally nigari (see page 381), the magnesium-rich brine that is the last liquid to drain from sea salt as it dries once it precipitates out of seawater. The resulting solids are pressed into blocks of varying textures. *Silken tofu* has a soft, custardy texture;

GERMAN: salz • **GREEK:** alati • **HAWAIIAN:** pa'akai • **HEBREW:** melach • **HMONG:** ntsev •

---

firm tofu, the workhorse of the family, is widely available, sold in off-white blocks immersed in water. Packages or containers of tofu should be refrigerated, and once they're opened, the water should be changed every day. You can also buy *pressed tofu*, which has a dense texture rather like a medium cheddar or Jack cheese, or you can make it yourself from firm tofu by placing a small weight on top and letting it drain for six hours.

TOGARASHI: *See* Shichimi

TURMERIC: A rhizome related to ginger and galangal, turmeric (*Curcuma longa*), which is native to the Indian subcontinent, is one of the oldest documented spices. Fresh turmeric has a fine orange-brown skin and a bright orange interior; turmeric powder is bright yellow. Both forms will stain your hands and work surfaces, so beware! Because it is now being grown in many places turmeric is widely available as whole rhizomes as well as in its powdered dried form. Traditionally used as a dye, turmeric has a strong earthy taste and is used in cooked dishes in South Asia and elsewhere. Turmeric has long been known by Ayurvedic practitioners to have antibacterial and anti-inflammatory effects.

VIETNAMESE CORIANDER: Known as *rau ram* in Vietnamese and *pak chi vietnam* in Thai, *Persicaria odorata* is a perennial herb, a succulent with thick, reddish stems and narrow pointed leaves. It has a distinctive aromatic flavor and is widely used in Southeast Asia in salads or added to soups at the last moment.

WAKAME: *Undaria pinnatifida* is a species of kelp (seaweed) that grows in the colder areas of the Pacific Ocean and has been harvested for centuries in Japan and China and the area. Wakame is relatively high in calcium and iodine. It's sold in dried form in Japanese and Korean groceries.

WASABI: A Japanese plant that grows in water, *Wasabia japonica* is related to both horseradish and mustard, all of them brassicas. The rhizome is ground to a paste to make a pungent condiment, also called wasabi. Most of the wasabi available commercially is a mix of horseradish and food coloring. True wasabi has a more complex flavor.

YUZU: A wild citrus tree, *Citrus junos*, that traveled from somewhere in the China-Tibet region to Japan many centuries ago, yuzu produces small aromatic fruits that turn yellow as they ripen. Both the juice and zest are used in cooking and are now sought after by Western cooks and chefs because of their distinctive sweet-tart-aromatic flavor.

ICELANDIC: salt • **IRISH:** salaan • **JAPANESE:** shio • **KANNADA:** uppu • **KOREAN:** sogeum •

RESOURCES

A bibliography can feel overly precise in this era of swirling multisource research factoids. As well as searching out books and articles in periodicals, we can now find information online in the form of PDFs or Wikipedia entries or YouTube videos of many kinds and many degrees of reliability. Many of the books and articles listed here are available online.

A few caveats: Because salt is such a huge topic, spanning many worlds in time and space, it goes without saying that this list is inevitably incomplete. And as I scan for information and understanding online, I find that it's all too easy to pick up a nugget of understanding from a source, whether in written or video or photographic form, whose whereabouts and attribution I don't note down. Though I have tried to include every source that I consulted for guidance, there may well be omissions.

The same goes for conversations over the years that have informed my understanding and the details of which are incompletely documented. My general statement of thanks on page 391 to all scholars of food, human history, and related fields who have mentioned or touched on the subject of salt in their thinking and research arises from the fact that over the years I've lived with ideas and questions about salt, sometimes subconscious questions, and thus can't accurately acknowledge all the people who have influenced my thinking and understanding.

Whole books have been written on salt history. For detailed delving, have a look at Samuel Adrian M. Adshead's *Salt and Civilization*; Mark Kurlansky's *Salt: A World History*; papers from the Salt Archaeology conferences; and writings by Olivier Weller, E. Anne MacDougall, Sally Grainger, and other historical anthropologists and salt archaeologists. Many papers and books on salt archaeology are available at www.academia.edu. A number are listed in this bibliography, but there are many more. Once you start looking, you risk falling headlong down a series of fascinating rabbit holes.

BOOKS AND ARTICLES

Abulafia, David. *The Boundless Sea: A Human History of the Oceans*. London: Allen Lane, 2019.

Adshead, S. A. M. *Salt and Civilization*. London: Macmillan, 1992.

Alford, Jeffrey, and Naomi Duguid. *Beyond the Great Wall: Recipes and Travels in the Other China*. New York: Artisan, 2008.

——. *Flatbreads & Flavors: A Baker's Atlas*. New York: Morrow, 1995.

——. *Home Baking: The Artful Mix of Flour and Tradition Around the World*. New York: Artisan, 2003.

——. *Hot Sour Salty Sweet: A Culinary Journey Through Southeast Asia*. New York: Artisan, 2000.

——. *Mangoes & Curry Leaves: Culinary Travels Through the Great Subcontinent*. New York: Artisan, 2005.

——. *Seductions of Rice: A Cookbook*. New York: Artisan, 1998.

Anderson, E. N. *The Food of China*. New Haven, CT: Yale University Press, 1988.

Aras, Nilhan. "Salt-pot/*Tuz Testisi*: A Salt and Terracotta Water Cooler from Turkey." In *Food & Material Culture: Proceedings of the Oxford Food Symposium on Food and Cookery, 2013*, edited by Mark McWilliams. Totnes, England: Prospect Books, 2014.

Armstrong, Julian. *Made in Quebec: A Culinary Journey*. Toronto: HarperCollins, 2014.

Asher, David. *The Art of Natural Cheesemaking: Using Traditional, Non-Industrial Methods and Raw Ingredients to Make the World's Best Cheeses*. White River Junction, VT: Chelsea Green, 2015.

Azkarate, A., and Plata A. Introduction to *Salt Production System of Añana, Valle Salado* by Alberto Plata Montero and Andoni Erkiaga. Universidad del Paîs Vasco, 2018.

Baker, Jenny. *Kettle Broth to Gooseberry Fool: A Celebration of Simple English Cooking*. London: Faber and Faber, 1996.

Benkerroum, Noureddine. "Traditional Fermented Foods of North African Countries: Technology and Food Safety Challenges with Regard to Microbiological Risks." *Comprehensive Reviews in Food Science and Food Safety* 12, no. 1 (January 2013).

Benkirane, Fettouma. *Secrets of Moroccan Cookery*. Casablanca: Taillandier-Sochepress, 1985.

KURMANJI: xwe • **KURDISH/SORANI:** khweh • **LAO:** keu • **MALAGASY:** sira • **MALAY:** garam •

Bilderbeck, Lesley. *Salt: The Essential Guide to Cooking with the Most Important Ingredient in Your Kitchen*. London: St Martin's Press, 2016.

Bitterman, Mark. *Salted: A Manifesto on the World's Most Essential Mineral, with Recipes*. Berkeley, CA: Ten Speed Press, 2010.

Bloch, David. "The Secret and Forgotten Salts Traded at the Silk Road's Frontiers: Byzantium's and Pre/Post-Islam's Impact upon the Fall of the Supreme Ottoman State." *Advances in Earth and Environmental Science* 2, no. 3 (August 21, 2021).

Bloch, M. R. "The Social Influence of Salt." *Scientific American* 209, no. 1 (July 1963): 89–98.

Brigand, Robin, and Olivier Weller, eds. *Archaeology of Salt: Approaching an Invisible Past*. Leiden: Sidestone Press, 2015.

Brobeck, Florence, and Monika B. Kjellberg. *Smörgåsbord and Scandinavian Cookery*. New York: Grosset & Dunlap, 1948. From the Experts' Choice Cookbooks series. Reprint of *Scandinavian Cookery for Americans*. Boston: Little, Brown, 1948.

Brown, Ian W. *The Red Hills of Essex: Studying Salt in England*. Tuscaloosa, AL: Borgo, 2013.

———. *The Role of Salt in Eastern North American Prehistory*. Louisiana Archaeological Survey and Antiquities Commission Anthropological Study no. 3, Baton Rouge, LA: Department of Culture, Recreation and Tourism, 1981.

———. *Salt and the Eastern North American India: An Archaeological Study*. Lower Mississippi Study Bulletin no. 6. Cambridge, MA: Peabody Museum, Harvard University, 1980.

Chang, K. C., ed. *Food in Chinese Culture: Anthropological and Historical Perspectives*. New Haven, CT: Yale University Press, 1977.

Chesterman, Lesley. *Chez Lesley: Mes secrets pour tout réussir en cuisine*. Montreal: Editions Cardinal, 2020.

Chou, Hsiao-Ching. *Chinese Soul Food: A Friendly Guide for Homemade Dumplings, Stir-fries, Soups, and More*. Seattle: Sasquatch Books, 2018.

———. *Vegetarian Chinese Soul Food: Deliciously Doable Ways to Cook Greens, Tofu, and Other Plant-Based Ingredients*. Seattle: Sasquatch Books, 2021.

Collingham, Lizzie. *The Taste of Empire: How Britain's Taste for Food Shaped the Modern World*. New York: Basic Books, 2017.

Cooke, Nathalie, and Fiona Lucas, eds. *Catherine Parr Traill's The Female Emigrant's Guide: Cooking with a Canadian Classic*. Montreal: McGill-Queen's University Press, 2017.

Crouzet-Pavan, Elisabeth. *Venice Triumphant: The Horizons of a Myth*. Translated by Lydia G. Cochrane. Baltimore: Johns Hopkins University Press, 2002.

Danopoulos, Evangelos, Lauren Jenner, Maureen Twiddy, and Jeanette M. Rotchell. "Microplastic Contamination of Salt Intended for Human Consumption: A Systematic Review and Meta-analysis." *SN Applied Sciences* 2, no. 1950 (2020).

Dash, Mike. "White Gold: How Salt Made and Unmade the Turks and Caicos Islands." Smithsonian.com, December 14, 2012.

Dethier, V. G. "The Taste of Salt." *American Scientist* 65, no. 6 (November–December 1977): 744–51.

Dempster, J .F., S. N. Reid, and O. Cody. "Sources of Contamination of Cooked, Ready-to-Eat Cured and Uncured Meats." *Journal of Hygiene* 71, no. 4 (December 1973): 815–23.

Dos Santos, Susan Plant. "Salt and Sugar in Portugal." In *The Anthropologists' Cookbook*, Jessica Kuper, ed. London: Routledge & Kegan Paul, 1977.

Duffy, Nikki. "Super Ingredients: Bottarga." *Guardian*, August 13, 2005.

Duguid, Naomi. *Burma: Rivers of Flavor*. New York: Artisan, 2012.

———. *Taste of Persia: A Cook's Travels Through Armenia, Azerbaijan, Georgia, Iran, and Kurdistan*. New York: Artisan, 2016.

Dunlop, Fuchsia. *The Food of Sichuan*. London: Bloomsbury, 2019.

———. *Revolutionary Chinese Cookbook: Recipes from Hunan Province*. London: Ebury, 2006.

Encyclopaedia Iranica. https:iranicaonline.org.

Erickson, Renee, with Jess Thomson. *A Boat, a Whale, and a Walrus: Menus and Stories*. Seattle: Sasquatch Books, 2014.

Fallon, Sally, and Mary G. Enig. "Australian Aborigines: Living off the Fat of the Land." *Price-Pottenger Nutrition Foundation Health Journal* 22, no 2 (1999) 574–81.

Fielding, Andrew Philip, and Annelise Mary Fielding. *The Salt Industry*. London: Bloomsbury, 2006.

FitzGibbon, Theodora. *A Taste of Ireland: In Food and in Pictures*. London: Pan, 1968.

———. *A Taste of Scotland: Scottish Traditional Food*. London: Pan, 1976.

Freeman, Susan Tax. "The Spanish Pig Preserved: The *Olla* and the Ham." In *The Anthropologists' Cookbook*, edited by Jessica Kuper. London: Routledge & Kegan Paul, 1977.

MALAYLAM: upp · **MALTESE:** melḥ · **MANDARIN:** yan · **MAORI:** tote · **MONGOLIAN:** davs ·

Fregly, M. S. "Salt and Social Behavior." In *Biological and Behavioral Aspects of Salt Intake*, edited by M. R. Kare, M. J. Fregly, and R. A. Bernard. New York: Academic Press, 1980.

Fuller, Dorian Q., and Cristina Castillo. "Diversification and Cultural Construction of a Crop: The Case of Glutinous Rice and Waxy Cereals in the Food Cultures of Eastern Asia." In *The Oxford Handbook of the Archaeology of Diet*, edited by Julia Lee-Thorp and M. Anne Katzenberg. Published online January 2016.

Grainger, Sally. "Garum, Liquamen, and Muria: A New Approach to the Problem of Definition." In *Fish and Ships: Production and Commerce of Salsamenta during Antiquity*, edited by Emmanuel Botte and Victoria Leitch. Aix-en-Provence: Publications du Centre Camille Jullian, 2014.

———. "Garum and Liquamen: What's in a Name?" *Journal of Maritime Archaeology* 13 (2018): 247–261. https://doi.org/10.1007/s11457-018-9211-5.

Gray, Patience. *Honey from a Weed*. London: Prospect, 1986.

Greene, Bert. *Greene on Greens*. New York: Workman, 1984.

Grigson, Jane. *Charcuterie and French Pork Cookery*. London: Penguin, 1967, 1970.

Hachisu, Nancy Singleton. *Preserving the Japanese Way: Traditions of Salting, Fermenting, and Pickling for the Modern Kitchen*. Kansas City, MO: Andrews McMeel, 2015.

Harding, Anthony. "The Prehistoric Exploitation of Salt in Europe." *Geological Quarterly* 58, no. 3 (2014): 591–96. https://doi.org10.7306/gq.116.

Hartley, Dorothy. *Food in England*. London: MacDonald and Jane's, 1954; 1974 edition.

Hathaway, S. J. E. "Take it with a Pinch of Salt? Thinking about the Cultural Significance of Producing and Consuming Salt." In *Food and Drink in Archaeology I: University of Nottingham Postgraduate Conference 2007*, edited by S. Baker, M. Allen, S. Middle, and K. Poole. Totnes, England: Prospect Books, 2008.

Hepinstall, Hi Soo Shin. *Growing Up in a Korean Kitchen: A Cookbook*. Berkeley, CA: Ten Speed Press, 2001.

Inner Wheel Club of Darjeeling. *Himalayan Recipes*. Darjeeling, n.d.

Katz, Sandor. *The Art of Fermentation: An In-Depth Exploration of Essential Concepts and Processes from around the World*. White River Junction, VT: Chelsea Green, 2012.

Kennedy, Diana. *The Essential Cuisines of Mexico*. New York: Clarkson Potter, 2000.

Kiernan, V. G. "Grains and Pinches." *London Review of Books* 14, no. 13 (July 9, 1992): 16–17.

Kim, Eric. "Think of Kimchi as a Verb." *New York Times*, July 2, 2020.

King, Niloufer Ichipuria. *My Bombay Kitchen: Traditional and Modern Parsi Home Cooking*. San Francisco: University of California Press, 2007.

Kingry, Judy, and Lauren Devine, eds. *Complete Book of Home Preserving: 400 Delicious and Creative Recipes for Today*. Toronto: Robert Rose, 2006.

Knight, Ivy. "What Happens When You Age Fish?" *Vice*, September 28, 2016.

Kurlansky, Mark. *Salt: A World History*. New York: Penguin, 2003.

Laudan, Rachel. *Cuisine and Empire: Cooking in World History*. Berkeley: University of California Press, 2013.

Laszlo, Pierre. *Salt: Grain of Life*. Translated by Mary Beth Mader. New York: Columbia University Press, 2001.

Lovejoy, Paul E. *Salt of the Desert Sun: A History of Salt Production and Trade in the Central Sudan*. African Studies Series no. 46. Cambridge: Cambridge University Press, 1986.

Luard, Elisabeth. *The Old World Kitchen: The Rich Tradition of European Peasant Cooking*. New York: Bantam, 1987.

Machlin, Edda Servi. *The Classic Cuisine of the Italian Jews: Traditional Recipes and Menus and a Memoir of a Vanished Way of Life*. Croton-on-Hudson, NY: Giro, 1993.

Maltby, Mark. "Salt and Animal Husbandry: Linking Production and Use in Iron-Age Britain." In *Integrating Zooarchaeology*, edited by Mark Maltby. Proceedings of the Ninth Conference of the International Council of Archaeozoology, 2002. Oxford: Oxbow Books, 2006.

Mann, Charles C. *1493: Uncovering the New World Columbus Created*. New York: Knopf, 2011.

Martin, Melissa M. *Mosquito Supper Club: Cajun Recipes from a Disappearing Bayou*. New York: Artisan, 2020.

McDougall, E. Ann. "The Sahara Reconsidered: Pastoralism, Politics and Salt from the Ninth through the Twelfth Centuries." *African Economic History* no. 12, Business Empires in Equatorial Africa (1983): 263–86. https://doi.org/10.2307/3601328.

———. "Salts of the Western Sahara: Myths, Mysteries, and Historical Significance." *International Journal of African Historical Studies* 23, no. 2 (1990): 231–57.

McFadden, Syreeta. "Uncovering the Roots of Caribbean Cooking." *The Atlantic*, January 2, 2019.

McGee, Harold. *The Curious Cook: More Kitchen Science and Lore*. San Francisco: North Point, 1990.

NEPALI: nuna · **PALI:** lona, lavana · **PORTUGUESE:** sal · **PUNJABI:** luna · **QUECHUA:** kachi ·

———. *Nose Dive: A Field Guide to the World's Smells*. New York: Penguin, 2020.

———. *On Food and Cooking: The Science and Lore of the Kitchen*. New York: Scribner, 1984, 2004.

McKillop, Heather. "Salt as a Commodity or Money in the Classic Maya Economy." *Journal of Anthropological Archaeology* 62 (June 2021).

McLagan, Jennifer. *Bitter: A Taste of the World's Most Dangerous Flavor, with Recipes*. Berkeley, CA: Ten Speed Press, 2014.

———. *Odd Bits: How to Cook the Rest of the Animal*. Berkeley, CA: Ten Speed Press, 2011.

———. *Fat: An Appreciation of a Misunderstood Ingredient, with Recipes*. Berkeley, CA: Ten Speed Press, 2008.

———. *Bones: Recipes, History, and Lore*. New York: William Morrow, 2005.

Meunie, Mme. Jacques. "Sur l'architecture du Tafilalt et de Sijilmassa (Maroc Saharien)." *Comptes rendus des séances de l'Académie des inscriptions et Belles-Lettres Année* 106, no. 2. (1962): 132–47.

Montgomery, David R., and Anne Bikle. *The Hidden Half of Nature: The Microbial Roots of Life and Health*. New York: Norton, 2016.

Moraba, Kareh. "The Story of Kashk." *Gastronomica* 16, no. 4 (winter 2016): 97–100.

Moxham, Roy. *The Great Hedge of India*. New York: Carroll & Graf, 2001.

Nummer, Brian A., and Elizabeth L Andress. *Curing and Smoking Meats for Home Food Preservation Literature Review and Critical Preservation Points*. Athens, GA: University of Georgia, Cooperative Extension Service, 2002.

Oseland, James. *World Food: Mexico City; Heritage Recipes for Classic Home Cooking*. Berkeley, CA: Ten Speed Press, 2020.

Parks, Cara. "Shaking Up Salt: Craft Salt Farmers Go against the Grain." *Modern Farmer*, December 16, 2014.

Passmore, Jacki. *The Encyclopedia of Asian Food and Cooking*. New York: William Morrow, 1991.

Perry, Charles. "Dried, Frozen and Rotted: Food Preservation in Central Asia and Siberia." In *Cured, Fermented and Smoked Foods: Proceedings from the Oxford Symposium on Food and Cookery 2010*, edited by Helen Sabieri. London: Prospect Books, 2011.

Phillips, Carolyn. *All under Heaven: Recipes from the 35 Cuisines of China*. Berkeley, CA: Ten Speed Press, 2016.

Ramachandran, Amini. *Grains, Greens, and Grated Coconuts: Recipes and Remembrances of a Vegetarian Legacy*. Lincoln, NE: iUniverse, 2009.

Redzepi, René, and David Zilber. *The Noma Guide to Fermentation*. New York: Artisan, 2018.

Robb, Peter. *Midnight in Sicily: On Art, Food, History, Travel, and la Cosa Nostra*. Boston: Farber & Farber/Farrar, Straus and Giroux, 1998.

Roden, Claudia. *A Book of Middle Eastern Food* (1968). New York: Vintage Books, 1974 (paperback edition).

Rudzinski, Russ. *Japanese Country Cookbook*. San Francisco: Nitty Gritty, 1969.

Sada, Luigi. *La cucina pugliese*. Rome: Newton Compton, 1994.

Sandler, Nick, and Johnny Acton. *Preserved*. London: Kyle Books, 2004, 2009.

Santa Maria, Jack. *Chinese Vegetarian Cookery*. London: Rider, 1983.

Selbitschka, Armin. "The Early Silk Road(s)." In *Oxford Research Encyclopedia of Asian History*, edited by David Ludden. New York: Oxford University Press, 2018.

Schwartz, Randy K. "Searching for the Pre-Expulsion Foods of Spain." *Repast* 17, no. 1 (winter 2001): 7–11.

Scott, James C. *The Art of Not Being Governed: An Anarchist History of Upland Southeast Asia*. New Haven, CT: Yale University Press, 2009.

Shih, Rich, and Jeremy Urmansky. *Koji Alchemy: Rediscovering the Magic of Mold-Based Fermentation*. White River Junction, VT: Chelsea Green, 2020.

Shockey, Kirsten K., and Christopher. *Miso, Tempeh, Natto and Other Tasty Ferments: A Step-by-Step Guide to Fermenting Grains and Beans*. North Adams, MA: Storey, 2019.

Shurtleff, William, and Akiko Aoyagi. *The Book of Miso: Savory Soy Seasoning*. Lafayette, CA: Soyinfo Center, 1976, 2018.

———. *The Book of Tofu*. Brookline, MA: Autumn Press, 1975.

Siegień, Ekaterina Maximova Paulina. "The Pomors." *New Eastern Europe*, December 19, 2019.

Simmons, Alexy. "Salty as Sailors' Boots; Salt-Cured Meat, the Blessing and Bane of the Soldier and the Archaeologist." In *Cured, Fermented and Smoked Foods: Proceedings from the Oxford Symposium on Food and Cookery 2010*, edited by Helen Sabieri. London: Prospect Books, 2011.

Sobral, Jose M. "Salt Cod and the Making of a Portuguese National Cuisine." In *The Emergence of National Food: The Dynamics of Food Nationalism*, edited by Atsuko Ichijo, Venetia Johannes, and Ronald Ranta. London: Bloomsbury Academic, 2019.

Spence, Caroline. "Smuggling in Early Modern France." Master's thesis, Warwick University, 2010.

SANSKRIT: lavanamh, sikataa · **SHONA:** munyu · **SINHALA:** lunu · **SOMALI:** cusbo ·

Steinkraus, Keith H. "Lactic Acid Fermentations." Chapter 5 of *Applications of Biotechnology to Fermented Foods: Report of an Ad Hoc Panel of the Board on Science and Technology for International Development*. Washington, DC: National Academies Press, 1992.

Sutton, David C. "The Stories of Bacalao: Myth, Legend and History" in *Cured, Fermented and Smoked Foods: Proceedings from the Oxford Symposium on Food and Cookery 2010*, edited by Helen Sabieri. London: Prospect Books, 2011.

Tamang, Jyoti Prakash. *Himalayan Fermented Foods: Microbiology, Nutrition, and Ethnic Values*. Boca Raton: CRC, 2010, 2019.

Tan, Cecilia. *Penang Nyonya Cooking: Foods of My Childhood*. Singapore: Times Books, 1992.

Taylor, Harden F. *Principles Involved in the Preservation of Fish by Salt*. Appendix II to the Report of the US Commissioner of Fisheries for 1922. Bureau of Fisheries Document No. 919. Washington, DC: US Government Printing Office, 1922.

Thiam, Pierre, with Jennifer Sit. *Senegal: Modern Senegalese Recipes from the Source to the Bowl*. New York: Lake Isle Press, 2015.

Thibault, Simon. *Pantry and Palate: Remembering and Rediscovering Acadian Food*. Halifax, NS: Nimbus, 2017.

Twitty, Michael. *The Cooking Gene: A Journey through African American Culinary History in the Old South*. New York: Harper Collins, 2017.

——. "Stinking Fish, Salt Fish, and Smokehouse Pork: Preserved Foods, Flavor Principles and the Birth of African American Foodways." In *Cured, Fermented and Smoked Foods: Proceedings from the Oxford Symposium on Food and Cookery 2010*, edited by Helen Sabieri. London: Prospect Books, 2011.

Vogel, Hans Ulrich. "Types of Fuel Used in the Salt Works of Sichuan and Yunnan in Southwestern China: A Historical Overview." In *Sels, eau et forêt d'hier à aujourd'hui*, edited by Olivier Weller, Alexa Dufraisse, and Pierre Pétrequin. Paris: Presses Universitaires de Franche-Comté, 2008.

Waheed, Nayyirah. *salt*. Self-published, CreateSpace, 2013.

Warren, John K. "Gourmet Salt NaCl or Halite: Origins and Culinary Variety." *Salty Matters* (blog), January 31, 2020.

Weller, Olivier. "First Salt Making in Europe: An Overview from Neolithic Times." *Documenta Praehistorica* 42 (2015).

Wertheim, Bradley. "How Not to Die of Botulism." *The Atlantic*, December 2, 2013.

Whitsitt, Tara. *Fermentation on Wheels: Road Stories, Food Ramblings, and 50 Do-It-Yourself Recipes*. New York: Bloomsbury, 2017.

Wilkerson, Isabel. *Caste: The Origins of Our Discontents*. New York: Random House, 2020.

Williams, Eduardo. *The Salt of the Earth: Ethnoarchaeology of Salt Production in Michoacán, Western Mexico*. BAR International Series 2725. Oxford: Archaeopress, 2015.

Wolfert, Paula. *Couscous and Other Good Food from Morocco*. New York: Harper & Row, 1973.

Yu, Su-Mei. "A Lamentation for Shrimp Paste." *Gastronomica* 9, no. 3 (August 2009): 53–56.

BLOGS & ONLINE INFO

COOKING BLOGS

Cooking With Koji
Recipes and info about koji and things Japanese, by a writer in Australia.

Dassana's Veg Recipes
A blog by Dassana Amit.

Just Hungry
Makiko Ito, author of *The Just Bento Cookbook: Everyday Lunches to Go*, provides generous explanations of Japanese recipes and techniques.

Maangchi
A useful and refreshingly informal blog by Maangchi, who is knowledgeable and an excellent explainer. It's a good introduction to Korean traditional cooking and preserving.

Practical Self Reliance
An interesting site by a woman who homesteads in Vermont, with instructions for home-curing egg yolks, guanciale, etc.

RealCajunRecipes
Brandon Abshire and Chrissy Lemaire offer a succinct set of instructions for drying shrimp Cajun-style in their post "The Art of Drying Shrimp."

Science Meets Food
A blog posting on this site gives a useful simple explanation of the glutamates involved in producing the umami and kokumi taste sensations, with a description of how they interact.

SALT HISTORY, SALT HARVESTING, SALTING TECHNIQUES

Anderson, Dan. "Salt and Midwestern Slavery." *Food Tells a Story* (blog).

Blonder, Greg. "Salt Brine Curing Calculator." Genuine Ideas, January 2017.

SPANISH: sal • **SWAHILI:** chumvi • **SWEDISH:** alati • **TAMIL:** uppu • **TAJIK:** namak • **THAI:** gleua •

"Eastern Carpathians: A Story of a Lost Dacian Hillfort."
Published online January 2016.

Early salt exploitation in Romania north of Bucharest.

Feldmar, Jamie, and Liza Corsillo. "9 Chefs on Their Favorite
Sea Salts." *The Strategist* (blog). *New York*, March 20,
2019.

Gainsford, Peter. "Salting the Earth." *Kiwi Hellenist* (blog),
December 12, 2016.

A blog by a classical scholar living in New Zealand. This
entry is about the salting of the earth at Carthage, the
reverse of the myth: salt as fertility.

Ginise, Patrick. "Salting Steaks before Grilling."
TheGrillingLife.com, April 11, 2020.

Lindeman, Scarlett. "Why You Should Incorporate Sal
de Gusano into Your Home Cooking." *Epicurious*,
September 6, 2019.

Meathead, "The Science of Salt." Meathead's AmazingRibs
.com, n.d.

Schiller, Tom. "Sea Salt." Oishi So Japan, January 1, 2016.

"The 300-Year-Old Sea Salt Making Tradition of Utazu."
Google Arts and Culture, n.d.

Wolke, Robert L. "Kosher Salt." *Washington Post*, October
4, 2000.

Zimmerman, Michael B., and Kristien Boelaert. "Iodine
Deficiency and Thyroid Disorders." *Lancet Diabetes and
Endocrinology* 3 (2015): 286–95.

FOOD SAFETY

"Botulism: Control Measures Overview for Clinicians."
Centers for Disease Control and Prevention, October 6,
2006.

Botulism advice.

"How Not to Die from Botulism." nwedible.com.

Terrific online graphic presentation for home canners about
botulism.

World Health Organization. "Botulism" (fact sheet), January
10, 2018.

Zoutman. "Preventing Botulism with Pickling Salt," n.d.

MEAT CURING

Desmazery, Barney. "Salted Egg Yolks." BBC Good Food,
n.d.

Eat Cured Meat, eatcuredmeat.com.

Great explanations and descriptions of options if you want
to get deeply into curing.

Frame, Andy. "Cured Meat Is In, but Is It Safe?" *Food Safety
News*, September 6, 2012.

Schwarcz, Joe. "What Is Saltpeter Used for, and Is It True It
Reduces 'Carnal Urges?'" McGill Office for Science and
Society, March 20, 2017.

About saltpeter and meat preservation.

Sontag, Elazar. "Bacon, Pancetta, and More: Cured Port
Products and How to Cook with Them." Serious Eats,
October 28, 2019.

Discusses differences between various cured porks.

Wright, Matt. "Charcuterie: Nitrates and Nitrites."
Wrightfood (blog), July 13, 2010.

About meat cures, nitrites, curing salt, safety, etc.

FERMENTATION ADVICE

Fenley, Kaitlynn. "How Much Salt Should You Use to
Ferment Vegetables?" Cultured Guru, March 27, 2018.

"Measuring and Using Salt in Fermenting." Fermentation
Recipes, n.d.

Mennes, Mary E. *Make Your Own Sauerkraut*. Publication
B2087. Madison: University of Wisconsin–Extension,
1994.

"Try Salting. It's an Easy Way to Ferment, Pickle, and Store
Vegetables." Home Preserving Bible, n.d.

Great guide to salt-preserved vegetables.

Workman, Dion. "Making Miso." Permaculture Research
Institute, February 4, 2012.

TIBETAN: tshwa • **TURKIC LANGUAGES:** tuz • **URDU:** namak • **VIETNAMESE:** muối • **WELSH:** halen

---

ACKNOWLEDGMENTS

This book has taken me on a thrilling and humbling journey. Along the way, I've been helped by both friends and chance-met strangers, and I've learned from countless writers and researchers. I've been learning about foodways for decades, and those lessons continue to resonate. As with other books, I've drawn on past experiences as well as on more recent research to shape the recipes and stories here. I'm grateful to many people from travels past—travels that have over time given me an understanding about salt. I feel fortunate to have had those earlier travels and projects, especially given the limitations that the pandemic imposed on travel.

My first thanks are to Lia Ronnen, publisher of Workman and Artisan, who had confidence in my sketched proposal for the book. I am very grateful for her generous and collaborative approach throughout the editing and design process.

More recently, thanks to Nancy Harmon Jenkins for being a fun (and deeply knowledgeable) traveling companion on my salt-focused trip to Sicily and then, with her daughter Sara Jenkins, for including me in the olive-picking crew in Teverina, near Cortona. And thanks to Mary Taylor Simeti and her family in Sicily for their generous hospitality.

Big thanks to Annie Kemp, who drove me to eastern Essex and explored that landscape with me, from the delicious oysters of Mersea to the impressive details of the Maldon salt-making operation.

When ceramic artist and small farmer Caroline Watanabe read that I was hoping to travel to Japan's Noto Peninsula, she offered her help, and then invited me to stay with her. She embraced my endless questions and guided my time in Noto with generous energy. Thank you, Caroline. And thanks to scholar and writer Elizabeth Andoh, who welcomed me to one of her cooking classes in Tokyo and gave me very helpful advice about Japanese salt-preservation traditions, and to Saratwadee Assasupakit for welcoming me to her place in Osaka.

Tyler Dillon gave me background information on the incredible salt terraces in Maras, Peru. Thanks to his friends Jeremy Flores Ochoa and Tatiana Mendoza in Maras for answering my many questions about local plants, foods, and history.

Big thanks to Kathy Wazana for many conversations over the years about Morocco and the complex history of its population, which helped give me greater understanding when I traveled there, and to Lousine Ouichou of Kasbah Tiguemi N'oufella for conversations about the history of the Telouet area.

Thanks to many salt makers and salt workers: Andrew Shepherd, founder of the Vancouver Island Sea Salt Company, and owner Scott Gibson explained their operation, located on a stretch of coast near Oyster Bay, and Philippe Marill of Salt Spring Sea Salt showed me his flavored salts. The management of Maldon Sea Salt company generously welcomed me to visit and photograph their brine-gathering area of the Blackwater River estuary and, at the plant, allowed me to shovel the freshly crystallizing salt out of the hot brine, heavy and wet, in a hot steamy room. It was a valuable opportunity to feel the muscular effort and the demanding labor that goes into salt production, even in modern times.

And thanks to the people of the salt-making village of Bo Kleua in northern Thailand who tolerated my camera and my questions. People in and around Kampot, Cambodia, kindly answered questions about the salt ponds history and the current issues they face. Big thanks to the salt makers along the west coast of the Noto Peninsula, and the guide at the salt museum, who answered my many questions about the traditional methods of salt making there. I am grateful to the salt workers at Lac Rose, in Senegal, who long ago allowed me to photograph them and answered my questions about pay and working conditions; to the salt workers in Khatch who allowed me to photograph them; and to the salt workers in the Maras terraces who answered my questions and allowed me to photograph them. Thanks to the personnel at the Salinas de Añana in Basque Country for their explanations.

Conversations with friends and the relatives and friends of friends, and with many people in the food world, have informed me at every turn. People have been very generous with their salt stories and experiences, with information about salt-preserving traditions in their family, opinions about their favorite salt, and explanations of why salt is their favorite flavor. Thanks to Jeff Koehler for his story of traveling up to the Khyber Pass lying on a huge block of salt; to Shayma Saadat for conversations about Khewra salt and qurut; to Robina Aryubwal for information about the use of kashk in Afghanistan; to Sean Chen, scholar and inquiring mind, for advice on brined eggs; to Potz for his story of gathering salt in northern Sri Lanka; to Jim Oseland for recommending an excellent documentary on the salt makers of Colima in Mexico; to Kay Plunkett-Hogge for tales of Gozo; to David Matchett for photos of Gozo; to Tasmana

Ayoub for describing her Afghan father's salted meat tradition as it continues in Toronto; to Dali Kuprava for describing the Svanetian-style salted dried meat her father used to make in their apartment in Tbilisi, and to many more.

And thanks to those who brought or sent me salt from various places, including Ilse Wong for the salt called sugpo asin, from Pangasinan in the Philippines; Ruth Shamai for an array of sea salts; Isaac Turner for salt from Japan; Shayma Saadat for salt from Pakistan; Bartosch for salt from Poland; Simon Thibault for salt from Nova Scotia.

We depend on salt makers for our salt, but also on importers and the shops who stock it and are curious about finding new salts. Aziz Osmani of Kalustyans in New York City is one such seeker, who helps expand everyone's food horizons, and there are many more. Be sure to look for them and to thank them.

Over the last decade and more at the Oxford Symposium on Food and Cookery, I've made good friends whose lived experience has broadened my understanding of the ways people think about food, and about food preservation and tradition. Special thanks to director Ursula Heinzelmann, chair Elisabeth Luard, and trustee David Matchett. My thanks to all Symposiasts for welcoming me into their generous-minded and intellectually curious community. I urge anyone who has not attended, either in person or virtually, to consider participating.

Specific Oxford Food Symposium-related thanks to Zita Cobb for her description of the salt cod and other traditions of Fogo Island; to Harold McGee for his keynote and explanations of the ways in which salt interacts with plants to affect what we smell; to Andiswa Mqedlana, a Symposium Young Chef awardee from South Africa who talked about the spiritual and medicinal importance of ingredients, including Baleni salt; to Tim Charles and Jonathan Gushue for the Fogo Island Split Pea Soup recipe; and to the authors of many papers given over the years at the symposium that you'll find listed in Resources.

Thanks to those who shared recipes, or gave me permission to adapt their recipes: Dina Fayerman, who introduced me to kapusniak (Polish sauerkraut soup) and gave lots of other valuable recipe advice; Dawn Woodward, whose recipe is the backbone of the miso-chocolate chip cookies; Cassandra Kobayashi, who developed the brilliant brittle recipe; Gord Sato for his salted cucumber pickles. Big thanks to Shubhra Chatterji, aka @historywali, who generously gave me very helpful information about pisi loon, the Uttarakhand flavored salts.

Huge thanks to Cassandra Kobayashi for steering me with a firm hand; to Dawn Woodward for sharing her wisdom on baking with unsifted flours; to Hilary Buttrick for insights about Chinese and Japanese food traditions, and for conversations about language; to Penny Van Esterik for sending me papers about prehistoric salt making in Thailand and Laos and for salt conversations; to Mennat-Allah El-Dorry for information about evidence of early Egyptian bottarga/batarekh art and processes; to Edmund Rek for valuable flavor combo advice; to Ivy Knight and the late John Bil for helping me understand fresh fish and what happens as it ages; to Haig Petrus for tasting my basturma; to Cameron Stauch for advice on duck breast prosciutto; to Simon Thibault for Acadian salted onions advice and discussions; to Elisabeth Luard for introducing me to thinly sliced dried bottarga on buttered toast, with a squeeze of lemon; to Lesley Chesterman for recipe advice; to Karen Burke for caramel education; to my cousin

Diana and her husband, Bob, with whom I stayed in Comox; to Fern Somraks and Tamar Babuadze, and to travelers who have been on my immersethrough trips in Burma, Georgia, and Thailand; to Deb Olson of Laramie Travel for all kinds of support and wise advice; to Lillian Burgess for introducing me to spruce tips and permaculture ideas; to Michael Poskanzer for the use of his ice cream maker; to Jennifer McLagan for meat conversations; to Birgitte Kampmann in Copenhagen for inviting me to share several of these recipes (Bacala Mantecato, Bacalao Tortilla, and Miso Cookies) in an online Kitchen Lab cooking session, and to the participants for their enthusiasm and their questions; and to Anne MacKenzie, Cameron Stauch, and Tina Ujlaki, for test-driving recipes and giving very helpful and generous feedback.

We all depend on those who grow and process our food and bring it to market. I am grateful for all I have learned from the people at Sanagan's Meat Locker, my local butcher; at Hooked, the local fish store; and from the farmers and other vendors at the Wychwood Barns farmers' market, whom I depend on for fresh produce and other foods.

Through the pandemic, the deadline for delivery of the manuscript for this book helped keep me grounded. So did the dear friends in Toronto with whom I went on a long walks or on bicycle excursions, or met for horizon-widening conversation: Julia Bass, Hilary Buttrick, Dina Fayerman, Ana Ferraro, Kim Galvez, Trisha Jackson, Anne MacKenzie, Jennifer MacLagan, Judy Nisenholt, Carol Off, Ethan Poskanzer, Sandy Price, Susie Reisler, Lorne Richmond, Shayma Saadat, Gord Sato, Rebecca Shamai, and Cathy Yolles. Big thanks.

As always, when I send off a book manuscript, I'm aware that it needs trimming and tidying. That job takes patience and good judgement. This time I was very lucky to have Martha Holmberg's help with the hands-on editing and shaping. The other essential editing contribution came from copy editor Judith Sutton, who has no equal. She has copyedited every book I've done, starting with *Flatbreads & Flavors*, and all of them are much better because of her meticulous work. Huge thanks.

In the beautiful golden light of September, photographer Richard Jung and a wonderful team worked in the less-than-ideal space in my kitchen to create the studio photographs in the book. Enormous thanks to Richard, whom I first came to know when he made the photos for *Hot Sour Salty Sweet*. He brought the team together: food stylist Lindsay Guscott and her assistant Sean O'Connor, and prop stylist Andrea McCrindle. Ksenija Hotić joined us as a general helper and soon became Richard's assistant and note-taker. The skill, patience, and good judgement that everyone brought to the shoot radiate from the photographs. Big thanks to you all.

I am very grateful to Ethan Poskanzer and Judy Nisenholt for taking such good care of Richard Jung while he was here in Toronto.

The last stages of turning a manuscript into a book involve a team of designers, production managers, proofreaders, and more. I am very lucky to be so well taken care of. Big thanks to art director Suet Chong and designers Jan Derevjanik and Jane Treuhaft, to executive managing editor Zach Greenwald, to associate editor Bella Lemos, and to the rest of the crew.

Finally, as always, I am deeply grateful for the support and patience of the home team: dear Paul, who has lived with fridges and cupboards full of small jars of this and that, and has tasted recipes, come on trips, and been encouraging throughout; and now-adult Dominic and Tashi, who have many years' experience of the book-making process and who continue to lovingly remind me, from nearby or far away, that I am always stressed as deadlines approach, and that things seem to turn out fine in the end.

INDEX

Note: *Italic* page numbers refer to pictures and captions.

Photographs copyright © 2022 by Richard Jung, except for photos on pages 4–5, 8, 20,
32–33, 40, 41, 67, 69, 94–95, 116–117, 120, 132–133, 136, 150, 154–155, 158, 177,
182–183, 206–207, 212, 226–227, 248–249, 258, 266–267, 284–285, 312–313, 318, 331,
338–339, 368, 371, 372, and 375 copyright © 2022 by Naomi Duguid

Library of Congress Cataloging-in-Publication Data is on file.

ISBN 978-1-57965-944-8

Design by Suet Chong and Jan Derevjanik

Artisan books are available at special discounts when purchased in bulk for
premiums and sales promotions as well as for fund-raising or educational use.
Special editions or book excerpts also can be created to specification.
For details, contact the Special Sales Director at the address below, or send
an e-mail to specialmarkets@workman.com.

For speaking engagements, contact speakersbureau@workman.com.

Published by Artisan
A division of Workman Publishing Co., Inc.
225 Varick Street
New York, NY 10014-4381
artisanbooks.com

Artisan is a registered trademark of
Workman Publishing Co., Inc.

Printed in China on responsibly sourced paper

First printing, September 2022

10 9 8 7 6 5 4 3 2 1